MW00991436

# MAKING WAR

# MAKING WAR

The 200-Year-Old Battle Between
the President and Congress over
How America Goes to War

## JOHN LEHMAN

CHARLES SCRIBNER'S SONS
*New York*

MAXWELL MACMILLAN CANADA
*Toronto*

MAXWELL MACMILLAN INTERNATIONAL
*New York Oxford Singapore Sydney*

Charles Scribner's Sons
Macmillan Publishing Company
866 Third Avenue, New York, NY 10022

Maxwell Macmillan Canada, Inc.
1200 Eglinton Avenue East, Suite 200
Don Mills, Ontario M3C 3N1

Macmillan Publishing Company is part of the Maxwell Communication Group
of Companies.

Library of Congress Cataloging-in-Publication Data
Lehman, John.
    Making war: the 200-year-old battle between the President and Congress
over how America goes to war/John Lehman.
        p.  cm.
    ISBN 0-684-19239-X
    1. War and emergency powers—United States—History.  2. Executive
power—United States—History.  3. United States. Congress—Powers and
duties—History.  4. World politics—20th century.  5. World politics—19th
century.  I. Title.
KF5060.L44  1992
342.73′062—dc20
[347.30262]              91-39228

*To Robert Strausz-Hupé,*
*scholar, diplomat, mentor, friend*

# Contents

# Contents

# Preface

"Power corrupts; absolute power is really neat!" So joked Donald Regan, President Reagan's all-powerful chief of staff. The 1987 Gridiron Dinner audience roared with laughter because they knew it was true. So, too, did the classically educated gentlemen who wrote the U.S. Constitution. They knew also that Lord Acton's pre-Regan aphorism "Absolute power corrupts absolutely" was equally true. Franklin, Madison, Jefferson, Hamilton and their fellow drafters of the American Constitution disagreed on many things, but all agreed that there should be no absolute seat of power in the new government. Dispersal of the police and military powers—the tools of tyranny—was a high priority, and they achieved it by dividing them among three separate branches. But some feared the possible tyranny of the legislature—as in Cromwell's Parliament, for example—while others feared the creation of a despotic executive like George III. They could not agree on how precisely to allocate those powers. The Constitution is therefore not precise, with grants of power to each that overlap and even contradict, setting up a permanent struggle between the branches and leaving events and politics to determine who rules. The framers consciously chose to give up police, military, and diplomatic efficiency in order to prevent the consolidation of authority and the corruption of absolute power.

As we shall see, there is no perfect or preordained balance between President and Congress on national security, and recourse to the third branch—the judiciary—has resolved only small facets of the issue. There are only the barest of limits to the divided and overlapping powers specified by the Constitution, and there are the diverse practices of successive generations. The balance has usually been set less by legalities than by politics, more by urgent problems than ingenious theory. In short, the "invitation to strife" issued by the founders has been answered and attended by both president and Congress. Often the Minuet has ended with blood on the floor.

As for war, experience of eighteenth-century government and the Revolution itself had taught the Founding Fathers that Congress could not run a war effectively; that authority must fall to the executive. But they also resisted an executive whose powers, like those of a monarch, could bring the country to war without congressional consent.

Given the role of force in foreign policy, Congress would usually be inclined to restrain executive warmongering. Despite an international reputation for bellicosity, the people of the United States have always disapproved of getting entangled abroad and almost never favored initiating hostilities. Their representatives in Congress have nearly always reflected this aversion. Once involved in hostilities, however, popular opinion historically swings overwhelmingly behind the prosecution of force, with Congress falling in line with public opinion. In the decade prior to World War II, for example, the American people and Congress opposed and blocked FDR's attempt to build up war-making capability to deal with the growing threat posed by Japan and Nazi Germany. Efforts to fortify the Philippines, train an army (the entire U.S. Army was still smaller on Pearl Harbor day than the Marine Corps is today), and expand the army and air corps were voted down year after year because the people wanted no war. Even as late as 1940, the renewal of draft authority passed by only one vote, and even that was only a year's extension. Once the war began, however, the pendulum slammed hard over to the president in support of the war effort.

During World War II the executive reigned supreme; Congress, to paraphrase Gilbert and Sullivan, "throughout the war did nothing and did it very well." After World War II, the onset of the Cold War left the executive with much of the hot war prerogatives. Both the Korean and Vietnamese conflicts were waged without formal declarations of war. But the war in Vietnam, like the war in Korea, enjoyed congressional support only so long as the war appeared to succeed, that is, had clear objectives, acceptable costs, and a foreseeable date of probable conclusion. Once our objectives were not attained, even had there been a declaration of war instead of the Tonkin Gulf Resolution, Congress would not have continued to support it.

For the last thirty years the struggle between president and Congress has intrigued me as an amateur political historian, and for the last twenty-three years I have found myself a frequent participant at what in Pentagonese is called the "forward edge of the battle area." In my early years in Washington I found it most perplexing to try to fit the practice I saw (wide-eyed) going on all around me to the neat constitutional theory taught confidently at university.

What theory, for instance, neatly covers Congress's pushing reluctant presidents into war in 1798 and again in 1898 and presidents ignoring and defying Congress while using military force in 1950 and 1990? How do we reconcile Robert McNamara's being praised and honored for lying to Congress about secret commitments to withdraw missiles in Turkey and the criminal prosecution of CIA officials for not telling Congress about secret missile deals in Iran-Contra?

When the Constitution was written, war was seen in terms of the threats it posed to liberty and the burdens of expenditure it necessarily imposed. Military force involved battles between hundreds, occasionally thousands, of trained combatants. After the Civil War introduced the era of "total war," involving not hundreds but hundreds of thousands of casualties along with the strategic destruction of cities and economies, the issues of whose role it is to decide and control the use of military power became much graver. Fifty-five million people died in World War II, a conflict that saw the first casualties of nuclear weapons of truly mass destruction. In this era, our own, war and the threat of war became the central focus of politics. This book is an attempt to consider the interaction of military adventures and American politics, to understand what happens, how and why.

It is not intended as an exhaustive history or a treatise on

constitutional theory. We revisit those events in American history
that have shaped current practice and review the theories and
the legal judgments that have framed the debate. The largest
part of the book deals with the last two decades of events in which
I was a participant. I have tried to be completely objective, but
the reader will have little trouble placing me along the spectrum
of debate. I have been a "strong president man" when in the
executive branch and a "strong Congress man" when out of the
government in political opposition. Most writers on the subject
have similar patterns of shifting perspective. Arthur Schlesinger,
who published *The Imperial Presidency* during the Nixon presidency, wrote persuasively in the *Wall Street Journal* arguing
against President Bush's right to use force in Iraq without congressional authority, which is what President Truman had done
in Korea in 1950. In response to the charge that he had strongly
supported the actions of President Truman, a fellow Democrat,
Schlesinger answered, "I was wrong." Perhaps.

Instead of beginning with *The Federalist* and the newly popular
exercise of imagining the original intent of the framers, we plunge
directly into our most recent war, Operation Desert Storm. I
believe it is the perfect showcase to display the incredible process
of how we go to war. We begin by reviewing the history of our
involvement in the Persian Gulf these two centuries past. I have
not constructed an exhaustive chronology, but have rather made
a selection of events that I believe shaped our official attitudes.
When Saddam Hussein invaded Kuwait in August 1990 and President Bush said, "This will not stand—this aggression against
Kuwait," the world watched riveted as the slow march to war
began. Rarely in history has the traditionally complex and secret
interaction of diplomacy, military mobilization, and domestic politics leading to war unfolded so deliberately and visibly. Much will
be written elsewhere about the remarkable diplomatic success of
the Bush administration in leading the United Nations and in
forging a disparate coalition. Much more will also be written
about the brilliant high-tech military campaign itself and the
accomplishment of the military leaders, beginning with President
Bush, who led it—and of President Reagan, his Pentagon leaders,
and his Republican and Democratic supporters in Congress who
together rebuilt the U.S. military following the post-Vietnam collapse of the 1970s.

I touch only briefly on the fighting itself, and while not resisting the temptation to make clear certain military lessons, I concentrate instead on the intense prewar maneuvering between President Bush and the leaders of Congress. This opening chapter relieves the reader of waiting in suspense to learn the book's conclusions: Desert Storm demonstrated that once again, after two decades of congressional imperialism, a strong president has primacy in national security as long as he is successful.

With our most recent war vividly in mind, I go back to the thinking of the writers of the Constitution to seek some understanding of the enigmatic language with which they spread the national security and war-making powers between the branches. We review what the wiser scholars and political historians have had to say and then review the case law and legal opinions on the issue.

Finding no agreement but many conflicting insights from these sources, we look in the next two chapters at what presidents and Congresses have actually done in the first two hundred years after the Constitution was written. It is a selective history (leaving out, for example, most of the Civil War, an internal insurrection) beginning with military action in 1801 against the Bashaw, a pirate ruler of Tripoli, and ending with a military strike in 1986 against Mu'ammar Qaddafi, another pirate ruler of Tripoli.

The constitutional consensus we failed to find in law and theory eludes us also in historical practice. Some presidents were dominated by Congress; others dominated. Some presidents refused to act without congressional authorization; other presidents took military action without even informing Congress.

Beyond war, the making of international agreements and treaties has been a major field of battle between the branches since the Constitution was written. Agreements, treaties, and diplomacy in general have often been portrayed by opponents of the use of force as alternatives to making war. Certainly all wars are in a sense the result of the failure of diplomacy. But very often diplomacy has failed when it has not been backed with credible military capabilities. The twenty-year American effort to end the arms race through diplomacy and the negotiation of strategic arms agreements is explored in chapter 5. The interaction of Congress and the executive through the treaty process was far more important to the outcome of this endeavor than American interaction with the Soviets. The unusual debate over the Toma-hawk cruise missile provides the focus on how the process really works.

Easily the greatest source of congressional power in the endless constitutional struggle is one not even mentioned in the document, the power of investigation; or, as it is viewed by the executive, the power of inquisition. Backed by legislative and appropriation powers as well as subpoena power, this indeed is the counterbalance to executive conceits in national security affairs. The sixth and seventh chapters review the origins of this power and the response to it within the executive branch. The permanent tension between Congress's need to know everything that is relevant to its legislative responsibilities in national security and the executive branch's need to maintain confidentiality and secrecy over sensitive military and intelligence information has, for the most part, achieved what the framers intended. But the record overflows with abuses on both sides. In the post–World War II period, the excesses of the executive branch (since giving virtually every official authority to classify information culminated in the highly visible abuses of secrecy to cover malfeasance and chicanery in the 1960s and 1970s) led to a period of what I see as even grosser excesses by Congress, the legacy of which is with us to the present day. A flood of disclosures of operational military information that should have remained secret arose from congressional committees during the later period of the Vietnam War, and the widespread leaks of sensitive intelligence matters by members of congressional oversight committees have led to a paranoia in the executive branch and a refusal by foreign governments to risk the sharing of intelligence or of confidentialities.

The disappearance of any standards of confidentiality in Congress has led also to the common leaking of embarrassing information from personnel and FBI files of executive nominees, leading in 1990 and 1991 to the universal revulsion at congressional behavior during hearings about the nomination of John Tower to be secretary of defense and Clarence Thomas to be a justice of the Supreme Court.

But the most damaging and disturbing of all the excesses in the current imbalance between investigation and secrecy has been the emergence of what amounts to the criminalization of the political process. The perfect case study of abuse by both branches leading to absurdity is Iran-Contra. The executive, Ronald Reagan, avoided a fight in the proper policy arena—Congress—finding instead secret, back-channel support for the Contras against the prohibitions of the Boland Amendment, an act of Congress. This led to creation by Congress of an endless and budgetless criminal prosecution of low-level executive officials by a special prosecutor.

The two-centuries-old weakness of the executive branch—to fall for the lures of covert action as a way to evade partnership with Congress—is explored in chapter 8, which is a detailed look at our relations with Panama and Manuel Noriega leading to the invasion of 1989.

Just as the first chapter demonstrates that President Bush has reasserted primacy over national security affairs, as demonstrated in Desert Shield and Desert Storm, the final chapter on the power of money demonstrates that Congress still has the final say on national security policy because of its control of the power of the purse. Congress has used this power to stop presidential military action, to change it and mold it as actions unfold, and has especially used it to modify defense policy and programs to its own partisan and constituent priorities. It is in this latter role that a new phenomenon and indeed a new fourth branch of government has been born. Congress has increased its staff exponentially, and the staff has in turn vastly increased its involvement in overseeing the minutest detail of executive spending. During the debate over the most recent defense budget, Congress rewrote or modified more than two thousand individual items. With congressional staffs now at a level equivalent to three army divisions, it is impossible for members of Congress to understand, much less rein in, what these powerful bureaucrats are doing. The most accurate assessment of this absurd situation was best expressed by the chaplain of the Senate during debate on the defense budget in 1985. He opened the Senate session with the following prayer: "Father in heaven, I confess not knowing enough about what is happening here to pray relevantly. . . ." Nor is any secretary of defense or his senior officials much wiser about the details of the more than thirty thousand pages of detail that make up his budget submission every year. The budget is the

joint creation of 560,000 procurement career officials, who, together with the three divisions of congressional careerists, have
become what is nothing less than a fourth branch of government.
It is this phenomenon (when combined with the media, they are
termed by some "the iron triangle") that needs to be addressed
in the future and that looms larger than any imbalances that
scholars have perceived between the powers of the executive and
Congress. The greater part of the substance of governance in this
country has flowed unobserved into the reservoirs of this new
and unchecked center of power.

# Acknowledgments

My former colleague on the National Security Council staff, Bill Stearman, who continues his unique career combining scholarship and statecraft, teaching and writing at Georgetown University while serving with the National Security Council, is responsible for my undertaking this book. It was his idea, and his continuing encouragement and critique brought it into being. It was, moreover, Jeffrey Cimbalo, his brilliant young graduate assistant, who labored over the past two years as my research assistant in finding and verifying acts and events and assisted in the drafting.

My longtime friend and counselor Dr. Harvey Sicherman was invaluable in helping me learn and understand what really happened in Central America and the Middle East.

Edward T. (Ned) Chase, senior editor at Macmillan/Scribners, did not let our friendship interfere with his excellent and occasionally blunt editing. Bill Goldstein provided considerable input to the improvement of the text.

Mark Geier, my administrative assistant, and my secretaries, Elizabeth Kelly and Barbara Majett, worked hard and successfully in keeping the many drafts flowing and in order.

To all of these friends I express my deep gratitude.

# MAKING WAR

# 1

## Desert Storm

On the evening of February 25, 1991, sixty-six U.S. Army Black Hawk helicopters sped at 155 miles per hour only ten feet above the desert floor of the Arabian Peninsula. Deep in Iraq, the helicopters halted to discharge 1,000 troops from the 101st Airborne Division. "The Screaming Eagles have landed in the Euphrates Valley," radioed the brigade commander to his division command post. Soon the main highway connecting Baghdad with the Iraqi command center located in Basra had been cut.[1]

Two days later, 270,000 U.S., British, and French soldiers, spearheaded by 1,500 tanks, began a massive flanking attack that obliterated Iraq's best armed forces, the Republican Guards. Beginning on January 16, six weeks of air war and then a final hundred hours of ground war methodically reduced the world's fourth-largest army to a desperate rabble of fleeing soldiers and junked metal. Saddam Hussein's conquest had been shattered by one of history's most successful military actions, which caused over a hundred thousand Iraqi casualties. Only 137 Americans died in the fighting, nearly one in four from friendly fire. Fewer than forty aircraft were shot down. Two warships were damaged by mines.

This most one-sided battle in modern history had been the least expected. It had all the makings of a geopolitical fantasy. Iraq conquers Kuwait. The United States makes war on Iraq at the head of an international coalition. Saudi Arabia allows half

1

a million Western troops to repel another Arab state from its soil. And perhaps most amazing of all, Congress authorizes the president to make war at a time and a place of his own choosing.

Individuals, timing, and popular opinion all played crucial roles in this astounding story. George Bush's will and skill throughout the Gulf crisis surprised and pleased most Americans. He was aided by an exceptional act of villainy committed by an exceptional rogue. Saddam Hussein not only filled this role; he obviously loved it. Finally, the time—the immediate post–Cold War era—and the place—the Persian Gulf—provided a unique opening for the exercise of American leadership. The United States still had the global military power to deal with a Soviet threat and was able to use those forces against Iraq without fear of Soviet intervention. And most Americans seemed to believe that U.S. interests in keeping the Gulf free of hostile domination was worth a fight.

The result was to transform America itself, giving the nation a long-overdue tonic that would clear away the Vietnam hangover. As the hugely victorious campaign exorcised the ghost of Vietnam from the military, so presidential, congressional, and public support for the war locked the closet on another Vietnam skeleton. The Gulf war would be popular. The president and Congress would achieve rare, if reluctant, harmony, rendering irrelevant the Vietnam-era War Powers Resolution, designed to checkmate the White House in the use of force abroad. The war would thus reconfirm American leadership abroad and presidential primacy in foreign policy.

## A Crisis Long Coming

The story of the Gulf war begins with the unsettled relations among all of the Gulf states and who among them would be the leader in the region. Iran brought oil, population, and an imperial history as her claim. But the Persians of Iran were separate ethnically from the Arabs; and their Shiite Islamic religion was considered a heretical sect or, at best, inferior to the dominant Sunni faith of most of the Arab Muslims.

On the Arab side, both Saudi Arabia and Iraq were states of

very recent origin. Saudi Arabia was the product of conquest by the Saudi family and the Wahabi sect, an austere variation of Islam unique to the peninsula. Thinly populated, Saudi power derived from oil wealth and control of the mosques at Mecca and Medina.

Iraq had both wealth and population, but it lacked political coherence, having been cobbled together by the British after World War I out of several very different Ottoman provinces. There was an imperial history centered on Baghdad, but it was Sunni. The majority of Iraqi citizens were either ethnic Kurds, who wanted their own ways and their own state, if they could get one; or, mostly, Shiite Muslims, who, although Arab, did not care for Sunni overrule. To make the matter even more troublesome, the sacred sites of Shia Islam were found in Iraqi territory, an irritant to Sunni-Shia relations in Iraq and, of course, across the border with Iran.

Adjacent to these large rivalrous states were Kuwait, Bahrain, Oman Qatar, and the United Arab Emirates (UAE). The five each had colorful histories as traders and pirates, large revenues from oil, and small populations whose work was done by imported labor and foreign experts. They needed "big brothers" from inside or outside the region to survive. For much of the last century, that brother was British. More recently, America, with much hesitation and some fumbling, has assumed that role.

American involvement in the Persian Gulf is indeed very recent. During the first hundred years of our Republic the only significant activities in the Persian Gulf were fishing, pearling, and piracy. It was Great Britain, whose trade with India grew in importance during the period, that found it necessary to take military action against the pirate fleets. This led in 1820 to a general treaty with the tribal sheikhs of the western and southern coasts to suppress piracy and the slave traffic. London thus extended its empire to the Gulf and began to assume responsibility for the region's security.

The security established in this "Trucial" system (The term came from the agreements establishing truce with the sheikhs) was quite selective. Pirates based in Iran were outside the system, and those sheikhs within the system were constrained only against British and Indian shipping. Therefore, Yankee traders seeking to gain a foothold in this trade had no protection from Great Britain during most of the nineteenth century and were fair game. Yankee commercial interest, let alone their military interest, in the region were distinctly not welcome by the Brits, and the appearance of an American flag in the Gulf was an extreme rarity right up until World War II.

One of the most significant events during this century was the discovery by the British of major oil deposits in southwestern Iran in 1908. Development of the fields was slow at first but accelerated rapidly during World War I. Oil was discovered in 1923 in Iraq but was developed at a slower pace. Oil in commercial quantities was not discovered on the Arabian Peninsula until 1938, in southeastern Kuwait, and was not seriously developed until after World War II, when Arabian reserves proved to be vastly larger than those of both Iran and Iraq. By 1953, Kuwait had risen to become the largest producer in the Gulf, a position it held until it was eclipsed by Saudi Arabia in 1965. The early years of oil exploration in the Gulf were dominated by the British, with minor participation by other European consortium members. American participation did not become substantial until the late 1930s. Thus commenced American involvement in the Persian Gulf.

World War II brought the Gulf into major focus as a superpower arena. The newly developed oil fields in Persia and Iraq became essential to the Allies, and the Gulf became critical as the warmwater port essential to Russia's war effort. The Soviet Union quickly occupied the northern Iranian province of Azerbaijan, and the Allies took over administration of the principal Gulf ports. By 1943 the Soviet Union was receiving more than 1 million tons a month of beans and bullets from the Allies through Iran. The memory of this experience was never far removed from Soviet foreign-policy making in the postwar period.

Azerbaijan proved to be one of the first crises of the Cold War when Stalin violated the occupation treaty signed in 1942 with Great Britain. Both parties had committed to withdraw their forces from Iran six months after the end of hostilities. The Americans and British withdrew, but the Russians did not. Instead, they demanded oil concessions equal to those of the British and American companies and began organizing popular uprisings in northern Iran. President Truman sent a very strong demarche in March 1946, demanding immediate withdrawal of Russian forces. The Soviets backed down, and by May 6 the Red Army had departed, and the Soviets had suffered their first Cold War defeat.

The Russian hand was seen again by some British and Americans in 1951 with the coming to power in Iran of Mohammed Mossadegh. While supposedly an Iranian heading an Iranian nationalist movement in wresting power from the shah, considerable Communist influence was alleged as he proceeded to nationalize the Anglo-Iranian Oil Company. By the summer of 1953, the State Department had concluded that Mossadegh was moving into the Soviet orbit. The United States cut off all aid to Iran and with the British made possible a successful coup by Shah Reza Pahlavi, for which he was provided military equipment and full communications support by the United States.

Since the discovery of oil in Iran, American companies had been trying to break into the field. They failed because of dedicated British opposition. The shah now showed his gratitude and established a new international consortium, giving the British 40 percent of the oil and five American firms 40 percent; the Dutch and French divided the remaining 20 percent. The Soviet Union received its second defeat of the Cold War in the Gulf, and American involvement there was firmly established.

Despite the unwelcome intrusion of American oil companies and a modest U.S. Navy presence, British hegemony remained essentially unchallenged after the war. In 1961 the British showed their willingness to protect their interests when they hurriedly sent forces to protect Kuwait against Iraqi threats. All of this changed, however, in January 1968, when the Labor Government of Harold Wilson announced that the United Kingdom planned to withdraw all military forces from east of Suez and would close all military bases in those regions within three years. This diplomatic thunderclap began several years of considerable turmoil in which Soviet interest in the area was vigorously increased.

In July 1969, recently inaugurated President Richard Nixon stopped in Guam on his way to an inspection tour in Vietnam and Thailand. There he announced a policy first called the Guam

Doctrine, later known as the Nixon Doctrine, which he later defined as follows:

> I began with the proposition that we would keep our existing treaty commitments, but that we would not make any more commitments unless they were required by our own vital interest.
>
> In the past, our policy had been to furnish arms, men, and material to help other nations defend themselves against aggression. That was what we had done in Korea, that was how we had started out in Vietnam. But from now on, I said, we would furnish all of the material and economic and military assistance to those nations willing to accept the responsibility of supplying the manpower to defend themselves.[2]

At the same time, Henry Kissinger, Nixon's new national security adviser, had concluded a classified survey of the area and a study of American bases and commitments abroad. This translated in the Gulf to an effort by the United States to organize a new security system in the wake of the British departure. It was called the "Twin Pillars." We would rely on our ally, the shah of Iran, to provide the muscle on one side and our other ally, Saudi Arabia, to provide money and influence on the other side. Iraq, which by that time had been gripped by a Baathist (which means Renaissance) revolutionary regime closely allied to the Soviets, was an obvious target of the scheme.

The first project I was assigned, in January 1969, as a new junior staff member on the National Security Council (NSC), was a study of American military bases abroad. A major survey of worldwide basing, called the Woods-McClintock study, had been done at the end of the Johnson administration, and using this as a basis, Kissinger assigned Richard Allen, who had just been appointed as his deputy, to recommend new base openings and closures to support the Nixon Doctrine. Dick Allen had been Nixon's national security adviser during the campaign, and when Kissinger was appointed over him as the national security adviser to the president, there was, to say the least, a certain awkwardness. The assignment to work on the worldwide base structure was, for Dick Allen, the equivalent of being sent to China to explain American policy to the Chinese—one by one. But for me, as Allen's twenty-six-year-old assistant, it was a most exciting assignment. After several trips abroad and six months of study, we concluded there was a major need for a new American base in the Indian Ocean to support the American military forces soon to be required to fill the vacuum in the Persian Gulf left by British withdrawal. After close looks at former British bases, such as Aldabra and Gan, we settled on Diego Garcia in the Chagos archipelago in the middle of the Indian Ocean.

On my first visit to Diego Garcia, I was amazed to find such a perfect naval base. A coral atoll twenty-two miles around, it had a deep lagoon in the middle able to take the latest and deepest-draft naval and logistics ships. The decision was soon made to build the base here, and an agreement was reached with the British to expedite construction.

After initial opposition from the dovish Senate Foreign Relations Committee, construction on Diego Garcia began on a modest scale. When I visited the base in 1972, it was like a scene from a World War II movie, with Seabee construction battalions and tented barracks. The base expansion was accelerated after the 1973 Arab-Israeli war and the sudden scare brought about by construction of a Soviet military base in Somalia, on the Horn of Africa. The threat of a Soviet advance in the Gulf was again perceived when they supported the ouster of Haile Selassie I from Ethiopia by a pro-Soviet junta. The 1973 war was followed by an Arab boycott of states supporting Israel and a quadrupling of the oil price by the OPEC cartel. Stability in the Gulf continued to deteriorate in the mid-seventies.

These geopolitical concerns were not nearly as high in the priorities of the Carter administration. President Carter campaigned on a strong platform of commitment to human rights around the world. The shah was a particular target of those in the new administration deeply concerned by human rights violations.

Historians will long argue whether the forces that brought the Ayatollah to power would have prevailed even if Washington had not undermined the shah. The unbridled arms buildup in Iran promoted by the United States and West Europe brought a flood of arms salesmen and loose money, creating deep resentment— and support for the fundamentalist Ayatollah. But there can be no doubt that the Carter administration's ideological hostility toward him hastened his fall. When it soon became clear that the shah could not last, the administration received indications from the Iranian military that it intended to seize power to prevent the Ayatollah from gaining control. The administration immediately dispatched Gen. "Dutch" Huyser to inform the Iranian military that the United States would actively oppose any attempt by them to seize power. The result of it all was one of the truly monumental mistakes of our policies in the Gulf. The U.S. itself facilitated the triumph of the Ayatollah Khomeini, America's archenemy, who dreamed of a new Islamic empire built on the ruins of Western influence and interest and made the shah's human rights policies look like a model of enlightenment.

Within the year, the magnitude of the disaster became clear to the Carter administration, and in January 1980 the president enunciated the Carter Doctrine. In his last State of the Union address he said, "Let our position be absolutely clear: any attempt by an outside power to gain control of the Persian Gulf region will be regarded as an assault on the vital interests of the United States of America. And such an assault will be repelled by any means necessary, including military force."

Thus was declared the policy that would be the basis for Operation Desert Storm.

The Carter administration began a hurried effort to implement its doctrine, including the establishment of the Rapid Deployment Force. Except for the creation of a headquarters staff in Tampa, Florida, and the appointment of a commander, Gen. P. X. Kelley (a brilliant leader and later commandant of the Marine Corps), the change of administrations a year later left implementation of the Carter Doctrine to the administration of Ronald Reagan.

## Gulf Policy in the Reagan Administration

At the Republican National Convention in July 1980, Ronald Reagan's defense policy positions were incorporated in the Republican platform, which hotly criticized Carter's foreign and defense policies but nonetheless endorsed its emphasis on a strong defense of the Gulf. The Gulf was a central focus of the initial Reagan NSC policy directives and was a principle justification for the large increase in the size of the U.S. military put forward by the Reagan administration.

In the very first Reagan defense budget, the enlargement of the army from thirteen to sixteen divisions begun in the Carter administration was expanded even further—to eighteen active and ten reserve divisions, for a total of twenty-eight fully equipped divisions. For the air force, an increase of its strategic programs as well as a major tactical modernization and expansion necessitated thirty tactical air wings, a total upgrade of the F-111 force, an entirely new attack strike version of the F-15, the completion of the "Have Blue" stealth fighter program begun in the Ford administration and put into production under President Carter, the building of an entirely new tanker fleet of KC-10 aerorefuelers and a new fleet of C-5B heavy lifters, and a major expansion of the Marine Corps amphibious assault capability by more than 70 percent.

Focused on the Gulf, the most ambitious rebuilding of our strategic sealift since World War II was undertaken. It included the building of thirteen huge maritime prepositioning ships. These ships were filled with equipment and weeks of supplies at combat consumption rates for three full marine brigades. It included the modification of eight fast containerships to carry a full army armored division at thirty knots, cutting the time from the United States to the Persian Gulf from four weeks to two weeks. We began a huge program to build offloading equipment, causeways, lighters, and crane ships, enabling very rapid unloading virtually anywhere in the Gulf. We began an ambitious expansion of the Ready Reserve Force of mothballed break-bulk cargo and containerships, expanding from 36 to 121. All of those sealift programs made Operation Desert Storm possible.

At the same time as the army and air force buildup, the navy was expanded from thirteen to fifteen carrier battle groups, with the additional two earmarked for the Gulf. Four battleship battle groups were added to the force structure, with a major focus their ability to reach virtually all of the important targets in the Gulf with their Tomahawk cruise missiles or sixteen-inch guns.

It was this significant expansion of all of the services focused on beefing up American presence in the Gulf that earned such withering criticism from Congress during the 1980s. Yet without it, Operation Desert Storm would have been impossible.

The Reagan buildup of U.S. forces for use in the Persian Gulf had few historical parallels. The USS *Vincennes* was the first U.S. Navy ship to visit the Gulf, calling at Muscat in 1800, and ironically, the modern Aegis cruiser USS *Vincennes* that shot down the Iranian airliner in 1988, just a few miles from Muscat. This incident had taken place while Vincennes was under attack by Iranian missile boats during the "tanker war" of 1987–89. Since the United States was protecting tankers that were carrying Iraqi oil from Iranian attack, we found ourselves on the side of Saddam Hussein, a tilt that had consequences in 1990.

The USS *Peacock* had captured four British ships near the Gulf during the War of 1812, but there is no recorded U.S. naval activity in the region from that time until Theodore Roosevelt's Great White Fleet passed through in 1908. It was not until 1941 that the U.S. military came to the Gulf to stay.

After initial battles in the Indian Ocean between the Japanese and Royal navies during World War II, the Persian Gulf was recognized by 1942 as the second most important entrepot to the beleaguered Soviet Union. The U.S. military entered the theater to convoy supplies to the principal Iranian ports.

The Persian and Iraqi oil fields immediately became very important to the Allied war effort. By 1942, James Forrestal, then under secretary of the navy and later secretary, spearheaded planning for permanent access to Persian Gulf oil at the end of the war. Forrestal was convinced that, based on its known oil reserves, the United States would not be able to provide for its domestic and defense needs in the postwar period. Despite concerted British opposition during the war, by its end, four American oil companies had gained very strong footholds in the Gulf. In fact, Standard Oil of California and Texaco had already gained control of all foreign concessions in Saudi Arabia and Bahrain.

From the end of the war, in the years before it was put under the War/Defense Department by the 1947 National Security Act, the Navy Department argued strongly for a major emphasis on maintaining American power in the oil-rich Gulf. The War Department objected strenuously. Its strategy focused entirely on central Europe, arguing that the Gulf and the western Pacific were distractions from the confrontation sure to occur in Europe in the emerging Cold War. With the National Security Act of 1947 and its subsequent amendments, this strategic perspective

10

effectively superseded the view of the Navy Department. Nevertheless, because of the dependence of the Pacific fleet on Kuwait and Saudi oil products, the navy maintained a small presence at Bahrain throughout the Cold War period.

Following the 1973 Arab-Israeli War and subsequent oil boycott, the U.S. naval presence in the Persian Gulf was significantly increased. At the end of the official U.S. involvement in the Vietnam War in 1973, the navy had expected easing of the deployment schedule that had been destroying its morale and readiness. Instead, the fleet was cut from one thousand to five hundred ships, with no letup in deployments, with those in the Gulf of Tonkin now replaced with permanent carriers in the vicinity of the Persian Gulf. With the fall of the shah in 1979, the requirement was doubled to two carrier battle groups patrolling what came to be called "Gonzo Station."

When the Reagan administration came to power in 1981, a major effort was made to augment the U.S. naval presence by securing base rights for the army and the air force in Egypt, Somalia, Sudan, and the Gulf States. While no direct base rights were made officially available in the manner, say, of the Philippines, the Reagan administration spent $10 billion upgrading facilities in those countries to enable rapid deployment of American air and ground forces in the event of war. Saudi Arabia was assisted in building some thirty-two air bases to U.S. standards.

Other than modest naval training exercises the only actual military operation carried out in the Gulf by the United States during the Carter years was the ill-fated Desert I rescue attempt. That sad affair offered in my judgment an accurate insight into the hollow strength of American military might that was a result of the ill-advised retrenchment that took place under Republican and Democratic presidents after Vietnam.

The major military buildup that we in the military leadership of the Reagan administration believed to be a prerequisite to a new foreign policy was accompanied by a sustained diplomatic effort to organize large-scale multinational exercises involving all of the friendly states in the region and all of their combined land, sea, and air forces.

In August 1985, after doing reserve duty on the USS *Midway* in one such exercise in the North Arabian Sea, I traveled to the

Gulf to confer with our commander of MIDEASTFOR (Penta-gonese for Middle East Force, the small naval contingent based in the Gulf since the close of World War II) and with the emir of Bahrain. We flew an S-3 jet from the *Midway* to Manama, Bah-rain, through the Strait of Hormuz and then along the Trucial coast to Bahrain, which lies in the western part of the Gulf be-tween Qatar and Saudi Arabia.

As the huge American-built naval and air force base at Bandar Abbas in Iran appeared on the radar scope, I thought back to my early visit to that base in the early seventies. In my lieutenant's uniform and returning from my annual active duty in Vietnam, I had hitched a fourteen-hour ride on a P-3 patrol plane from Thailand to Diego Garcia and then on to Iran. I was dropped in Bandar Abbas and stayed the night in the brand-new bachelor officer quarters (BOQ). It was much better than a U.S. Navy BOQ. Among the more amusing features, however, was a water spigot rather than toilet paper, as specified, so I was told, by the local mullah. My six-hour flight to Tehran in the back of an Iranian C-130, with a crowd of Kurdish refugees being relocated as part of the newly signed agreement between Iran and Saddam Hussein, was equally instructive.

The S-3 has an excellent surface search radar, and as we flew in the night over the Gulf, it was amazing to see the hundreds of targets on the radar scope. On an average day there are 450–500 surface ships in the Gulf. In addition there are many hundreds of drilling rigs that on radar look just like ships. I realized how difficult it must be for attack pilots to distinguish between friendly and unfriendly targets in the tanker war that was then raging between Iran and Iraq. Looking down at the Gulf was like looking up at the stars: the lighted rigs stretched in all directions, some in seeming constellations as large as towns. Later in 1987, the USS *Stark* was to pay the price of that confusion when she was hit by an Exocet missile fired by an Iraqi pilot focusing on what he thought was an Iranian target. The captain of the *Stark* was fully equipped with all the necessary defenses needed to defeat the Exocet but for some reason did not use them. Forty-seven sailors died.

As soon as we landed at Manama, the aircraft became totally covered by fog. Flying at 25,000 feet, the plane became very cold;

at 9:00 P.M., the temperature on the ground was 105 degrees Fahrenheit, with 95 percent humidity. I couldn't see to taxi. Emerging from the cool cockpit into that steam bath was a shock. Fighting a war at that time of year would be a nightmare for ground forces, as both Iran and Iraq had learned the hard way. Taking advantage of the chaos brought to Iran by the shah's fall, Saddam Hussein, the ruler of Iraq in early 1979, immediately attacked Iran. The Ayatollah's propaganda among Iraqi's Shiite Moslem population provided the rationale. Saddam Hussein simply tore up the 1975 agreement on the disputed Shatt-al-Arab waterway between Iran and Iraq, as five of the then twelve Iraqi divisions marched into Iran, seizing the territory adjacent to the waterway and laying siege to the significant Iranian oil port of Abadan.

But Saddam has miscalculated. He had no real campaign plan and no political objectives much beyond the abrogation of the 1975 agreement. Iraqi military strategy was therefore nonexistent; its army's goal merely to hang on to captured territory.

By July 1982, the Iraqis were defending their own territory against inspired waves of Iranian attacks; the Ayatollah had rallied Iranians to a holy war. Then the will of the Iraqis stiffened as they began to realize the value of firepower deployed from well-prepared defensive positions. It was the lesson of World War I trench warfare all over again. After two seasons of slaughter, the Iraqi lines still held. And despite serious setbacks, the Iraqis (aided by growing assistance from the West) gradually gained the upper hand.

Confronted by this massive breakdown of the status quo in the Gulf, the Western powers could hardly disguise their relief. The two powerful states most hostile to Western interests were at war with one other, yet each had to pump oil for American and Western consumption in order to finance the conflict.

The Iranians increased their sales through ports on the Persian Gulf. The Iraqis, blocked from exporting through the Gulf, persuaded the Gulf Arab states to swap oil. Iran retaliated by attacking Kuwaiti tankers—more than one hundred by the summer of 1987—carrying such swapped oil. President Reagan then intervened against Iran by ordering the U.S. Navy in July 1987 to begin escorting Kuwait's tankers in the Gulf, under the

13

fig leaf of having them reregistered under the U.S. flag. Just like President Roosevelt in 1940, he did not consult with Congress. President Reagan was clearly in violation of the War Powers Act's "imminent danger" clause.

In 1988, almost exactly a year after the attack on the *Stark* during the escorting, another frigate of the same class, the *Samuel B. Roberts*, hit an Iranian mine. There were heavy casualties. In retaliation, an attack was ordered by President Reagan against Iranian naval targets. Several patrol boats and one frigate were sunk, and another frigate was heavily damaged by A-6 carrier aircraft. The frigate was the first combat kill for the "skipper" laser-guided bomb that we had sped into the inventory. It was to serve in far greater numbers and equal effectiveness in Operation Desert Storm. It was during that engagement that the *Vincennes* accidentally shot down the civilian airliner. During the entire two-year period of the "tanker war," when the United States regularly escorted tankers reflagged under American registry, Kuwait refused to allow American helicopters engaged in minesweeping even to refuel in Kuwait.

During this period, valuable lessons were learned in how to effectively operate military forces in the Gulf. After the *Stark* incident, the Pacific Fleet commander, Admiral James Lyons, had been very critical of the too long chain of command and the impracticality of responding to developing crises in the Gulf from a large bureaucracy in Florida. He pointed out that the chain of command stretching far across the Atlantic had led the *Stark* to completely misinterpret the rules of engagement worked out in Florida. When Operation Desert Shield was launched in August 1990, one of the first decisions taken by Central Command CINC (commander in chief) Norman H. Schwarzkopf was to leave the bureaucracy in Tampa and move his headquarters and a small staff to Saudi Arabia.

Fearing Soviet rather than Iraqi aggression, we had been given the time during the general Reagan defense buildup to put a Rapid Deployment Force together in the Gulf. Through assistance to the Afghani Mujahedin, we were able to prevent Soviet success in Afghanistan. And in the Arabian Peninsula, the Saudis and their smaller Arab neighbors began to gravitate closer to an America they saw recovering its spirit and grip.

But something else was also happening. War had galvanized the Baathist regime. Wartime facilitated mobilization and control. Saddam also drew upon his external support to finance both guns and butter—a veritable Iraqi economic boom in the midst of the war. The war served not only to consolidate the Islamic republic of the Ayatollah; it also strengthened what one Iraqi called "the Republic of Fear" under Saddam Hussein. Little understood by American strategists was the price the United States would later pay for their support of Saddam's regime.

The American and Western policy toward Iraq had about it the overripe aroma of pure power politics. It was surely not Iraqi good behavior that aroused Washington's support. In fact, Saddam's regime had a relentless record of antagonism toward the United States. Iraq had organized the Rejectionist Front against the Camp David Accords; it had a well-documented record of supporting terrorists; it was allied to the USSR. In June 1981, there had been a further incident. Israel had raided and destroyed a French-built nuclear complex. For this, the government of Menachem Begin earned international censure and had to suffer a temporary delay in the supply of U.S. F-15 fighter jets. But the Israelis' assessment that Saddam was indeed bent on developing nuclear weaponry was widely shared.

However dangerous Saddam had been, or would become from 1982 onward, the shared Iraqi-U.S. interest in defeating the Ayatollah forged an increasingly close alliance.[3] Taken off the list of terrorist states on its promise of restraint (the Abu Nidal gang was expelled in 1983), Iraq was the beneficiary of "Operation Staunch"—the U.S. effort to deny arms supplies to Iran. In 1984, full diplomatic relations were reestablished, leading to major sales of U.S. commodities, such as wheat, and billions of dollars of credit. There were rumors in Washington that select military intelligence was also being shared.

Saddam's military, more than his people, were the beneficiaries of Western largesse. Saddam bought Mirage fighters and Exocet missiles from France, mines from Italy, radar from Brazil, and spare parts wherever he could find them. The Germans, whom the Iraqi policy had favored even when the Nazis were in power beginning in the 1930s, supplied munitions as well as communications gear, fortified bunkers, and chemical-weapons plants.

15

German technicians helped Iraq upgrade its Soviet-supplied Scuds. South African artillery equipped the Iraqi army with weapons of longer effective range than those in any Western arsenal. All told, $13.4 billion of Western arms were sold to Iraq between 1982 and 1989, financed by "loans" from Saudi Arabia and Kuwait. All of it was added to a huge supply of Soviet weapons, tanks, helicopters, jet aircraft, and bombers and an air defense system, amassed during the 1970s. During the 1980s, Iraq emerged as the fourth-largest army in the world.

The end of the Iran-Iraq war in 1988 left Saddam with a stronger grip on Iraq, a profitable relationship with the Western powers, and an expanding influence in the Gulf. But he was also left with a mountain of debt, a population mourning half a million war casualties, and a huge military machine. The United States and its allies were anxious to see Iraq pursue a more constructive course postwar. Our diplomats earnestly explained how a "reformed" Iraq would prosper.

To Washington's chagrin, Saddam preferred to settle scores first. He went after the Kurds, destroying hundreds of their villages, and used poison gas against them—a weapon he had already tested in combat against the Iranians. There were diplomatic protests but no sanctions. (A Senate sanctions bill was sidetracked successfully by the Reagan administration.) Then Saddam entered the Lebanese civil war, sending arms to General Michel Aoun, who had vowed to fight the Syrians.

Preferring the lighter side of this record, American advocates of Saddam could point to his reconciliation with Egypt, allowing Cairo to reenter the Arab League, and his support for King Hussein of Jordan, who in turn promoted Iraq as a good investment. The Iraqi ambassador to the United States also cut a popular and effective figure, touching many constituencies once considered enemies of Iraq. There were even rumors that secret Israeli contacts had been made. Then Washington's bungling of the Iran-Contra affair left the United States with little choice except to continue to cultivate Baghdad. The ties dating from the war had been reinforced by commercial contacts and diplomatic exchange.

But there was one flaw in all of this. It did not work for Saddam. There was about him what an Egyptian diplomat called "a craziness." Described once as the "Don from Takrit" because of his love for the *Godfather* movies, Saddam had his own dramatic story to tell. Born into peasant poverty and an unwanted child, Saddam grew up in the Sunni heartland. Already a gunman before twenty, Saddam was an early member of the Baathist party of Iraq. Like its counterpart (and deadly rival) in Syria, the Iraqi Baathist party offered a Middle Eastern version of several European political philosophies, none of them democratic. This potted "Arab socialism" attempted to translate the old unity of the Islamic world, which was based on a common faith, into a secular, state-controlled, "socialist" destiny.

Saddam always justified his violence with Baathist ideology, but no one ever took that seriously. He had (and by all accounts still has) a peasant's cunning in dealing with the more sophisticated. Like most men skilled at violence, that aspect of power is never far from his calculation—or his experience. All of the officially propagated stories about Saddam (and the rumors) glorify his capacity to endure pain and to maim or murder his opponents—even among his relatives.

Having ascended to power over his rivals in Iraq's thirteenth (and last) coup, Saddam applied his proven methods of security nationwide. One observer estimated that in the Republic of Fear half the people belonged to the Baathist party and half the entire population was employed by the government, the army, and the military. Or as a *New York Times* reporter was told by a European diplomat familiar with Iraq, "There is a feeling that at least three million Iraqis are watching the eleven million others."[4] Truly, as one human rights groups put it, "a nation of informers."

Aside from his own murderous instincts, what Saddam had in Iraq was a country the size of California, with great natural wealth (oil) and a diverse population of 17 million. Of these 17 million, Saddam's power rested ultimately on the Sunni 20 percent; much less on the Shiite, 55 percent; and in opposition to the Kurdish, 20 percent. In peacetime, he could not sustain his dictatorship, his vast military, his plans for superweapons, and a growing economy simultaneously. Oil prices were not high enough. Lenders and investors were more impressed with Iraq's debt and mismanaged economy. Something—or someone—had to give, and it was not going to be Saddam.

As Iraq began to run short of money and the population grew

irritated at continuing privations, a great change occurred. The urgency of Saddam's financial situation merged with what he believed was a strategic opportunity. On February 19, 1990, he explained to a meeting of the Arab Cooperation Council in Baghdad that the demise of the Soviet superpower meant that the Soviets were no longer a challenge to the United States. It was therefore time for the United States to get out of the Persian Gulf. Three days later, in Amman, at an Arab League summit, Saddam got very specific on another matter. He wanted Iraq's $30 billion in debt owed to the small Gulf States canceled and $30 billion more in cash from them.[5]

Thus began what John Kelly, assistant secretary of state for Near Eastern affairs, called the "Spring of Misbehavior." Britain recalled its ambassador when a British journalist named Farzed Bazoft was tried and hanged for espionage. In late March, ominous evidence mounted of Iraqi's military activity. There were plans to build a "supergun" capable of hitting Israel, designed by an artillery genius named Gerard Bull; he was killed in Brussels, presumably by Israel's Mossad on March 22. Then came the news of smuggling by the Iraqis of special weapons capacitators; of eight Scud launchers located in western Iraq that could hit Tel Aviv; and finally, on April 2, a declaration by Saddam that he had binary chemical weapons: "By God we will make fire eat half of Israel if it tries anything against Iraq."[6]

These statements and evidence of Iraqi embezzlement on the grain credits agitated the State Department sufficiently to conduct a policy review, or at least to argue for one. Under NSC supervision, a study some months earlier had confirmed that the previous "tilt" toward Iraq should continue. This conclusion was not seriously disturbed by the new situation. While the credits were suspended for financial reasons, nothing else was done.

Experience has taught me that so-called policy reviews never come to anything if the attention of the main policymakers and their chief aides is not captured by the problem. Even in the best of times, it requires a herculean effort to consider anything short of the crisis of the day. And in the spring of 1990 the dismantling of the Soviet empire in Eastern Europe, beginning with German reunification, had seized the attention of Washington and the world.

This having been said, the fact remains that the executive and the Congress never signaled Saddam that his misbehavior had a price. Saddam's April speech was denounced by State as "outrageous." But the five senators, led by Minority Leader Bob Dole, who saw Saddam shortly thereafter, adopted a different tone. They were impressed with him, and they told him so. They said that anti-Iraqi sanctions being considered in Congress would be defeated. They sympathized with Saddam's critique of the press. (Saddam, like most dictators, assumed that the U.S. press was government controlled. Two months earlier he had angrily denounced a USIA [United States Information Agency] broadcast about the fall of Romania's tyrant as being too suggestive of advocating his own overthrow.) They left, Senator Dole later recalled, assuring Saddam of U.S. interest in better relations.[7]

The Gulf States were not concerned about Saddam's nationalist rhetoric, all of which they had heard or uttered themselves on previous occasions. They did move on his financial complaints by passing the bill on to the consumers, and on April 17 the Saudis, Kuwaitis, and the UAE decided to lower output in the hope of raising prices. OPEC (Organization of Petroleum Exporting Countries) ratified this strategy in an emergency meeting on May 3, and eventually, on July 10, the price was fixed at $21.50—a $5-a-barrel increase.

Saddam was not satisfied. He began to focus on Kuwait, accusing the emir of waging "economic warfare" against Iraq through overproduction. Then, on July 17, Saddam demanded compensation for a $14 billion drop in revenue, allegedly caused by Kuwaiti cheating—not only overproduction but stealing oil from the Rumaila field, which straddled the border—an act Saddam claimed was part of a broader U.S. conspiracy to cut Iraq down to size. Moreover, for the first time, he threatened military action over the Rumaila issue. More than a division of Iraqi troops began moving toward the border.

The Kuwaitis were alarmed, but not unduly. Iraq had a history of trying to lay its hands on Kuwait when it needed money. The most serious previous threat occurred in 1961, when Kuwait, after gaining independence, renounced its security treaty with Britain. After an Iraqi army assembled to seize Kuwait, the British equivalent of a rapid deployment force was dispatched. The

Iraqis backed off, and the then dictator, Abdul Karim Qassim, humiliated, was killed in a coup eighteen months later.

In 1990, the British were not available. But an "Arab Solution" seemed to be. Just as the Arab states had patched matters up between the two after the 1961 episode, leading to Iraqi recognition of the border and a large Kuwaiti "loan" to Iraq, so some such agreement might be reached this time. As befitted the stakes, President Hosni Mubarak of Egypt and King Fahd Ibn Abdul Aziz of Saudi Arabia lent their personal prestige to the task.

The other Arab state threatened by Iraq, the UAE, went a step further. On July 24, in response to a UAE request, the U.S. navy deployed six combat ships as part of a joint air-refueling exercise with the UAE's small air force. There were no specific U.S. defense treaties with Kuwait or the UAE, but the State Department observed that the United States "remains committed to supporting the individual and collective self-defense of our friends in the Gulf."

The very modest American refueling exercise brought Saddam to conduct one of the more celebrated exchanges in our recent diplomatic history. On July 25 the American ambassador to Iraq, a career officer named April Glaspie, was summoned on one hour's notice for her first interview with Saddam, a man who rarely saw ambassadors at all.

Glaspie was adjudged later to have taken too soft and ingratiating an approach. Whatever the mood music, a careful reading even of the Iraqi version of the interview indicates that Glaspie sent the only message she could send to Saddam: that the United States, especially President Bush, wanted better relations with Iraq and that the United States was disturbed because growing numbers of Iraqi troops were gathering on the Kuwaiti border. And the response was vintage Saddam: He complained about a U.S. conspiracy. But he also delivered what his foreign minister called "good news." As he had told Mubarak, so he would tell Bush: Iraq would not move against Kuwait so long as negotiations were continuing.[8]

Thus, relieved by Saddam's apparent affirmation of the "Arab Solution"—a negotiated fleecing of Kuwait—Glaspie left Baghdad for a long-desired vacation.

The next day, Kuwait agreed at an OPEC meeting in Geneva

to lower its quota once more in support of higher prices—$21.50 a barrel.

Saddam had apparently won. He had forced OPEC and his immediate neighbors into a large price increase based on his need alone; the Americans were not protesting. Now everyone expected the "negotiation" between Kuwait and Iraq to produce a combination of debt cancelation and hard cash for Baghdad.

Saudi Arabia provided the place. In Jidda, on the last day of July, King Fahd of Saudi Arabia urged the Iraqi and the Kuwaiti representatives to settle their differences in a brotherly way that would reflect credit on the Arabs. The Iraqis laid their demands on the table, including the cessation of Kuwaiti pumping from the Rumaila field, the effective control of two Kuwaiti islands at the entrance of the Shatt-al-Arab, a $10 billion compensation for oil pumped from the Rumaila field, and the presence of the emir in Baghdad to agree to the deal. The Kuwaitis refused. Before haggling could begin, the Iraqis walked out.

Now that negotiations were over, Saddam considered himself no longer bound by his pledge of restraint. He had achieved strategic and tactical surprise. Kuwait's armed forces, no match in any case for Iraq, had stood down from alert so as not to "provoke" anything. Washington had been advised by its best Arab friends—President Mubarak, King Fahd, and King Hussein— that in this dance between Kuwait and Iraq it was best to be the wallflower and let the Arabs handle it as they had in the past. On August 1, with U.S. intelligence agencies trying to calculate mathematical probabilities of invasion by the 100,000 troops and 300 tanks now massed at Kuwait's border, the State Department told Iraq's ambassador in Washington that "disputes must be settled peacefully."

Few officials in Washington or elsewhere expected there to be an invasion. Fewer still expected Iraq to seize all of Kuwait, far beyond Saddam's initial territorial demands. But beginning at 2:00 A.M. on Thursday, August 2, Gulf time, the Iraqis swept rapidly through Kuwait, reaching the vicinity of the Saudi border before the day was out. They captured most of Kuwait's Western-supplied military hardware, including two I-Hawk batteries.

A year before, Saddam had personally given the emir of Kuwait Iraq's highest award in gratitude for his help against Iran. Now

Saddam declared that Iraq had intervened to assist a popular uprising against the corrupt emir. A "provisional government" of Kuwaiti "patriots" was announced, but none of its members was named.

---

Saddam's action had confounded Washington's assumptions about his purposes. But what did it mean? What should be done about it? And what could be done about it?

The state seized by Saddam was not exactly an American household word. Kuwait was a small place that had been ruled semi-independently for two centuries by a commercial and trading oligarchy headed by the al-Sabah family. Oil made it a prize, relieved its 600,000 citizens of the need to work, and launched it upon the uncertain course of a nation weak and wealthy.

Kuwait's diplomacy, heavily influenced by a large resident Palestinian population, had not been notably friendly to the United States.

In fact, Kuwait was not very popular in the Arab world or elsewhere. Few of the million foreign workers who did Kuwait's chores and ran its society were allowed the benefits of citizenship. Few of the beneficiaries of Kuwait's largesse abroad felt any gratitude. Saddam had been one, and his seizure of Kuwait was popular in Baghdad. Yassir Arafat of the Palestine Liberation Organization (PLO) had been another. He supported Saddam with vigor and enthusiasm.

Kuwait itself therefore does not explain Bush's reaction to the invasion or his subsequent policy. Nor does oil. Saddam had taken pains to insist that Kuwaiti oil would continue to flow at OPEC's $21 price. So access to Persian Gulf oil was never really at issue.

Instead, it was the fear that Saddam, by seizing Kuwait, had taken a big step toward becoming the dominant Arab power and that this was a very dangerous development. Saddam might use the money from oil (Kuwait's oil doubled Iraq's reserves) to enlarge his military and his capacity to intimidate. Then America's friends and its interests would be at stake.

There was also a sense of what President Bush would call "a defining moment in history." He saw the waning of the Cold War as an opportunity to build a more peaceful world order. Saddam seems to have calculated that in the absence of a Soviet threat

America had no reason to fight for anything in the Gulf—so long as oil continued to flow. If Saddam's reasoning prevailed, then the United States could expect a rash of regional aggressions on the assumption that without the Soviets no vital U.S. interests would ever be at stake.

Finally, Bush, a combat pilot in World War II, was a man shaped by the metaphor of Munich and not of Vietnam. He believed deeply in America's power to do good; he saw in Saddam's aggression not only an obstacle to a better world but a replay of the perennial challenge of evil men to good men everywhere. George Bush would go to war against Saddam because he believed it was the right thing to do.

After an inconclusive NSC meeting on August 2, the president decided to keep a speaking date in Aspen, Colorado, where his subject was America's new defense strategy in a post–Cold War world. There he met British prime minister Margaret Thatcher, who was attending the same conference. The Iron Lady added steel to Bush's instincts. After the war, awarding Thatcher the Medal of Freedom at the White House, Bush would relate that at a crucial early stage of the crisis she had uttered words he would never forget: "Remember, George, this is no time to go wobbly."[9]

There were, in fact, plenty of pressures to go wobbly and to do so early and often. Bush had to reverse his own prolonged policy of seeking accommodation with Saddam. He had to overcome the widespread feeling that he would not go to war because he lacked the will to do so. He also had to face down a decade of American disasters—the shah, Lebanon, Iran-Contra, the Americans still held hostage in Lebanon—in the Middle East. And then there was the legacy of Vietnam—the fear of military quagmire, rising casualties, loss of public support, congressional rebellion. Iraq was not Grenada or Panama, where a quick and easy victory would silence the opposition.

Diplomatically, Bush had to find support among the oil consumers in Europe and Japan, who, although our allies, had rarely followed our lead in the Middle East. Then there were the local states. Their rule of thumb was simple: Let the Americans deter "over the horizon" to protect against a Soviet threat. But in the absence of that threat would they accept U.S. forces?

Bush had to be sure that the Soviet Union was indeed no

threat. Gorbachev was at a very delicate moment, on the eve of adopting the most radical plan yet for *perestroika*. He had just yielded his Eastern European empire by agreeing with Chancellor Helmut Kohl that a unified Germany could become a full member of the North Atlantic Treaty Organization (NATO). How far could he go in condemning Iraq, a longtime Middle East ally? And how long could he associate so closely with U.S. policy in doing so?

There were the economic costs. Opposing Iraq through economic embargo was certain to deny the oil markets Iraqi and Kuwaiti oil—a shortfall of 2–3 million barrels daily. If this could not be made up, the price would skyrocket. The economics of many nations would be badly damaged, with resulting pressure to let up, thereby confirming Saddam in his conquest.

Finally, there was a potential human drama. Hundreds of thousands of foreigners worked in Iraq and Kuwait. Thousands of them were Europeans, and perhaps thirty-eight hundred Americans were in Kuwait. Saddam might make them hostages. What would the United States do?

When the NSC convened, on Friday morning August 3, for its second Gulf session, to discuss all of this, some steps had already been taken. UN Resolution 660, condemning Iraq and demanding immediate, total, and unconditional withdrawal, had passed 14–0. The United States had frozen Iraqi and Kuwaiti assets and imposed a trade embargo. Secretary of State James Baker, who had been in Irkutsk, Soviet Mongolia, on a visit with the Soviet foreign minister, went on to Moscow, where he secured a joint condemnation of Iraq and a freeze on Soviet arms shipments to Saddam.

But the big immediate problem facing the president and his advisers was a straightforward matter of military force. Even to make an embargo against Saddam successful would require acts of war: closing down Saudi and Turkish oil pipelines and enforcing a naval blockade. The Saudis, above all, would be subject to military reprisal. Iraqi troops were already on the border, and not much stood between them and the main Saudi air base on the Gulf side, Dahran. The United States would have to get the Saudis to agree to a major U.S. military presence even if only economic sanctions were to apply.

The upshot of the Friday NSC and successor meetings on Saturday and Sunday was a far-reaching presidential decision: As Bush put it on August 5, "This will not stand—this aggression against Kuwait." The United States moved forward rapidly to secure the broadest international sanctions against Iraq and to deny Saddam the fruits of his victory: the oil and money of Kuwait, the intimidation of his neighbors, and eventually the conquest of Kuwait itself.

---

After a short hesitation, the Saudis agreed to receive Secretary of Defense Dick Cheney on August 6. The king and the royal family were facing the ultimate nightmare: a military challenge to their survival that could be resisted only by accepting a huge Christian army to save them. Cheney brought photographs of the Iraqi forces on the Saudi border; he said the president was ready to send over 100,000 troops; and he told the king that he should not call for American help when it was too late, as the Kuwaitis had done after the invasion began. To American surprise, the king agreed. He and the family had concluded that Saddam was after much more than Kuwait.[10]

Plan 90–1002 contained the Pentagon's strategy for defending Saudi Arabia. The first thing that Gen. P. X. Kelley had done when he was appointed commander of the Rapid Deployment Force in 1980 was to draw up a strategy for defending the key Gulf oil regions. During much of the 1980s, the idea was to defend Iran from a possible Russian grab. With the Cold War over, however, attention shifted to the growing threat to the Arabian Peninsula represented by Saddam Hussein. Throughout the 1980s contingency plans were developed and refined in exercises and in war gaming; as the forces and equipment bought during the Reagan administration buildup were deployed, the contingency plans became more focused and realistic.

By the time the Bush administration came to power, the full Rapid Deployment Force was in place and ready. There were twenty-six prepositioning ships in Diego Garcia, thirty-two modern airfields in Saudi Arabia, and earmarked forces in the army, marine corps, navy, and air force that had been trained extensively in desert warfare. The overall strategy of defense had benefited greatly from the reform debates of the 1980s, in which General Kelley had been a principal participant. The plans were based on using the tremendous advantages of command of the seas and the air to avoid a war of attrition on the ground. Ground forces were configured and trained for maneuver based on fast mobility and combined air, ground, amphibious, and naval operations. The marines were to be the initial heavy forces put in place, with units from Camp Pendleton on the West Coast of the United States and Camp Lejeune on the East Coast being flown to meet the tanks and equipment shipped in the prepositioning ships from Diego Garcia. Initial air superiority would be provided by aircraft carriers and air wings ferried from the United States. A force of about 120,000 was to be the initial operating force, with steady reinforcement from the United States and Europe as the need was required.

It was this plan that was ordered implemented by President Bush in August 1990.

On Wednesday evening, even as U.S. forces were arriving, the president told the American people that America would be defending Saudi Arabia. On the next day, he wrote Congress of his action, stating that the troops were not "in imminent danger of hostilities." This was consistent with the War Powers Resolution and did *not* set that act's clock ticking—it mandated a forty-five-day countdown, after which the Congress had to either support deployment made "in imminent danger of hostilities" or cut off the operation.

But was the president's action consistent with reality? What the administration had most to fear was an attack on U.S. forces before they were ready, an attack Saddam could justify as the Saudis inflicted sanctions on him. Indeed, a month later, on September 16, Bush said publicly that Iraq and the United States were "on the brink of war." Even more telling was an administrative action on September 20 that gave the forces deployed to Saudi Arabia "imminent danger" pay.[11]

It was thus abundantly clear from a very early stage that the president was putting U.S. forces "in harm's way"—even imminent harm's way. Under these conditions, the War Powers Resolution could have either been triggered by a more accurate presidential notification to Congress—obviously not forthcoming—or a congressional debate on the issue. That did not take place. Nor was there any effort in Congress to start the clock. Bush was therefore able to operate in the initial stage of the military buildup quite free of congressional constraint, even though he did not hide his overall objective: Saddam's incursion "will not stand."

———

Immediately following his invasion of Kuwait, Saddam had emphasized that oil would continue to flow, and he promised that his troops would start withdrawing within a few days, once the new government of Kuwait had assumed control. He reiterated the possibility of an "Arab solution" but of course would not even attend an Arab meeting if its purpose was to condemn him.

Within a very few days, much of Saddam's scheme had gone awry. The emir of Kuwait had escaped; Kuwait's $100 billion hoard of foreign assets was beyond Saddam's reach. President Mubarak of Egypt and King Fahd of Saudi Arabia were deeply shocked. They saw in Saddam's actions, King Hussein's defense of Iraq, and Arafat's immediate support for the invasion a vast plot of which they, too, were to be the victims. And they were determined to fight.

After a brief hesitation, Saddam's hated rival President Hafez al-Assad of Syria also joined the opposition, burying decades of anti-Western rhetoric. Iran also denounced Baghdad. And Turkey's president, also overcoming long-settled habits, took his country into the anti-Iraq coalition, closing Iraq's other oil pipeline to its markets.

With his Arab foes and the United States together standing against him, Saddam doubled his bet. If the Arabs would not accept a puppet government in Kuwait, he would annex Kuwait—which he did on August 8, declaring it Iraq's nineteenth province. If the Americans were sending a division to Saudi Arabia, he would increase Iraqi forces in Kuwait by 50,000. And then, on August 9, Saddam sealed Iraq's borders, preventing any foreigners from leaving. They were now "guests."

These actions did not intimidate his Arab opponents. The Arab League, second only to the Organization of American States (OAS) in its famous reluctance to do anything, voted 12–9 on

August 10 to send Arab troops to Saudi Arabia, with Egyptian and Moroccan troops leading the way. Again, Saddam tried to counter the move. He declared a holy war and for the first time "linked" Iraq's seizure of Kuwait with the Syrian presence in Lebanon and Israeli military occupation of Jerusalem, the West Bank, and Gaza. Finally, on August 15, he agreed to meet Iran's conditions for ending the state of war, essentially returning to the original 1975 pact he had torn up ten years before at the cost of hundreds of thousands of Iraqi lives. Iraq was freeing a quarter million soldiers for duty in the south.

Thus, fourteen days after the invasion, the basic lines of struggle were set. In the first phase, from August until November, Iraq would deploy its considerable army to hold Kuwait while enduring a political and economic siege by a growing opposition. Saddam, without ever saying he would withdraw, probed for a price at the expense of the weakest member of the coalition—Kuwait—and the most vulnerable regional political target—Israel. He also upped the ante continuously. He called for the overthrow of King Fahd and President Mubarak. Iraqi forces were increased to maintain a healthy surplus over the allied forces now coming into the region by air, land, and sea. Western hostages were first displayed and then posted to strategic locations, "to deter war," as the Iraqis said. Iraqi "superweapons" were displayed and tested; simultaneously, Saddam's generals constructed a huge, multiple reinforced redoubt around Kuwait that seemed to leave the allies no choice but a bloody frontal assault.

The United States, for its part, would deny Iraq every fruit of its aggression (except its physical occupation of Kuwait) while building up a large military force, supplemented by Arab and European contingents, to defend Saudi Arabia. Washington would try to hold Moscow from responding to any diplomatic openings by Baghdad, and multilateral economic assistance would be used to hold to a minimum any damage to members of the coalition's interests.

Beneath it all, however, lay two very different calculations: (1) on President Bush's part, that Saddam, if faced with a choice of political defeat or military disaster, would choose political defeat; the key problem for Bush was therefore to convince Saddam that he did indeed face that choice—that the threat of war was serious.

(2) And on Saddam's part, that President Bush, if faced with war as the only way to defeat Iraq, would choose a diplomatic solution that allowed Iraq some reward rather than risk great loss of American life. The key problem for Saddam was therefore to convince President Bush that nothing short of a bloody war would defeat him and that a compromise was therefore the Americans' best way out even if Iraq emerged with the advantage.

Saddam proved more persuasive than George Bush—to Saddam's everlasting regret. Saddam seems to have believed that a big force buildup on the part of the United States in Saudi Arabia was a kind of political trap. It would be too big to be tolerated by the Arabs if it did nothing but defend Saudi Arabia, yet it would never be used against him because of the potential casualties and political fallout both in the Middle East and within the United States.

Whatever the Iraqi calculations, the United States was given the opportunity to send the entire Rapid Deployment Force of Central Command to the area. Not too long after the Force had been established in 1980, with a mission headquarters in Tampa, Florida, the late Sen. Scoop Jackson had joked that it was neither rapid nor deployable nor a force. But by the end of the Reagan defense buildup it was a very serious, rapid, and deployable force; five army divisions, two carrier battle groups, three marine brigades, two thousand aircraft—about 20 percent of the entire U.S. military force. It had cost about $40 billion to put in place.

Had Saddam waited a year or two, much would have been different. The end of the Cold War had sharpened the congressional knives, and the defense budget was headed for a free-fall. But he could not wait. With exquisite timing, Saddam chose to challenge the United States while we still had the military created to win the Cold War in place. And then having challenged us, he dug in and gave us time to set up our forces most effectively.

During this period of relative weakness on the ground, the United States deployed formidable diplomatic and economic assets. Within a month, the UN Security Council had authorized economic sanctions and the patrols to enforce them, condemned the hostage taking, declared the annexation of Kuwait null and void, expanded the embargo to include air traffic, and held Iraq liable for damages.

Saudi Arabia and the UAE, eventually with OPEC consent, increased their oil output by over 2 million barrels a day. Once more the oil market responded more to fears of future cutoffs than it did to present supply. From $21 on August 2, the price shot up to $33.63 within six weeks, eventually rising to nearly $40 by late September. It remained in the $28 to $35 range, rising and falling on rumors of war or peace, until finally plummeting to under $20 a barrel on January 18, 1991, two days after the air war began.

A still more remarkable spectacle was what the traveling press called "Operation Tin Cup." On a trip between September 5 and September 13, Secretary of State Baker and other cabinet officers solicited allied financial support to the tune of $16 billion for those members of the coalition in economic need and for the costs of what the Pentagon had called Operation Desert Shield. Turkey, doubly injured by the pipeline closing and the end of the Iraqi imports, was especially anxious. So was Egypt, which soon benefited from U.S. debt cancellation and Saudi cash.

The Saudis and the Kuwaitis were forthcoming. The British and French were contributing troops and some aid, through the energing European Community (EC). Germany put on an odd performance: superb assistance on the ground (especially after November, when the United States decided to move its European armor to the Middle East) but grudging financial aid, an uninformed and at first hostile public opinion, and public foot dragging over NATO's commitment to Turkey. And the Japanese, most dependent on Gulf oil of all, treated the U.S. requests as a kind of trade negotiation with only partial merit on the American side.

Throughout Operation Tin Cup and thereafter, the halls of Congress echoed with complaints that the allies were not doing enough. Having looked away from the issue of "imminent danger" because defending Saudi Arabia seemed popular, Congress positively demanded an erosion of its most valuable power—control of the purse strings. Desert Shield and later Desert Storm would be the first major U.S. war financed largely by contributions from abroad, solicited by the executive and paid into the treasury, with Congress cheering on.

Eventually, it would be claimed that $50 billion of the $65 billion cost of it all would be pledged by the allies.[12] But in the beginning payment seemed slow and done with poor grace. The Gulf War gave definitive proof that we waited too long to call in payments when the burdens of Gulf security should have been shared equitably from the start.

———

In this early phase, Saddam had been unable to arrest the U.S. buildup, the UN political isolation, or the economic embargo. His crude display of hostages backfired, and the Iraqis were soon releasing women and children in the hope of creating a "peace constituency" of families anxious for the safety of their husbands, fathers, and brothers. American public opinion and the U.S. Congress supported President Bush's actions.

Still, the United States faced a fundamental difficulty. The signal it wished to send that the alternative to Iraqi withdrawal was disaster—including military disaster—lacked as yet the military clout to make it credible. It may have lacked the diplomatic clout as well. For much of that depended on whether the unusual U.S.-Soviet partnership would hold and whether the Soviets were indeed determined that Iraq should not profit from its actions.

On September 9, President Bush met President Gorbachev at Helsinki—at the former's request. A joint agreement pledging to reverse Iraqi aggression and containing unconditional demands on Iraq was duly reached. It was designed to erase the impression left by Moscow's proposal of September 4 for a massive international conference to take up all Middle East issues—perilously close to Saddam's own call several weeks earlier.

Despite the stated agreement, at the press conference Gorbachev said something else. President Bush had confessed to Gorbachev that, on principle, the United States had long sought to exclude the USSR from the Middle East, especially the Arab-Israeli peace process. But a new day was possible given Moscow's constructive approach. This position, actually welcomed by the Israelis, if not Mr. Bush's critics at home, was less remarkable than Gorbachev's artful exposition of the Soviet position. He was ready to take up a constructive involvement on all questions. A conference might be useful. But in any event, force was not the proper way to get Saddam out of Kuwait.[13]

This disagreement on the use of force at the summit was aggravated by two confusing events that occurred on either end of it. Secretary Baker had described to Congress on September 4 the potential for a Persian Gulf version of NATO, the implication being a large, permanent U.S. military presence—precisely what the president had told the American people and the Saudis we did *not* want. Then, on September 17, U.S. Air Force chief of staff Gen. Michael Dugan talked about taking the war—if there was one—to "downtown Baghdad." He was sacked forthwith.

What did the Americans really want to do? It fell to French president François Mitterand to clarify this confusion by offering Saddam a specific way out. At the annual convocation of the UN General Assembly on September 24, Mitterand suggested that a definitive Iraqi commitment to withdraw from Kuwait could trigger a "negotiation" that might not be limited to the Kuwaiti issue. Mitterand then left New York and maintained a discreet silence about the meaning of his words. Six days later, Saddam replied, setting preconditions that included no return to the pre–August 2 situation, the withdrawal of all Western forces, and the creation of a Palestinian state. The next day, October 1, President Bush told the United Nations that an Iraqi withdrawal from Kuwait could open new opportunities not only in the Gulf itself but in finding a solution to Arab-Israeli problems.

With oil prices continually falling and expectations of a negotiated settlement rising, the magic words "withdrawal from Kuwait" were still not to be heard from Saddam. Gorbachev tried hard to elicit them. To the disturbance of Foreign Minister Eduard A. Shevardnadze, who was still warning publicly of war, he sent Yvgeny M. Primakov, a long-standing aide who knew Saddam personally, to force the words. He could not.

These diplomatic feelers, which never quite touched, were suddenly overtaken by violence. Already the UN discussions had been disturbed by increasing evidence that the Iraqis were looting Kuwait—right down to its toilets and toilet paper. A surprisingly strong Kuwait resistance was being ruthlessly suppressed. Mrs. Thatcher tried to focus the United Nations on this problem, although it took to the end of October before a resolution could be adopted.

The more disturbing violence came from Jerusalem. Saddam had wanted to shift the entire international focus of discussion from his aggression to what the Arabs considered to be Israeli aggression. His cause was wildly popular among the Palestinians, and the PLO's terrorist capabilities were assumed to be at his disposal. On October 8, a Palestinian counterdemonstration, organized to oppose the claims of a small Jewish group on the Temple Mount, turned into a stone-throwing riot suppressed by Israeli gunfire. Nineteen Palestinians died.

Following a U.S.-led UN Security Council condemnation of Israel for excessive violence, the council was tied up for weeks with the issue. On October 21, a Palestinian killed three Israelis with a knife in Jerusalem as revenge. This cycle of violence redoubled the arguments of those who believed that any American attack on an Arab army would surely ignite popular passions in the region. The Arab governments, however, were careful to distinguish between Israel and the United States, resisting a PLO attempt to get Arab League condemnation of American aid to Israel. The coalition held, even as the "Israeli diplomatic card" was played. It has been said that diplomacy is the art of saying "nice doggie" til you can find a rock. The rock was now almost in reach.

## November Firestorm: The "Offensive Option"

On October 8, the Egyptian and Syrian governments announced that their forces were deploying to defend Saudi Arabia, to free Kuwait, and not to attack Kuwait. That meant more than ever that the military campaign would be a U.S. exercise. Indeed, the president's objective had been to convince Saddam that the use of such force could "not be ruled out."

Aside from the difficulty in coordinating the diplomatic signals, there was the question of military adequacy: While the United States and its allies had been pouring forces into the region, the Iraqis had not been idle. The numbers alone are instructive.

By the end of August, Iraq had 265,000 troops, 1,500 tanks, 1,200 armored personnel carriers, and 800 artillery pieces in place in the Kuwait theater. Against these stood 50,000 U.S. troops, 70 ships, and 300 aircraft. By early October, the Iraqis had deployed 430,000 troops; the U.S., 200,000, plus 30,000 Arab troops, a UK division, and 4,000 Frenchmen. And then, in early November, the United States had 250,000 in place.

The plan, of course, had as its primary objective the defense of

Saudi Arabia. The American-led coalition possessed command of the seas and could achieve early command of the skies, although it was outnumbered by the Iraqis on the ground. But by mid-October, the political judgment in Washington was that Saddam had not gotten the message from the force in place: that is, he still did not believe he faced military disaster if he failed to leave Kuwait.

Ironically, the allied force now in place was quite sufficient to eject Iraq from Kuwait and even to unseat Saddam Hussein from power. But the U.S. military had promoted the idea that Iraq's fifty divisions were seasoned, highly effective combat forces equipped with the most up to date high-tech weapons. This had never in fact been the case. While Iraqi troops had performed well in the static trench warfare of the Iran-Iraq war, they had never demonstrated any real capability in combined-arms warfare. Moreover, it was a foregone conclusion that the U.S. Navy, Marines, and Air Force would establish total air superiority within hours of military action.

There was therefore a large gap between what was really required militarily in the Gulf region and what was necessary to create the image, through the media, of "overwhelming force." There was a danger, however, that deploying a force beyond 250,000 troops would by itself significantly increase the likelihood of heavy casualties.

But President Bush needed time to demonstrate to the United Nations and to his hastily formed coalition that he was going the last mile to find a diplomatic solution, and time, in turn, provided the opportunity to indulge the endless need for more generated by the military bureaucracy. And as the size of the force in the Gulf grew, the seriousness of the intent of the president grew with it.

There were ominous signs that Kuwait itself was being "transformed." After widespread looting and the ruthless suppression of resistance, the Iraqis were encouraging Iraqis to move into Kuwait. Meanwhile, as the diplomacy of the last several weeks had indicated, Saddam was trying to split off from the coalition the French or the Soviets. Given the already proven potential for trouble over the Israeli-Palestinian conflict, managing the coalition was becoming an exhausting, accident-prone exercise.

A rough political-military timetable was also emerging. Winter in the Gulf was the best time to make war. But the winter was short; by late February and March, heavy rains could turn the desert to mud. Dust storms and electrical disturbances could seriously hamper operations, and unruly seas would obstruct any amphibious exercises. Then came the "hajj"—the pilgrimage season in Saudi Arabia, when more than a million Muslims would go to Mecca. It followed that if the United States waited and Saddam delayed, a campaign might have to be delayed through another summer.

Gen. Colin Powell, chairman of the joint chiefs of staff (JCS), his staff, and Gen. Norman H. Schwarzkopf, head of Central Command and the theater commander, did not see the quarter-million-man force as enough. Publicly and privately, additional troops were justified as necessary to assure victory and hold down casualties. There was a further argument that the force was "too light," that is, lacking in the heavy tanks and armor to take on the Iraqis. And finally there was the ever-present desire "to avoid another Vietnam"—not to rely on reinforcement later or the promise that victory would be secured if only another 100,000 men were dispatched.

In August, the idea of 100,000 Americans in Saudi Arabia had taken one's breath away. Yet the president had accepted it, and so had King Fahd. Now, in October, General Powell wanted to double the force, to take America's best armored units from the German plains and its aircraft carriers from the Atlantic and the Pacific. He seemed to want to approximate the approach of the U.S. operation against Panama in 1989: a truly overwhelming force.[14]

The president accepted the plan, no doubt to the surprise of the JCS. On October 29, Secretary of Defense Cheney indicated that more troops would be sent to the Gulf. In anticipation, the headquarters staff for two more corps had already been put in place. Shortly thereafter, on November 4, the Pentagon issued a call-up of reserve combat units, the Congress having extended the call-up time to 360 days.

Secretary of State Baker was dispatched on another exhausting round of consultations, this time to prepare the coalition for the doubling of American troops. Discussions were started on a UN resolution approving the use of force, if necessary. A further $13 billion in aid for countries affected by the crisis was pledged.

Before Baker could return from his mission, however, the president called a sudden press conference, broadcast nationwide, on the afternoon of Thursday, November 8. With little preliminary notice to anyone, President Bush announced the new U.S. deployment, stating categorically that it would give the coalition an "offensive military option." This announcement ignited a major political row within the United States. The coalition may have been ready for an "offensive option," but were the American people? And what about Congress?

Until November 8, Congress had taken a role largely supportive of the president's initiative. Both houses had denounced Iraq, approved of the president's defense of Saudi Arabia, and cooperated on extending reserve call-up authority. The president's assertion on October 30 that the military option was "not imminent" had relaxed Republicans anxious about midterm elections and seemingly forestalled debate over the potential for war, even though the very dispatch of troops and the operation of sanctions could have very easily have involved the United States; Saddam, after all, could have attacked.

Instead, the Democrats had busied themselves with a more enjoyable task: forcing the president reluctantly to agree to raise taxes in order to reach a compromise on a budget. He had done so in violation of a campaign pledge but had failed to secure for the Republicans any spending cuts from the Democrats in exchange. This had been a stunning blow to congressional Republicans, leading many to open revolt against White House leadership. In the November elections, the Republicans lost seats in both Houses, although not in great numbers.

Now Bush's announcement about the Gulf provided the opportunity for Democrats to charge him with warmongering. Leading Democrats accused him of flaunting public opinion and failing to consult Congress. Others claimed that by not rotating the forces in place while calling up reserves, Bush would build the force to the maximum by late January, after which he would have to "use them" or "lose them"—lose the edge because the troops deployed in August would be fatigued for lack of relief and recreation in the austere conditions of Saudi Arabia.[15]

Whatever the condition of the troops, it was open season on George Bush. The Catholic bishops, the National Council of Churches, pundits of many stripes, and the usual anonymous Washington sources argued that the strategy of containment and sanctions would be enough to bring Saddam to his knees. A certain rhetorical bumbling hurt the administration: The president favored impromptu press exchanges rather than formal speeches, and in these forums he justified the buildup on moral, political, and economic grounds but never with oratorical fervor or carefully explained reasoning. On November 13, Secretary Baker intoned that U.S. jobs were at stake, occasioning a memorable Herblock cartoon depicting "Baker of Arabia" urging the unemployed to follow his camel into the desert. The next day, Bush met with the bipartisan congressional leaders and was berated about Congress's right to declare war. He whipped out a copy of the Constitution and told them he understood that, but "it also says that I'm the commander-in-chief." But in the meeting he averted the calling of a special session by assuring them that he would consult Congress before using force—but he did not say that he would seek their authorization.[16]

These embarrassments were exploited by Saddam when he announced, on November 18, a staged release of *all* hostages to be completed by March 25 if nothing "mars the atmosphere of peace." Then, the next day, he called up another 250,000 men to offset U.S. reinforcements. A swirl of rumors suggested that Iraq was suffering seriously from the sanctions, although little evidence could be seen by those reporters allowed by the Iraqis to inspect the Baghdad markets.

Where was public opinion? Although in the wake of November's confusion Bush's personal approval ratings on the Gulf had slipped to nearly 50 percent, there was an underlying and astonishing consistency to the polls: Approval for the use of force to free civilian hostages *always* exceeded 60 percent. The same number supported the dispatch of American forces to the Gulf. While opinion on when to use force varied, 54–65 percent always supported the *eventual* use of force. The real kicker, however, was this: In mid-November, an ABC/*Washington Post* poll found that while the president had lost twenty percentage points of approval, as Americans questioned his explanation for his actions,

59 percent still supported him. Of the 36 percent who disapproved of his actions, nearly half disapproved because he was moving too slowly against Iraq![17]

## The President and Congress

On Thanksgiving Day, President Bush visited the troops in Saudi Arabia. His speech to them offered a long-sought-after, coherent explanation of events, justifying briefly but cogently that freedom was at stake, as was economic security, and that innocent lives hung in the balance. The threat of Saddam's nuclear potential was invoked, and in contrast to UN presentation the month before, the president reiterated what his secretary of state had been saying publicly and privately: There would be no linkage, no deals rewarding aggression, only unconditional withdrawal by Iraq.

Yet there was a heavy blow that day. British prime minister Thatcher resigned, forced out by a party revolt that was both sudden and shocking. Only two weeks before she had delivered in Parliament the clear signal that President Bush was trying so hard and so ineffectively to send: ". . . either [Saddam] gets out of Kuwait soon, or we and our allies will remove him by force."[18] One of her final acts while in power was to dispatch another 14,000 British troops to the Gulf, lifting the total to 30,000. Her successor, John Major, swiftly reaffirmed Thatcher's policy on the Gulf.

As Secretary of State Baker labored skillfully to rally international support behind a UN resolution on the use of force, the president's policy was subjected to withering scrutiny by congressional Democrats. Congress had already gone into recess before the elections in early November. On November 14, seeking to redeem the faltering of congressional support created by his announcement of a possible offensive action, Bush asked the leaders of Congress to convene a special session for the purpose of debating his war aims—if he could be assured that Congress would support him. Both Sen. Edward Kennedy and Sen. Richard Lugar had called for such a session, each for different ends. But the Democratic leadership refused, saying that hearings would have to be held first. The initial hearings would be run by Sen. Sam Nunn, chairman of the Armed Services Committee, who had suddenly surfaced as a leading *opponent* of the "offensive option."

Nunn was usually accused by his liberal colleagues of excessive support for the military. In this case, he adroitly adopted Pentagon and JCS cautions, reflected in the request for more troops, to the political realities of the Democratic party. Some Democrats were opposed to the use of force altogether, being either pacifists by conviction or fearful of the legacy of Vietnam. Others, like Nunn, were convinced that the strategy of containment and sanctions should be pursued for a longer, unspecified period, and that the president was moving too fast. All were agreed that *Congress* held the power under the Constitution to authorize war. By emphasizing the need to wait on purely pragmatic grounds, Nunn gave the Democrats a welcome credibility on the issue without forcing the party as a whole to decide the metaphysical issue of whether American military power should be used under any circumstances.

Nunn's hearings began on November 28. The administration refused to send its top witnesses first because it feared the impact of the hearings on UN discussions, then coming to their head, on a resolution authorizing force. In effect, the president was making it clear that he thought UN authorization for war more valuable than congressional approval of his actions. Yet this delaying tactic gave critics of his military policy a field day, and they were powerful and serious. Former Secretary of Defense James Schlesinger supported sanctions, and he had a reputation as a "hawk." Former JCS Chairman Adm. William Crowe led off the military testimony. Although he would later recant his position, on that occasion he was certain that sanctions would work and that any alternative was unwise and could cost American lives. Gen. David Jones, another former JCS chairman, agreed. Cap Weinberger, true to his often stated principle of never using U.S. force unless every other option had failed, emphasized the political risk of the Arab uprising that might come in the wake of war. Henry Kissinger alone spoke of the costs of delay, supporting the president. Others favored the half measure, an "air war only," despite the fact that this might not be enough to drive Iraq out of Kuwait.[19]

The hearings contributed to the development of an astonishing situation. For on November 29, after a final feverish full-court press by both President Bush and Secretary of State Baker, the UN Security Council accepted the American reasoning that Saddam was not taking UN warnings seriously enough. UN Resolution 678 now authorized members to use "all necessary means" to enforce earlier resolutions if Iraq did not leave Kuwait by January 15, 1991. Thus, the American buildup of military might and the UN authority to use it were in tandem. At the Soviets' insistence, a six-week "pause for peace" had been given to Saddam so that, in Moscow's view, a final round of diplomacy could take place.

But at this very moment, the Nunn hearings were giving the world and Saddam—an avid watcher of CNN—the distinct impression that the president in seemingly inverse proportion to his support abroad, lacked the support he vitally needed at home.

President Bush's abrupt announcement of November 8 that he might use the "offensive option" had ignited a congressional fire that now threatened to burn out of control. The day after the successful UN vote, Friday morning, November 30, the president moved abruptly to put this fire out. Reportedly adopting an idea put forth by the secretary of state, he proposed an exchange of visits—Secretary of State Baker would go to Baghdad, and Iraqi foreign minister Tariq Aziz would come to Washington—in the hope of persuading Saddam to relinquish Kuwait.[20] The idea, as Bush explained it, was to go the last mile, to "have Baker look him in the eye," to convince Saddam of how serious a situation he faced.

———

The president's sudden willingness to open direct high-level contact with the Iraqis met with great approval from his Democratic critics, which was reflected in public opinion polls. But at a meeting with congressional leaders on November 30, Bush's requests for an expression of support for Baker's mission and the UN resolution were parried by the Democrats, who said that the president should "take the initiative" in asking Congress for support *after* the results of Baker's talks. They insisted that offensive action *must* be approved by Congress. On this the president did not agree. In his opinion, his right as commander in chief allowed him the tactical decision of *when* to take the offensive.[21] Like Presidents Johnson and Nixon, Bush believed that however vague his authority to actually send forces abroad, once they were there, his powers as commander in chief covered whatever course of action he decided for them, without any need for Congress to approve or disapprove.

Another point arose. House Minority Leader Robert H. Michel warned that if the president should delay the use of force in favor of sanctions, the crisis might still be on as the 1992 presidential campaign season began. Could there be a pledge by the Democrats not to attack the president on foreign and domestic policy if troops were still in the desert? This, too, the Democrats parried. Why couldn't the president defend himself by noting that he was following a Democratic policy, that is, letting the sanctions work?[22] The exchange had an element of farce. The reality was that if the president followed Senator Nunn's advice to avoid force and let sanctions work for a year or two, the 1992 election would find Saddam still in Kuwait, a half million Americans still in Saudi Arabia, the economy in shambles, and the Democratic candidate—perhaps Nunn himself—brutalizing the president for inaction. Unlike some of his top advisers, the president saw this eventuality clearly. He knew that sanctions would take longer to succeed than political support could last.

The suggestion of November 30 had failed to achieve its immediate purpose. The Democrats would not support the president if he used force. The atmosphere had changed, but not the Democrats. Meanwhile, the coalition had been shaken as never before. For what Bush seemed to be proposing was a negotiated outcome that inevitably meant compromise—something for Saddam. This was the very situation American diplomacy, closely allied with Saudi and Egyptian positions, had sought to avoid. Worst of all, the initiative suggested that Bush's domestic support was too weak to support a big, costly conflict, and therefore Baker the deal maker was coming to Baghdad to work out the compromise.

Thus encouraged, Saddam set about to exploit the opportunity President Bush had seemingly supplied him. The Algerian president, Chadli Bendjedid, had been waiting to help launch an "Arab solution." He was now encouraged to open a separate channel to the Saudis, who would not want to be caught late coming to a deal. Saddam was also determined to show that President Bush's proposal really did mean compromise. So as he whiled the time away releasing groups of hostages to an assortment of intermediary nations, he also indicated that Secretary Baker would not be welcome before January 13—two days ahead of the UN deadline.

The White House and State Department seized the chance to abort the initiative. No negotiations were intended, they said, and certainly not on January 13. Instead, the secretary of state was to deliver this "message": Withdraw peacefully from Kuwait or run the risk of being thrown out. Thanks to Saddam's inept response to the U.S. advance, the United States was able to evade the coalition-shaking consequences of what appeared to be an offer to negotiate a compromise. Reinforced by this fresh evidence of American resolve, on December 14 the Saudis rejected an "Arab solution" by refusing to meet with Bendjedid.

Far more important for relations between the White House and Congress, however, was the continued doubt over when the military would be ready. Cheney and Powell both got their chance before Nunn's committee on December 3, and both assaulted the sanctions argument. No one could say when sanctions might finally work or at what point the United States should conclude they hadn't worked. In the meantime, U.S. forces would be sentenced to an indefinite stay in the desert and the Gulf. Waiting now could turn into inaction later, and yet, as the vice-president, Dan Quayle, said, "A moral price" would be paid as Kuwait disappeared into Iraq and the Iraqis grew better prepared. This was a theme both the president and secretary of state reiterated. It was amplified by a Central Intelligence Agency (CIA) judgment that sanctions, while effective in disrupting the Iraqi economy, would not seriously impede Iraq's war machine for at least nine months.[23]

Colin Powell took the argument a step further. He said that if the decision were made for war, U.S. strategy would include a ground attack. An assault by air power alone could not guarantee victory, and there was no point in starting a war that did not provide for certain victory.[24]

These assertions reinforced the Democrats' belief that the administration was bent on a bloody ground war, and soon. On December 4, the House Democratic Caucus therefore insisted that Congress must give "affirmative approval" before any U.S. attack. Democratic members of the Senate Foreign Relations Committee accused the administration of rushing to war. But the heaviest blows against the president's effort to keep the pressure on Saddam kept coming from the U.S. military. On December 14, Powell told the House Armed Services Committee that it might be late February before U.S. forces were ready. And General Schwarzkopf allowed two days later that the war with Iraq might last more than six months. Finally, on December 19, Schwarzkopf's deputy, Lt. Gen. Calvin Waller, said that the army would not be combat ready until early or middle February.[25]

The president was now engaged in political war on multiple fronts, and the message from each front suggested that the January 15 deadline could not be seriously enforced—the United States and its allies would not be ready to attack, or so the U.S. military suggested, and a long and bloody ground war seemed inevitable if war were to occur at all. Congressional Democrats, the majority of whom did not want to use force at all, had rallied behind the seemingly pragmatic position taken by Senator Nunn: Wait for sanctions to work.

Then, on December 20, Soviet foreign minister Eduard Shevardnadze resigned, warning of an imminent Soviet dictatorship by Gorbachev or "someone else." Gorbachev, together with Shevardnadze's successor, a Soviet Foreign Ministry professional, Alexandr Bessmertnykh, hastened to assure Washington that Soviet Gulf policy had not changed. Nonetheless, the departure of the Soviet foreign minister, like the loss of Thatcher, revived hope in Baghdad that the American position had been weakened.

Partly to offset the impact of these developments, the president began to use strong language. "If we get into an armed situation, he's going to get his ass kicked!" was Bush's analysis on December 20.[26] Cheney, in the Gulf, told the troops three days later that the "days are drawing closer when we may be forced to resort to military force."[27]

The lame-duck 101st Congress had adjourned for good at a controversial time, with members variously complaining about the cost of the prolonged crisis, the allies' uncertain willingness to pay their share, and the president's threatening language. But nonetheless Saddam's continued rampage in Kuwait, together with his obvious demands for diplomatic gratification and his threats against all and sundry, made him an ally of the president in his demand for congressional support. The president had been talked out of a special session in November because his advisers assured him that he might lose. Now the question was whether winning by only a small margin would really be a defeat.

———

Congress may not have been prepared to ratify the president's position on the use of force before its adjournment, but individual members were still willing—and able—to undercut the threat of force. Sen. Robert Dole, the Republican leader, irritated at what he thought was a petty disagreement over dates, phoned the Iraqi ambassador in Washington to find out whether there was flexibility; there might be, he was told. Two days later, on Sunday, December 30, he declared that the "American people aren't quite there yet . . . not yet committed to war."[28] On the same day, House Armed Services Committee chairman Les Aspin saw the logic of the situation leading inevitably to war; he stressed the need for diplomacy, not dates or deadlines. And Rep. Lee Hamilton, another key Democrat and chairman of the House Foreign Affairs Subcommittee on the Middle East, said of Dole's pronouncement: "right on target."[29] It is interesting to note that all these comments were solicited and disseminated via television, which facilitated a kind of congressional debate perhaps impossible to sustain within the houses of the legislature.

In effect, key members of Congress of both parties were urging the administration to take up the Baker mission once more, even at the risk of undercutting the president's emphasis on the threat of force. The logic here was the same that underpinned Bush's original motive—solidifying public opinion and dispelling the idea that the president wanted war. The inherent contradiction of also signaling Saddam that President Bush lacked domestic support for war proved of secondary concern, even though it meant that Baker's leverage was basically impaired. And oddly enough, it was perhaps this very signal that led Saddam to renew the negotiations over dates. By January 3, 1991, when Congress reconvened, the rendezvous was set: Baker and Aziz were to meet in Geneva on January 9.

Until Baker met Aziz, there had been no formal debate in Congress over the Gulf policy. Now, as the newly elected 102nd Congress met, they resolved to keep it in session but not to debate.

George Mitchell and Foley, opposed as they were to going to war, were also determined to avoid any blame for undercutting Baker with a formal debate. Instead, they would keep quiet in the Capitol while individual congressmen were free to say what they wanted outside the chambers. Only on the issue of the clear necessity to obtain congressional permission to start an offensive would they be loud and clear.

Thus continued the congressional pattern of evading the issue. Troops in the Gulf were not on a picnic; in theory the war powers clock should have begun to tick the moment it was clear that "hostilities" might be "imminent." It could have been argued that such a condition existed almost from the beginning of deployment back in August; certainly the Pentagon had treated it that way. But Congress refused to wind the clock, and the president would not do so unless he knew it would tick his way.

This limbo was of the Hill's own making, for a debate could have been held at any time after August. Yet it was not, the Democratic leaders having decided that the soon-to-be-disbanded 101st Congress should not debate the authorization of war. As for President Bush, he never indicated at any time that he felt legally bound to get congressional permission to act. His discussions with congressional leaders, whether on November 14, November 30, or later in January, both before Baker's mission and after it, derived solely from his view of their political prudence rather than their legal necessity. He wanted to signal to Saddam that as president and commander in chief, he had the nation's full support and that he would make war with as full support as possible. But George Bush, a man disturbed by congressional inroads on presidential prerogative and quick to use his veto power, had no intention of coming this far, only to let the Democrats determine the outcome. That was political reality.

The majority in Congress did not want war, did not want to obstruct one if necessary, and certainly did not want to look like an ally of Saddam's in the process. The safest course was to line up behind the Nunn position: Let's be tough but let the sanctions do the job. The Democrats therefore took their ironic stand: Not a decision to declare war itself, for none was asked, but a decision on whether the United States should "take the offensive"—a tactical issue that reasonably belonged to the commander in chief even if the power to decide to go to war did not. It was a position that appeared increasingly to give all of the game to Saddam unless negotiations started—which even then might give much of the game to Saddam!

Thus, contrary to the administration's hope, the Baker mission would indeed trigger congressional action, but not of a kind likely to improve the secretary's leverage in convincing Saddam that America was serious.

Henry Hyde, the articulate Republican conservative from Illinois, caught this dilemma in a handwritten note he passed to Secretary Baker: "You'll never get the affirmative you want from Congress unless your mission to Baghdad fails—and I pray to God it doesn't!"

Failure meant, of course, that Saddam would refuse to leave Kuwait. Did success, however, mean a departure with the advantage for Iraq? In advance of the January 9 meeting with Baker, the Iraqis played their old game: hinting at settlement possibilities if only the Israelis would be forced to pay a diplomatic price and the Kuwaitis a territorial and financial price.

The Baker-Aziz meeting, held in a Geneva hotel, lasted much longer than expected, but not because either party's positions were changed. Baker handed Aziz a letter from President Bush for Saddam that "informed" Saddam of the consequences of refusing to withdraw when the "pause of good will" ended on January 15.[30] Aziz read the letter and refused to accept it; it was "incompatible" with the dignity of his president. The "discussion" was composed largely of statements by both sides of their respective positions—at great length. But Baker noted and later publicized one fact: Aziz never mentioned Kuwait or withdrawal.

In Washington, before the ceremonial opening of the new Congress, President Bush had asked the congressional leaders once more, on January 3, whether he could expect a resolution of support. Again, no guarantees were offered. On January 7, the debate over the Gulf finally began. A day later, meeting with his advisers and lawyers on January 8, the president reviewed his prerogatives. Both he and various congressional leaders had been sloppy under the pressure of events: The president at one time said that sending young Americans to war was an agonizing decision that should only be asked of the president. Foley and

Mitchell had declared later that war needed the permission of Congress.[31] All were wrong.

The truth, of course, is that making war was a shared power. In practice, a formal declaration of war had been made on five occasions, each time after the war in question had already started. Yet the real power of Congress was one not of declaration but of the purse. The president's real power was that of strategy and tactics, not of declaration itself. In short, a war could occur without a declaration (as had happened many times in two hundred years), but it could not be fought if Congress refused to supply the funds for it.

Reportedly, Secretary of Defense Cheney, among administration officials the only veteran of Congress aside from the president himself, opposed asking Congress for a resolution of support for "all possible means."[32] He argued that if the president in fact got it, it would not guarantee later support if the war went badly; if he did not get it, he would be badly hurt already for lack of support. The only reason to seek it, therefore, would not be constitutional but political.

The president decided to take the risk, and his letter asking Congress for a resolution of support was basically a political act. To make that quite clear, on January 9, the day after he sent the letter, Bush said he did not need congressional authorization to act in support of the UN resolutions.[33] There were grounds for arguing that in fact the United States and its coalition partners were *already* at war with Iraq: Sanctions and blockades were acts of war; the American troops in Saudi Arabia, the U.S. Navy, or our aircraft could have been under attack from the day they arrived; an ultimatum had been served up by the United Nations. And, of course, the president could always have done just what the War Powers Resolution required: He could have written to Congress a letter stating that U.S. forces were in danger of imminent hostilities, fought the war, and then forty-five days later, waited for Congress to approve or disapprove his actions. Administration lobbyists relied heavily on the Truman precedent in Korea, smugly quoting the Democratic leaders in Congress in 1950, avowing that their Democratic president needed no authority from Congress to take military action.

Perhaps fearful of just such a tangle, fifty-six members of Congress, led by Ron Dellums, Democrat from California, had attempted to involve the third branch of the federal government in making war through a lawsuit. The basis of the suit was that the president's announcement of November 8 of "an offensive option" and the pattern of his actions created a "controversy" that demanded a court injunction to forestall presidential use of offensive force without congressional consent.[34]

In 1987, at the time of the reflagging of Kuwaiti ships in the Gulf, a similar suit, intended to prevent the president from ignoring the War Powers Act by failing to give notification to Congress of "imminent hostilities," had been rejected by a federal district court. That court cited diplomatic grounds—"the potentiality of embarrassment from multifarious pronouncements from various departments on one question." Now the administration argued against the Dellums suit on similar grounds of tactical interference with presidential prerogative. But this time the court acknowledged the justice of the congressional position—that the president's acts were preparing for an offensive military action properly described as "war making." And then the court concluded: ". . . it is therefore clear that Congressional approval is required if Congress desires to become involved." Here lay the rub: "It is only if a majority of the Congress seeks relief from an infringement on its constitutional war-declaration power that it may be entitled to receive it."[35] Of course, if a majority of Congress could demand an injunction from the Court, it could obviously take the more expeditious route of simply denying the president the money to act. In fact, nearly every one of the fifty-six plaintiffs voted in favor of a bill earmarking $2 billion specifically for Operation Desert Shield.

Thus, once again the courts avoided getting between the other two branches in allocating war powers.

———

The truly political element of the January debate was essentially how far the president could split the Democrats. Bush would be pressing the ideological fault line of a Democratic party still unable to reconcile its traditional military assertiveness with its newer McGovernite heresies. But the president also had to know that a substantial number of Democrats wanted to exorcise the political ghost of Vietnam as much as General Powell and others wanted to banish those same military demons. The president, in any case, was determined to do so, and he judged finally that Congress would not deny him support in a just cause.

Bush also benefited from two of the more powerful lobbyists of Congress: the Saudi ambassador Prince Bandar Ibn Sultan and AIPAC (The American Israel Public Affairs Committee), the Israeli lobby. Saddam's threats had brought Saudi Arabia and Israel together in a tacit alliance. Despite intense friction over the deaths of the Palestinians in Jerusalem and the subsequent UN condemnations, President Bush and Israeli prime minister Yitzhak Shamir had reached agreement that Israel would not make a preemptive strike against Iraq even though Iraq had made plain its intention to strike the Jewish state. A special communications line and information-sharing arrangement, together with an American pledge to intercept Iraqi Scuds aimed at Israel, had sealed the bargain.[36]

The debate in Congress did not finally revolve around the question of prerogatives; this issue had been diffused partly by the president's very decision to ask for support. A declaration of war was also not sought in the formal sense. It was simply a debate over whether Congress would support a possible war set to take place after January 15—the timing and tactics of which war making was left up to the president.

The Democrats, rallying around Senator Nunn's position, had fixed on an issue that did not appear to be constitutional but rather tactical. Should an offensive be authorized if necessary, or should the president be bound to a "contain and sanctions" strategy? The downside of this apparently reasonable approach now became obvious. It had been advanced in November as an easy way to beat Saddam without war. Now, sixty days later, Saddam was still defiant, and there was no evidence that sanctions were working. Would U.S. troops sit in the desert indefinitely, or would Congress itself set a deadline—obviously different from that set by the United Nations? The Nunn position therefore began to look like a bit of micromanagement at the expense of the troops, the president, and the United Nations.

Three resolutions were offered. The one supporting the president gave him authority to use force in support of the UN resolution once he formally notified Congress of his determination that

49

no other course would work. The other two resolutions were variants of the Nunn proposal: authorizing force to support the embargo, protect Saudi Arabia, and defend U.S. personnel while at the same time advising the president, nevertheless, that "sanction and contain" was the "wisest course."

The debate itself was in both houses free of partisan rancor. There was an unfortunate incident when the House leadership discovered that the House Committee on Foreign Affairs had a majority in favor of reporting out only the resolution supporting the president. A parliamentary and very partisan maneuver was required to get the opposing resolution onto the floor. Afterward, however, the debaters were careful to speak and to vote according to conscience, rather than party.

Speaker Foley spoke against the president, citing earlier and disastrous military experiences in Lebanon. He called the authorizing resolution "a virtual declaration of war," but he also declared that after the vote ". . . we are Americans here, not Democrats and not Republicans, all anxious to do the best for our country. . . ." Rep. Ted Weiss of New York wanted to reassert congressional constitutional authority by denying the president authority to pick the time and place of war—"the people make that decision"—evidently identifying Congress, rather than the president, with the people.

In the Senate, the newest senator, Paul Wellstone of Minnesota, gloried in his 1960s-era convictions, concluding finally that beyond all reason, his heart told him a decision for war was wrong. Less emotionally, Sen. Daniel Inouye, a World War II hero, advised the president that restraint and redoubled diplomatic efforts were signs of strength, not weakness. Sen. Robert Byrd, too, declared: "A superpower doesn't have to feel rushed." He criticized U.S. allies harshly for not doing enough: "It's a monstrous disgrace. . . ."

The president's supporters also offered a range of reasons. In the House, Rep. Bud Shuster reminded his colleagues of Saddam's chemical and nuclear programs, advising them that waiting, too, had its price if a war was ultimately necessary. Senator Dole asked: "Do we save lives by waiting six months or waiting a year?" Congress had been "AWOL," he said; the debate was late, and Congress was in danger of being only a spoiler of the president's strategy; constitutional prerogatives could not be invoked after they had been deliberately neglected. Dole said a vote in favor of authorizing force would give the president needed last-minute leverage to bring Saddam around.

Sen. Alfonse D'Amato excoriated the indefinite time already granted to Saddam and forecast more aggression later when it would be harder to stop. He could not understand how some supporters of Israel could fail to support the president when Prime Minister Shamir had made clear Israel's own support of the president's policy.

Among the Democrats, Sen. Charles Robb, a Vietnam veteran (and the son-in-law of Lyndon Johnson), endorsed the "rational actor theory" to support his vote for the president: ". . . if Saddam Hussein understands that we have not only the capability but the will to carry out such an attack if necessary, maybe he'll act rationally. . . ." Sen. Albert Gore confessed to an "excruciating" internal debate that left him of two minds. Yet in the end he also chose the argument of time; the United States could not simply ignore the UN deadline and then decide on another at some point later—especially given the unimpressive results of the Baker-Aziz meeting. It fell to Sen. Robert Graham of Florida to endorse the president's position for a reason not heard since before Vietnam: ". . . I believe that the president of the United States deserves to have presumption of correctness of his actions and that he especially deserves to have a prescription of correctness as it relates to matters of our national security and relations with other nations."[37]

On January 12, Congress voted to support the president. The administration had won, 250–182 in the House; 164 Republicans and 86 Democrats against 179 Democrats and 3 Republicans. It was much closer in the Senate: 52–47, with 43 Republicans joined by 9 Democrats against 45 Democrats and 2 Republicans. The president praised Congress for its debate and its vote. And he concluded that war was not inevitable but that Saddam must leave Kuwait without expectation of face-saving compromise or reward: "Let there be no mistake: peace is everyone's goal, peace is in everyone's prayers. But it is for Iraq to decide."

On January 14, the president signed the joint resolution authorizing him to go to war. There might still be political divisions over the wisdom of his course, but George Bush would face no uprising over constitutional prerogatives. With Saddam's assistance, he had made his case on the Hill, and he had won it. Desert Storm would soon begin.

At midnight January 15, the UN deadline expired. There was no sign of any change in Iraqi policy. Forty-eight hours later, at 2:30 A.M., January 17, the USS *Wisconsin* launched the first Tomahawk cruise missiles targeted against downtown Baghdad. At the same time, hundreds of U.S. and Allied aircraft began sorties against command-and-control centers of the air defense system of Iraq and to hit chemical and nuclear-weapons targets and fixed Scud launchers. The first phase of the air war had begun. The plan being executed involved destroying Iraq's air force and to undo systematically its ability to defend itself against the sustained air attack to follow. Averaging more than two thousand sorties a day between January 17 and February 23, the air attacks shifted away from the Iraqi air force and its equipment when it soon became apparent that the air force had been grounded or destroyed. Somewhat later, sorties were able to shift away from the rollback of Iraq's integrated air defenses and concentrate attacks on the infrastructure of the nation—its bridges, power plants, etc., supporting the forces in Kuwait. By the third week of the war much of the weight of the air interdiction was shifting toward dismantling Iraqi forces in Kuwait itself and against the positions of the vaunted Republican Guard held in reserve within Iraq. In addition, a great many sorties were directed to finding the mobile Scud units that continued to fire on Israel and Saudi Arabia, offering the only real war making Saddam was able to achieve.

Some 290 Tomahawk missiles were fired—from the battleships *Wisconsin* and *Missouri*, several Aegis cruisers, and two submarines—at high-value pinpoint targets in Baghdad and elsewhere in Iraq. The battleships also began to direct withering fire against the dug-in defense along the coast of Kuwait. Their sixteen-inch guns were able to engage targets more than twenty miles inland with 2,700-pound high-explosive shells delivered with pinpoint accuracy, thanks to the Pioneer drones that operated from the battleships to provide spotting.

At 4:00 A.M. on February 24 the ground offensive began with

an attack into Kuwait by two marine divisions led by a reserve battalion and accompanied by Saudi armored units. At the same time, the Eighteenth Airborne Corps and the Seventh Armored Corps conducted a huge flanking movement into Iraq. There were very light casualties, and over ten thousand Iraqi POWs were taken in the first twenty-four hours. The rapid advance led General Schwarzkopf to launch ahead of schedule further direct attacks by U.S. and UK armored units.

On February 25 and 26, with French and allied airborne units guarding the flank, allied armor turned eastward to strike Iraq's Republican Guards. The U.S. forces in Kuwait mopped up the crumbling Iraqi defenses while the U.S. division raced toward the Euphrates to block any escape by the Republican Guards.

On February 27, allied armor pressed their attack eastward on the Republican Guard divisions in northern Kuwait and southeast Iraq. Arab forces and the U.S. Marines took Kuwait City. At 5:00 A.M. Gulf time on the twenty-eight, President Bush declared that Kuwait was liberated and Iraq defeated and that the allied forces would suspend combat operations, 100 hours after the ground campaign had begun. At 0800 Gulf time, allied forces suspended all military operations. At the same time, Iraq delivered a letter to the United Nations saying it would accept all twelve United Nations resolutions passed the previous summer.[38]

## Lessons Learned

Desert Storm drove the final nail into the War Powers Resolution. After the president put forces in harm's way in August, the sixty-day cutoff required by the resolution came and went twice with neither branch paying any heed.

In the early months it was clear that a majority in Congress opposed military action, while the president was determined for it. The president claimed (largely on the Truman precedent of 1950) that he needed no authorization to go to war. In the end, the president dominated the outcome when Congress backed down and passed a resolution approving the use of force. They did so because they felt the pressure of strong public support for military action. Had it been otherwise, they could have blocked military action by including in the 1991 appropriation the words "no funds in this or any other act shall be used . . . etc." It was an almost perfect case study in how a government of divided and shared powers goes to war. It was an excellent case study also of how well the president, Congress, the press, and the public performed in providing for the common defense in the decade preceding Desert Storm. Some inescapable lessons emerge.

The first military lesson of the war is that military people must come first, equipment second. The success of Desert Storm was the success of the all-volunteer force. The quality of the people involved in Desert Storm was the highest of any military force ever deployed by the United States.

In 1980 the all-volunteer force was a failure. Political leaders of both parties were calling for a return of the draft, so poor was the performance, morale, and quality of the people in our armed forces nearly a decade after becoming all volunteer. But that year marked the beginning of a dramatic recovery, led in this case by Congress against the opposition of the executive branch. Opposed by the Carter administration, the Nunn-Warner pay raise and package of quality-of-life improvements boosted compensation by nearly 11 percent after years of frozen pay during double-digit inflation. In the next two years, the Reagan administration added successive raises in pay above inflation and thereafter kept military pay ahead of erosion from inflation. The bipartisan enthusiasm for the Reagan-led military buildup gave a tremendous boost to morale and produced a surge in military recruiting that almost swamped the system. Within a year it became highly competitive to be accepted into the enlisted ranks of all of the services. (Over 95 percent were now high school graduates.) The service academies suddenly became the most competitive and sought after undergraduate institutions in the country. This transformation began at the initiative of Congress, and while the executive branch of the Reagan administration became its enthusiastic champion, many of the more imaginative initiatives, like the Montgomery GI bill, continued to originate from congressional leaders.

The next most important lesson was the success of a new generation of strategy and high-tech tactical training. In the early 1980s the executive branch began a major upgrading of high-tech training facilities in each of the services. The army put almost $1 billion into the National Training Center at Fort Irwin; the air force computerized dogfighting and tactical training ranges at Nellis Air Force base and elsewhere around the country. The Navy Department put hundreds of millions of dollars into marine training ranges at Twenty-nine Palms, California, Yuma, Arizona, and the Navy Strike Warfare Center at Fallon, Nevada. At all of these ranges an environment was created that enabled combined service forces to train and fight in the most realistic environments, with every move and every weapon firing recorded and validated. The result was the elimination of uncertainty about which tactics worked and how to use them in effective strategies.

Throughout the 1980s there was a strong faction in Congress, led by a group called the Military Reform Caucus, that opposed the Reagan administration's emphasis on high-tech weapons rather than smaller, simpler, cheaper systems. The leadership of the Reagan Pentagon believed that it was far better to use the inherent advantages of American technological innovation and smart, high-quality, high-tech people to counter the ability of totalitarian regimes to field larger forces of cannon fodder and to accept attrition rates totally unacceptable in a democracy. It is far better in the Reagan view to spend extra money than extra lives. While it is true that the F-15E, for instance, costs about four times what the simpler, cheaper MiGs and Mirages in the Iraqi force had cost and the American M-1 tank about five times what the Russian M-60 of the Iraqi army costs, the results certainly showed the wisdom of the high-tech emphasis of the American forces: Expensive weapons, sometimes enormously expensive, were used to enable the conduct of a battle with a casualty ratio of 1:1,000. Ironically, it was the very high-tech weapons opposed by the military reformers that made possible the use of highly mobile and innovative maneuver warfare tactics that they had to their credit advocated throughout the 1980s. It was doubly ironic that the weapons that the American media ridiculed during the 1980s as wasteful and unworkable—the M-1, the Patriot, Maverick, Tow, Harm and Hellfire missiles, the Apache helicopter, the Tomahawk cruise missile, and the battleships—all performed brilliantly. The American networks and press were as surprised as Saddam Hussein. Both had believed their own propaganda.

Because it is so much less glamorous than airlift and because the aerospace industry is far larger and more powerful in Washington than the shipbuilding industry, sealift has always received scant attention compared to airlift in Congress and the executive. But in operation Desert Shield and Desert Storm, just as in all previous wars, over 90 percent of all matériel had to go by sea. Luckily, the Reagan administration had launched a major sealift program in 1981. As a result, we had eight 30-knot sealift ships to move the armored divisions from the United States to the Gulf, and we had some twenty-six ships prepositioned at Diego Garcia loadéd with equipment and supplies for three marine brigades and air force combat wings. All of those ships were procured, built, or chartered during the 1980s and enabled successful execution of the operation. By contrast, the favorite congressional pork-barrel program of maritime subsidies was something of a scandal. Most of the ships under American flag ownership that had benefited from some $600 million per year of congressional subsidy successfully evaded service in the Gulf. By contrast, more than four hundred foreign vessels were chartered by the Military Sealift Command during Desert Shield and Storm.

One of the real success stories of Desert Storm was the performance of the reserves. Reserve forces since World War II have been supported and equipped largely through congressional initiative. The executive branch, dominated by career active-duty military staffs, have not generally been sympathetic to the reserves. Whenever there has been a budget squeeze, the Pentagon has invariably proposed slashing the reserves far more than the active forces. More than 180,000 reservists served in Operation Desert Storm, flying combat missions in Air National Guard F-16s and navy A-6s, spearheading the marine tank attack into Kuwait, and augmenting virtually all of the air, ground, and sea forces. Had it not been for the congressional initiatives, support, and pressures against a reluctant Bush administration, that would not have been possible.

One cannot fail to conclude from the results that, however awkwardly, operating through the powers shared and distributed in Articles I and II, with the Reagan administration leading but with Congress making some singularly important innovations, a very effective defense capability was provided for the nation during the 1980s.

# 2

# Theory, Law, and Politics

War has been identified as that state in which a nation prosecutes its rights by force. Under such a definition, then, we have been at war in the Persian Gulf and in Central America for most of the past decade. Thus defined, war normally does not involve a declaration of hostilities or any kind of legal formalism. One study of conflict in Europe and America between 1700 and 1870 identified 107 cases of hostilities that began without declarations of war; only ten preceded by such declarations.[1] The U.S. Supreme Court in the *Eliza* case, arising out of an undeclared war with France in 1798, described the differences between formal declared war and the more common variety as being in the former case "solemn" and in the latter "imperfect war":

> If it be in declared form, it is called solemn, and is of the perfect kind; because one whole nation is at war with another whole nation . . . in such a war, all the members act under a general authority, and all the rights and consequences of war attached to their condition. But hostilities may subsist between two nations, more confined in its nature and extent; being limited as places, persons, and things; and this is more properly termed imperfect war; because not solemn, and because those who are authorized to commit hostilities act under special authority and can go no further than to the extent of their commission.[2]

A study done by the Library of Congress identifies over 210 cases of the use of U.S. armed forces abroad between 1798 and

1983. During the same period, however, the United States has actually declared war only five times, and four of those were made only after hostilities were already in progress. It is this broader phenomenon of war and the interaction between Congress and the executive in dealing with it that have formed the most interesting continuous theme of political debate throughout our nation's history.

## Who Should Be on Top: Congress or the President?

*Il faut que le pouvoir arrête le pouvoir.* With this simple axiom Montesquieu started the longest-running debate in American history. In a statement translating roughly as "one should set a thief to catch a thief," Montesquieu wisely perceived that governments of future corporate states would possess a power of a magnitude wholly unknown in his own time, requiring wholly new mechanisms for controlling government, if tyranny were to be avoided. He believed the answer was to be found in the practices evolved in Great Britain. He thought that the growth of democracy and stability in Britain was the result of the separation within its government of the major elements of sovereignty, the vesting in different branches of the essential functions of legislative, executive, and judicial authorities—and the keeping of each wholly separate.

In fact, like most foreigners, Montesquieu didn't understand what really went on in the British system. The great strength of the British constitution in his time, as it is now, lay in the *centralizing* of all three functions, as Thomas Hobbes had admonished, under one supreme authority where "the supreme determining power is upon all points the same."

When in due course Montesquieu became a leading light of the Founding Fathers of the United States, from among his many brilliant insights his one great misperception seems to have had the greatest inspirational power.

There will always be endless debate over what was the real intent of the framers on a great many points not clearly stated in the Constitution, but there is little disagreement that they all clearly intended to separate legislative, judicial, and executive powers. With their principal reference being the perceived tyranny of King George III, they sought to avoid creating the seeds of another tyranny by ensuring that sovereignty would not reside in a single place. As that most readable of constitutional writers Walter Bagehot has put it, they adopted instead the principle of having many sovereign authorities, hoping that their multitude might atone for their inferiority.

That seems about where consensus ended among the Founding Fathers. There is certainly no agreement on the important issue as to where the principal powers over foreign affairs, whether political or military, would reside, in Congress or the presidency. There are strong advocates of the primacy of Congress, the primacy of the presidency, and of the equality of both institutions, but the fragmentary records of the Constitutional Convention and the often contradictory arguments found in *The Federalist* and in speeches and commentaries written during the nation's formative years lend conclusive support to none of those positions. Emmet Hughes followed the tortuous progress of the formation of the idea of the presidency through Madison's notes and has frankly conceded:

> I am still not sure how a formal consensus on the Executive power was reached . . . as a summation of all labyrinthine debates of the Convention, this did not define: it deferred. With a truly peculiar restraint—of spectacular shrewdness—the Founding Fathers thus left the presidency, their most special creation, to be shaped by the live touch of history. And this could fairly be called their forever memorable gamble.[3]

Much of the bitter ratification debate of 1789 focused on the excessive power vested in the presidency. "How easy is it for him to render himself absolute!" said Patrick Henry. Yet even such critics of executive power as John Marshall spoke of the president as "the sole organ of the nation in its external relations, and its sole representative with foreign nations." The more vigorous federalists, such as Hamilton, Madison, Marshall, and Jay, at times argued forcefully for executive primacy (as in "Federalists Nos. 23 and 48" and the first letter of "Pacificas"). At other times, they implied support of congressional equality, as in "Federalists Nos. 69 and 75" as well as the "First Letter of Helvidius."

Whigs led by Thomas Jefferson believed in the firm subordination of the executive to "the Supreme Legislative Power," yet elsewhere Jefferson argued that "the transaction of business with foreign nations is Executive altogether."

It is abundantly clear that the contending views were never reconciled, and thus the Constitution and the so-called "conventions" of the constitution formulated two fundamentally inconsistent concepts. There is one conception of the presidency as existing for the most part to serve the legislative power, wherein resides the will of the people, and another conception of the executive's power as being subject only to specific and limited qualification.

In strictest constitutional terms, therefore, certain powers capable of affecting our foreign relations are conferred upon the president; other powers of the same nature, upon Congress; but which of the two branches shall have the dominant or final voice in determining the course of foreign relations in peace and war is not established.

There does, however, seem to be a prevailing view with regard to "solemn war" of the type discussed in the *Eliza* case; that view was expressed by Madison: ". . . those who are to conduct a war cannot in the nature of things, be proper or sage judges, whether a war ought to be commenced, continued, or concluded." The power to formally place the nation in a state of "solemn war" *ab initio* was undoubtedly intended for Congress alone.

But it is equally clear that it was intended, in Hamilton's words, that "if on the one hand, the Legislative have a right to declare war, it is, on the other, the duty of the Executive to preserve peace." Also, the powers to do so "ought to exist without limitation because it is impossible to foresee or define the extent and variety of the means which may be necessary to satisfy them." It is the president alone who is held constitutionally responsible for the nation's readiness to meet an enemy assault.

The answers to the most important questions of distribution of war powers were left for events to decide. Did the "power to repel sudden attacks" include the initiation of hostilities? What is Congress's power over the movement or deployment of the armed forces over which the Constitution gives them the power to raise, provide, maintain, and make rules for? Are these powers different during hostilities than they are in peacetime? And why does the

Constitution tell Congress to "maintain" a navy but only "raise" an army when needed?

Opponents of executive primacy can cite scores of instances in which all these questions were answered by unilateral executive action without authorization or interference by Congress, in which authority was asserted and exercised over military forces, including committing them to combat and deploying them worldwide.

Opponents will cite scores of instances in which the president sought advance approval for action and acquiesced in congressional prohibition. As Clinton Rossiter wrote: "Both the historical and Judicial precedents tell each principal in the great debate exactly what he wants to know."[4] There will never be a constitutional solution to this struggle, because each branch has indisputable rights that overlap; or as Hamilton described it, "joint possession." Because of the unreconciled differences among the drafters, the Constitution embodies two separate and incompatible concepts of executive power. All that the Constitution does is to confer upon the president certain powers over national security, certain other powers of the same nature upon the Senate, and still other such powers upon the Congress as a whole. The president is endowed with the sole power of "commander in chief," while Congress is directed "to raise and support armies," "to maintain a navy," to provide for "disciplining the militia, and for governing such part of them as may be employed in the service of the United States." No further guidance is provided.

What do these words really mean? Does "legislative power" include the right to exercise a surveillance or superintendence of the executive, including the deployment and the direction of military forces in the field? Does control of the purse strings include the right to refuse to raise armies and maintain navies at all or to cut off funds for their use once deployed in a conflict? Does the Senate's power to "advise and consent" to treaties include the right to abrogate "so far as the people and authorities in the United States are concerned" any treaty in which the United States is a party or to abrogate or refuse to implement executive agreements? Is the executive power of the passive variety described by John Locke and extolled by Thomas Jefferson, or is it the power to act "according to the discretion for the public good, without the prescription of the law, and sometimes even against it," as later exercised by Lincoln and the two Roosevelts. Do the laws that the president must faithfully execute include treaties, executive agreements, international law?

Cynics have seen a deep weakness in this constitutional contradiction. Walter Bagehot observed that the greatest weakness of the Constitution was not simply that it encouraged deadlocks between the president and Congress but that it yielded no solution to the situation and no formula for finding one. William Y. Elliot of Harvard surveyed two centuries of constitutional practice and found that the dysfunction had created in the structure and procedures of both branches an "unconscionable quantity of checks and balances" that resulted in enormous difficulties for efficient policy-making.[5]

Other observers, however, think it is just peachy. Looking at the same two hundred years, they see a validation of the "ingenious flexibility" provided by overlapping powers. They see the growth of the system that adapted readily to unforeseen military and diplomatic contingencies. They point to the amendment procedure as the evidence that the overlapping powers provided each generation with the opportunity to adapt the document and its system to historical experience and to contemporary problems.

But Justice Louis Brandeis has best articulated the real virtue of this inefficiency in his dissenting opinion in *Myers v. the U.S.*:

> The doctrine of the separation of powers was adopted by the convention of 1787 not to promote efficiency but to preclude the exercise of arbitrary power. The purpose was not to avoid friction but by means of the inevitable friction incident to the distribution of governmental powers among three departments, to save the people from autocracy.

That arbitrary power that Brandeis feared could, of course, exist in Congress as easily as in the executive.

The Constitution, wrote Bagehot, would long ago have been brought to a bad end by the overlapping distribution of its powers were it not for the American genius for politics, moderation and action, and regard for the law. "Sensible shareholders," I have heard a shrewd attorney say, "can work any deed of settlement; and so the men of Massachusetts could, I believe, work any Constitution."[6]

It has been said that the laws are no more and no less than what the courts will enforce. The courts, specifically the Supreme Court, have been very reluctant to intrude, however gingerly, upon matters involving allocation of powers between the branches of the Federal government, and especially those involving the powers to make war. Case law on the matter, therefore, is necessarily sparse. The court will not adjudicate "questions of a political nature," and such law as there is on the separation of powers has come before the court only when it has involved individual rights. Even when private litigation has brought the court face-to-face with an issue of national security powers, it has usually found a way to avoid deciding the case on any grounds that touch on the constitutional issue. And in those cases where it has, it has taken pains to limit the affect by using the most cautious, qualified, and ambiguous language. The overall attitude when dealing with the exercise of national security powers was reflected by Justice Robert Jackson in the *Korematsu* case in 1944 when he pointed out that the final arbiters of the validity of the actions of those who exercised constitutional powers are "political judgments of their contemporaries and . . . the moral judgments of history."

One major issue involved in the issue of primacy however, does seem to have received legitimacy from the court. The view of Alexander Hamilton and, later, Theodore Roosevelt that in the absence of restrictive legislation the president possesses a residual power to act in those gray areas of shared powers involving national security ". . . in the sense that the Executive may move within them until they shall have been occupied by Legislative action" received explicit support from a majority of the court in the 1952 *Youngstown Steel* case.

In the 1804 case of *Little v. Barreme*, Chief Justice John Marshall, speaking with reference to a vessel seized under an act of Congress, said ". . . that since Congress had acted in the matter the President was bound to follow its direction and that seizure had been illegal," clearly implying that if Congress had not acted, the president could have.

In the 1890 case of *In Re Neagle*, Justice Samuel Miller held that the constitutional phrase "to take care that the laws be faithfully executed" was not limited to the enforcement of congressional legislation but included "rights, duties, and obligations growing out of the Constitution and our international relations. . . ."

In the 1863 judgment that has been much examined in recent years, *The Prize Cases*, the court legitimized a broad exercise of presidential powers in emergency. It accepted the view that the president, without reference to Congress, can determine the existence of an emergency and act immediately. It accepted also the view that the president may commit the nation to military action without congressional approval.

The great landmark case in the substance of primacy in national security policy is *U.S. v. Curtiss-Wright Export Corporation*, 1936. The opinion was written by Justice George Sutherland, who was no friend of executive power and no admirer of FDR's. He was, interestingly, also former chairman of the Senate Foreign Relations Committee. In what amounted to a clear affirmation of presidential primacy, the court held that "the powers of external sovereignty do not depend upon the affirmative grants of the Constitution" and endorsed the existence of "the very delicate plenary and exclusive power of the President as the sole organ of the federal government in the field of international relations—a power which does not require as a basis for its exercise an act of Congress." The Court pointed out the special status of foreign affairs:

> . . . with its important, complicated, delicate and bountiful problems, the President alone has the power to speak or listen as a representative of the nation. . . .
> Congressional legislation must often accord to the President a degree of discretion and freedom from statutory restriction which would not be admissible where domestic affairs alone involved. Moreover, he, not Congress, had the better opportunity of knowing the conditions which prevail in foreign countries. . . .

Again speaking through Justice Sutherland in 1937, the court, in *U.S. v. Belmont*, held that the conduct of foreign relations, including the recognizing of foreign governments and concluding of international agreements, belongs to the executive alone. *Youngstown Sheet and Tube Company v. Sawyer* remains the most important example of the court invalidating actions taken by the executive branch under the presidential power to act in an emergency. While it is significant that none of his concurring colleagues agreed with his view of the source of presidential power, the opinion of the court rendered by Justice Hugo Black declares: "The President's power ... must stem either from an act of Congress or from the Constitution itself."

But in the more recent case of *Orlando v. Laird* the president's power to conduct operations in Indochina in the absence of formal authorization from Congress was upheld. The U.S. District Court held that "the reality of the collaborative action of the Executive and Legislative required by the Constitution has been present from the earliest stages" through Congress "appropriating the nation's treasure and conscripting its manpower."

In 1990 Cong. Ronald Dellums and fifty-five colleagues sought an injunction against President Bush going to war in Iraq. It was denied by the D.C. Federal District Court on the grounds that they represented only 10 percent of Congress, implying that if a majority had joined, it might have been granted.

One must conclude from the meager body of relevant cases that the questions of which branch has primacy has not been and will not be decisively resolved by the third branch of the government. But the weight of cases, such as they are, clearly leans toward endorsing presidential primacy.

———

While it is not necessary to agree with Jefferson that the transaction of business with foreign nations is altogether executive, it must be admitted that the nature of diplomacy, commerce, and defense, favors the executive. Negotiation, conflict, crisis, and the very real practices of other nations do not readily adapt themselves to the peculiarities of parliamentary process. The executive branch has attributes and capabilities that determine its powers and behavior. The nature of Congress is, of course, wholly different but no less determinant of its powers and behavior.

Until the Watergate era it was a fact of history that the expanded role of the federal government occurred almost entirely in the executive branch. In national security affairs this growth was enormously accelerated by World War II and the Cold War. The vast machinery of foreign and defense policy was lodged in the executive branch. A huge, permanent defense central planning bureaucracy was created to control what amounted to half of the nation's GNP in the war years. While its control now covers only 6 percent of GNP, its size has continued to grow over the past fifty years. By contrast, between the founding of the Senate Committee on Foreign Relations in 1816 and the so-called Watergate Congress of 1974, Congress expanded its institutions and staff only modestly. But since 1974 the institutions and staff of Congress have been quintupled and continue to grow at an annual rate even greater than the executive bureaucracy.

The vastness and variety of personnel resources and expertise found in the U.S. executive branch are unmatched by any organization in the world. The Pentagon alone has more than 3 million employees. While they are, of course, in theory employees of the federal government as a whole, in the context of the struggle between the branches for the control of war and national security powers they are squarely on the side of the executive.

In terms of expertise, the disparity is enormous. In the executive departments, the richness and sophistication in scientific, technological, military, diplomatic, statistical, medical, educational, geological, fiscal, legal, and sociological skills are truly awesome. Congressional staffs have a smattering of knowledge in all of these areas, but only a smattering.

The very continuity and longevity of an individual's career within the civil service and military have been the bane of presidents and cabinet officers, yet they provide an institutional memory totally absent in the notoriously transient staffs of Congress. The volume and complexity of international transactions and the decades-long durability and complication of international issues make this expertise an essential part of carrying out the process. There is a temptation in Congress to oversimplify, to be drawn, in Dean Acheson's words, "to courses high in debating appeal whose impracticalities are revealed only through considerable factual knowledge."[7]

An example of this expertise is found in military intelligence acquisition, the established, existing sources of which are an executive monopoly. Overt and covert production of information on conditions in foreign countries flows to the executive (sometimes) where it is digested into rational and usable information. Congress must depend on acquiring this secondhand from the executive branch or in much more random fashion from outside sources. Creation of the intelligence committees in Congress following Watergate has not changed this fact.

In theory, the greatest strength of the executive branch lies in what used to be called administrative unity: functional organization, unity of command, and internal discipline. These are the necessary attributes of problem solving, decision making, and policy execution. The orchestration and coordination of the many complex and controlled military, diplomatic, and domestic maneuvers in, say, the Cuban Missile Crisis would be impossible without a single determining energy. At least this is what the textbooks say, though anyone who has actually lived through a crisis in a position of responsibility can only smile at such a description.

One hundred senators and 435 representatives and their 39,000 staff members, these individuals and their independent committees and policy caucuses, possess none of the attributes of administrative unity. The slow and open deliberations of a democratic legislature are attuned to the process of compromise rather than decisive action. In Congress, controversy means delay and missed opportunities.

Another essential requirement for successful conduct of coherent national security policy is the ability to take a long-range view of situations, fashioning policy in light of long- and middle-range goals. Public opinion, to which Congress must be directly beholden, tends to lag far behind the facts of the international problems with which the executive must cope. Legislatures have a consistent habit of dealing with the future by legislating against the errors of the past. The great fanfares attending the repeal of the Tonkin Gulf Resolution and the passage of the Boland Amendments are examples among many.

One does not have to agree with the more florid boosters of the institution—that the presidency is the "sole crownlike symbol of the union"—to accept that the executive branch has a national constituency and is responsible to "the whole people," in Woodrow Wilson's phrase, whereas members of Congress represent local and regional constituencies in theory and in practice special interests and organized political action committees (PACs).

It has always been a fact of life that there is virtually no political profit for a congressman in the serious pursuit of national security affairs. The role of critic after the fact or of dramatic opponent, however, can produce useful publicity and "face" time on the evening news. And a latent American fondness for the bashing of "foreigners" has often exerted an obvious influence on congressional grandstanding. Only in the absence of opposition, interest, or consensus back home can a legislator be free to judge an issue by the larger national interest, and only then if he is free of the party whip, the pressure of a big contributor, or of the need to conform to committee disciplines. Most unsavory of all, of course, is that since the post-Watergate reforms, Congress had become particularly vulnerable to the powerful, narrow-interest PAC lobbies. The long hearings regarding the so-called Keating Five in the fall and winter of 1990–91 and the preposterous confirmation hearings on Judge Clarence Thomas in October 1991 demonstrated conclusively how pervasive the forces of narrow special interests equipped with PAC contributions have become.

The president, by contrast, along with the vice-president, as the sole nationally elected officials endowed with the unique stature which that entails, brings to the executive a mighty psychological power, the symbolic force of personalized leadership. It is the natural focus of the universal human desire to personalize trust. The more complex, distant, or dangerous the problem, the stronger the tendency to place trust in one man. Lincoln and FDR, for example, could never have acted with such independence of Congress had they not acquired the solid support that came with a near mythic position of trust. When that deep trust is lost, the executive has tended to become virtually powerless, as the administrations of Andrew Johnson, Herbert Hoover, Lyndon Johnson, Richard Nixon, and Jimmy Carter have demonstrated.

---

Woodrow Wilson was not exaggerating when he said that "inside the United States, the Senate is mostly despised," and it is quite true that the normal tedium of debate, incomprehensibility of procedure, and confusing array of elderly spokesmen vying for attention carry little danger of captivating the millions into an emotional allegiance to Congress. Indeed, it has proved to be highly dangerous politically for an individual member to confront a popular president. The lewd and vulgar low reached in the nationally televised Thomas hearings set a new record for public contempt of Congress with an 18 percent approval rating recorded in polls.

"The circumstances that endanger the safety of nations are infinite," wrote Alexander Hamilton in "Federalist No. 23." "And for this reason no Constitutional shackles can wisely be imposed on the power to which the care of it is committed." In such periods of danger presidents have normally found that their powers grow exponentially. While there have always been voices of dissent during war and crisis, Congress has never been disposed during periods of actual conflict to seriously challenge presidential actions of even arguable constitutionality. Neutrality acts and war powers resolutions are a Congressional luxury of postwar periods only.

Indeed the force of Congress during actual conflict has more often weighed on the side of bellicosity than on the side of restraint. The reasons are obvious enough: Popular opinion is always with the president in a crisis, and woe unto the congressman who lays himself open to the charges of "stiffening the resolve of the enemy," "pulling the rug from under the president," or "abandoning our soldiers in battle." Congressmen well know that in moments of crisis the president will always have the drop on them by being able to appeal over their heads directly to the people. Television and the press conference have made possible the strengthening of the president's bond with the public in a way that has no parallel for the 535 individual members of Congress. In 1933, it was quipped that FDR had "only to look at a radio to bring Congress to terms." More recently, Ronald Reagan used the media to great effect whenever he had problems with Congress over such things as his strategic defense initiative (SDI) or aid to the Contras. "Let [the president] once win the admiration and the confidence of the country," wrote Woodrow Wilson, "and no other single force can withstand him, no combination of forces will easily overpower him. His position takes the imagination of the country. He is the representative of no constituent but of the whole people."

In contrast, the deficiencies of Congress are so obvious as to need little repetition; yet its characteristic multifarious interests, diffuse authority, paucity of resources, thinness of expertise, lack of the hard data available to the executive, plodding and workaday procedures, freedom from secrecy, lack of continuity, and, above all, localism and parochialism are, ironically, also the bases of its power.

The sanction of elections ties members inescapably to the will and mood of the people. Every member must be responsive to the constituency he represents. In the executive, only the president is elected. The vastly powerful secretaries of state, defense and the military departments, the national security adviser and director of the Central Intelligence Agency (CIA) and their subordinates, respond to no constituency but the individual president. While elected by the "whole people," the president himself serves three competing constituencies: his bureaucratic government constituency, his partisan constituency, and his foreign constituency of allies and adversaries.

Congress is, in theory, the political matrix from which national security policy must be drawn. Theoretically, it alone is the institution capable of setting the boundaries of acceptable policy. In contrast with the initiative and executive functions requiring those virtues found in the presidency, Congress alone is organically suited to shaping the broad flow of foreign affairs in terms of directions, goals, and philosophy. Because the members are so close to the people, they must mold the popular understanding and support of good policy. It's a nice theory.

Congress monitors, reviews, questions, criticizes, challenges, defines, modifies, approves, vetoes, and provides or withholds the appropriations for executive action. It stimulates executive action through informal and legislative means and occasionally and usually with less happy results mandates and initiates policies and operations against strong executive opposition. Despite much rhetoric to the contrary, the activity and influence of Congress in foreign affairs is immense indeed, probably greater than that of any similar legislature in the world.

Each of the virtues of the executive noted above has a reciprocal and confounding counterpart among congressional attributes. Congressional freedom from the inertialike movement of the vast bureaucracy of government allows it a detachment from entrenched institutional viewpoints that inspires spontaneity of perception and the opportunity to view forests rather than trees.

---

It used to be that the very lack of armies of experts enabled the commonsense view of the layman to temper the often narrow specialist proposals of the executive. The most important issues of war and national security are not the proper preserve of technical and career specialists but should be amenable to the widely shared insights and common wisdom found among congressmen. Unfortunately, since the Watergate era, Congress has created its own entrenched bureaucracy, an eventuality that has greatly diluted the virtue of its native common sense. Moreover, until Watergate, Congress had a kind of expert talent not found in the executive: virtuoso politicians long in the tooth. The congressional leadership had tenure. Presidents came and went, but the powerful chairmen, whips, speakers, and party leaders were immortal. Individuals quite frequently held their posts a quarter of a century or more. They varied widely in education and wisdom but were invariably alike in political cunning, in their expertise in the dark arts of maneuvering against "the boys downtown." There used to be no such thing as a weakened Congress in the way the term has accurately been used to describe some presidencies. All that has changed, however, since the Watergate Congress abandoned the structures of seniority in the House; the party caucus in effect, the rabble, became king once again. Now chairmen are elected and insecure. The greatest source of congressional strength has been lost, particularly in the House. In order to remain as chairmen, those in power then must buy members' support by creating new subcommittees (each with staffs) for them to populate, greatly diluting the coherence and power of the full committees and their chairmen.

---

The corollary to the executive cult of the expert is the tyranny of secret information. The chaos of the classification system in the executive branch is legendary. In fact, however, all secrets that are really relevant to the responsibilities of Congress have always tended to reach the interested members (and usually the press)

71

with minimal delay. Because of the very openness of Congress, moreover, the public is usually guaranteed access to the really important data not otherwise available from, or willingly provided by, the executive. The revelations attending the proceedings of the committees chaired by Frank Church and Otis Pike in the Ninety-fourth Congress of 1975 as well as the many secrets flowing daily out of the Iran-Contra investigations in 1986–87 were recent cases in point.

"High prerogative" men of the executive are always quick to remind those who will listen that Congress isn't capable of acting with unity and dispatch, as required by the pace of international events. But in the legislatures, Hamilton wrote:

> promptitude of decision is oftener an evil than a benefit. The differences of opinion, and the jarrings of parties in that department of the government, though they may sometimes obstruct salutary plans, yet often they promote deliberation and circumspection, and serve to check excesses in the majority.

It is just such deliberation and circumspection that can restrain unwise initiatives on the part of a unified executive about to act with dispatch—as in the case of the Eisenhower move to rescue the French at Dien Bien Phu in 1954. (Though in light of the subsequent tragedy of Vietnam perhaps such a move could not have ended any worse for American interests.) In 1954, the deliberate skill and circumspect judgment of Georgia senator Richard Russell, who piloted a bitterly polarizing issue through the legislative process, helped Congress and the president create the kind of national consensus of gloriously broad generalities to which the wise and just then repaired; this was a democratic function of incalculable value. Unfortunately, without the seniority system and with the severe decline in the apparent quality of the members of Congress, there are no more Richard Russells to carry out this nearly indefinable function.

———

Most often in matters of war and national security it is the executive that proposes but the Congress that disposes. The activism of Congress in scrutinizing and modifying initiatives has always

72

horrified officials of the executive. This congressional role has received little scholarly or media attention because its methods are, as Madison described them: "at once more extensive and less susceptible of precise limits, it can, with the greater facility mask, under complicated and indirect measures, the encroachment which it makes on the coordinate departments." The executive gets all the headlines for initiating an Alliance for Progress or a SALT I treaty, but it is Congress that gives these proposals substance, and usually of a far different texture than that intended by the executive. I have heard this process likened to a boss first paying his employees, then luring them into a crap game during which he takes back all their pay.

———

While few congressmen can stand against a determined president who may propose grand policy schemes, the executive attention to these initiatives is then always delegated from the chief to his subordinates, and their ability to protect and defend the policies from major congressional surgery is entirely limited.

The isolationist legislation of the 1920s and 1930s, the violence annually wreaked on plans for foreign aid, the long opposition to recognition of mainland China, and the insulting restrictions on aid to Turkey (inspired by the Greek lobby) are well-known examples of the negative impact Congress may have on executive initiatives. Less widely understood are the initiatives and modifications of war and national security policy made by Congress itself. Congressional "war hawks," for example, pressed Madison into the War of 1812; McKinley, into the Spanish-American War. Later, it was Congress that led Truman to give aid to Taiwan. But Congress has proved to be most intrusive in its periodic efforts to change the structure and organization of the executive branch. The National Security Act of 1947, the creation of the Arms Control and Disarmament Agency in 1962, and Congress's annual reorganizations of the Pentagon are examples of what I mean.

A closely related dimension of congressional activism has been especially marked since the 1950s: overseeing administrative detail and superintending executive officials in their execution of policy and holding them personally accountable not to the executive branch they serve but to congressional committees. This has brought about an unprecedented role in recent years in the selection of nominees and the rejection of others for senior executive branch positions, often totally unrelated to issues of merit. Sen. Sam Nunn's garroting of John Tower's nomination as secretary of defense is a good example of this kind of assertion of "authority."

The primary source of congressional strength in foreign affairs is the deeply entrenched bonds tying the executive bureaucracy to the whim of Congress. Every congressman of any seniority has developed relationships with career civil servants, members of the military and foreign services, or intelligence officers throughout those agencies dealing in his area of committee or constituent interests. The length of such enduring symbiotic relationships typically stretches over three or more administrations. For the bureaucrat, the relationship yields benefits (or protection) to himself and to his little barony. It may assist in continuing promotions and even such comparatively mundane things as service academy appointments for relatives. The congressman, of course, gains access to information and an influence on the day-to-day application of policy. Nearly all of the chief political and permanent officers of the executive are also under constant temptation to do what the senior congressmen of their jurisdiction want them to do. They consult formally, informally, and often covertly; and their decisions regarding both policy and personnel are heavily influenced by these consultations. In subjecting executive policy and proposals to this off-line counsel and analysis on the part of advisers who owe no allegiance to the White House, there is a necessary, if imperfect, check and balance to the regal isolation of the president, for in all administrations, circumstances regularly conspire to exclude criticism from the Oval Office. No one, as George Reedy, Lyndon Johnson's press secretary, has succinctly pointed out, has ever invited a president in person to "go soak his head," but that inestimable function can be, and frequently has been, bravely performed on the floors of Congress, often with salutary effect.

# 3

# From the Shores of Tripoli to the War Powers Act

With as much inconsistency as there is in the theories and ideas of the Founding Fathers, it is small wonder that in practice the exercise of military power by Congress and the president has had no clear pattern. Neither branch can claim primacy on the basis of settled practice. The predominance of one or other of the branches has fluctuated in response to two determining factors: epic events and strong personalities. So much have dramatic events shaped the roles of each branch that some scholars believe that there are really two Constitutions: one for peaceful periods and another for crises.

Precedents were set early and pragmatically by the need to protect American commerce from being strangled between France and Britain during the Napoleonic world war. President John Adams asked a Congress, many of whose members were merchants and shipowners, for appropriations to expand and deploy the navy. "Congress responded on 1 July 1797 with an act empowering the President, should he deem it expedient, to man and employ the frigates *United States, Constitution*, and *Constellation, as he saw fit*."[1] By the turn of the century Adams had created a new cabinet-level department of the Navy, which assumed command of the some fifty combatant ships in service, a number that except for the Civil War remained relatively constant throughout the nineteenth century.

The principal enemy of the United States in 1800 was France, which refused to recognize American rights of neutrality and was busily grabbing Yankee merchantmen trading with the British, particularly in the Caribbean. In 1799 and 1800, the French captured 159 merchant vessels; the new American navy took 86 French prizes and recaptured 100 of the lost merchant ships. There was considerable pressure in Congress to declare war, but President Adams held off a formal declaration by deliberately following an ambiguous policy that he characterized as "neither peace nor war." Adams was the author of the important distinction found in the wording of the Constitution that distinguished "maintaining a Navy" but "raising" an army only when needed. Adams greatly feared a standing army. When Congress created a new provisional army at the behest of Alexander Hamilton, Adams feared it more than he did the French:

> I have always cried, Ships! Ships! Hamilton's hobby horse was troops! troops! with all of the vanity and timidity of Cicero, all the debauchery of Mark Anthony and all the ambition of Julius Caesar, his object was command of 50,000 men. My object was the defense of my country, and that alone, which I knew could be effected only by a Navy.[2]

Thus, the first war of the new United States was averted largely because of interservice rivalry.

Just as the quasi-war ended, Thomas Jefferson succeeded John Adams as president and made clear that his intention was to follow the military practices of Adams: "We mean to risk the safety of our commerce on the resources of our own strength and bravery in every sea."[3]

Since the American War of Independence, the rulers of the Barbary states Tripoli, Tunis, and Algiers had been a constant headache to Yankee traders, demanding ever-increasing amounts of tribute and seizing American ships when it pleased them. With the encouragement of both the British and the French, their depredations grew worse during this period of undeclared war, and Jefferson acted swiftly to deal with them once the "war" was ended. Using words that I myself might have used in my own testimony to Congress on fleet activities in dealing with Mr. Qaddafi of Libya in 1986, Secretary of the Navy Benjamin Stoddert in 1801 said: "It is conceived . . . that such a squadron cruising in view of the Barbary powers will have a tendency to prevent them from seizing on our commerce, whenever passion or a desire of plunder might incite them thereto."[4] The secretary of the navy's instruction to the squadron was very simple. They were to "protect our Commerce and chastise their insolence—by sinking, burning or destroying their ships and vessels wherever you shall find them."[5] A nice turn of phrase. Eight months after Jefferson ordered the initiation of hostilities, Congress recognized the existence of a state of war with Tripoli and authorized various presidential responses.

Thus, the very earliest precedents established one pattern that has often been followed since. To wit, the president initiates military action without congressional interference, often with ipso facto blessing if it has gone well. Such was the case with the Boxer Rebellion in 1900, the Mexican Expedition of 1915, the antisubmarine campaign in the North Atlantic prior to 1917, the Russian Expedition of 1918–20, the Nicaragua Expedition in 1926, the antisubmarine warfare campaign in the North Atlantic in 1940 and 1941, the occupation of Greenland and Iceland in 1941, the Korean action in 1950, the Bay of Pigs in 1961, the Dominican Republic in 1965, Lebanon again in 1982, Grenada in 1983, Tripoli again in 1986, the Persian Gulf in 1987, Panama in 1989 and the deployment against Iraq in 1990. These and scores of lesser skirmishes and deployments were acts of war undertaken by the executive with no formal and quite often no informal authorization or subsequent censure from Congress. In nearly all situations, however, there were strong voices of criticism and some hostile resolutions introduced in Congress. But all executive initiatives were finally either approved by some legislative act or acquiesced in by inaction.

In all of those crises that occurred while I was serving in the government, the reason that no authorization was sought from Congress was because none of us in the executive branch ever questioned that the president had the authority to act without Congress and usually no prior consultation was ever considered except in rare cases, with one or two trusted leaders, such as Scoop Jackson or John Tower, whose opinion President Reagan really did want. It was, of course, assumed that if the consultation extended beyond the trusted heavyweights, all of the information provided would be certain to leak from Congress to the press immediately. In fourteen years' service in the White House, State Department, and Pentagon, I never once heard that assumption questioned by any senior official of the executive.

———

But there is an entirely different stream of precedent that is not quite as strong but just as persistent in two hundred years of practice—the use or intended use of force where the executive felt the need, whether by politics or a lack of confidence to obtain prior authorization from Congress; and if he failed to get it, quietly to cancel the planned action. The War of 1812 was the first, quickly followed by the Florida expeditions of 1812 and 1816, war against Tripoli again in 1815, the attempted annexation of Texas in 1844, the Mexican War in 1846, the war with Spain in 1898, hostilities again with Mexico in 1914–17, full entry into World War I, troop deployments to Europe in 1951, assistance to the French in Indochina in 1954, Formosa in 1955, Lebanon in 1958, Cuba in 1962, Vietnam in 1964, Cambodian military assistance in 1971, aid to the Angolan rebels between 1976 and 1985, U.S. aid to the Contras from 1981 to 1987, and the launching of hostilities against Iraq in 1991.

Some events have a bit of both traditions. The American naval attack on Kuala Batu in Sumatra in 1832 was ordered by President Andrew Jackson after a U.S. senator demanded redress for seizure of a ship and its cargo of opium owned by the senator. The Whig party in Congress succeeded in passing a motion of censure against Jackson "for waging war without a Congressional declaration."[6] The recent war in Iraq started with the initial deployment of American troops without prior consultation with Congress and was accompanied by repeated claims by the White House that no authorization was required by Congress to launch a military operation to eject Iraq from Kuwait. Nevertheless, President Bush asked for and received from Congress a joint resolution approving military force in advance of the attack in January 1991.

The periods of presidential independence or preemptive moves in military affairs occurred, of course, during the terms of strong presidents, decisive men responding to unusual circumstances: Adams, Jefferson, and Madison in the vulnerable early days of the Republic; Polk in the Mexican War; Lincoln in the Civil War; Theodore Roosevelt on the Panama Canal; Wilson in World War I; Franklin Roosevelt in World War II; Truman in Korea. During these periods of crises, Congress proved unable to check wide expansions of executive powers of all kinds—approving, acquiescing, or retroactively authorizing the deployment of forces overseas, initiation of hostilities, suspension of elements of the Bill of Rights, and even the spending of unappropriated money.

Obviously, military powers were not shared during some of these periods. Were those executive actions constitutional? The presidents involved were certain that they were; Congress, while protesting some, approved others and repudiated none. The Supreme Court, in the few instances it was addressed, upheld the constitutionality of presidential action.

This intertwined history of alternating periods of presidential and congressional dominance over military affairs indicates that in large measure powers exercised by strong presidents in critical times do not rub off on the office itself. Instead, these periods have in each case provoked a reaction toward a more restricted presidency and an expanded congressional role. Congress has quite often expressed its pent-up criticism after such periods with devastating incursions on executive power. Jackson, for example, was followed by a series of shackled presidents (punctuated only by the brief interlude of Polk), culminating in Buchanan. Lincoln, too, was followed by a succession of presidents who were utterly powerless against Congress in matters of national security. The assertiveness of Theodore Roosevelt and Woodrow Wilson brought on the rejection of the League of Nations, the Neutrality Acts, and the triumph of isolationism imposed by Congress. Franklin Roosevelt left Truman an office that was promptly forced to swallow a rapid succession of ever more noxious doses of disarming and disruptive legislation until fear of Stalin came to the rescue. But the combination of the Vietnam War and Watergate caused by far the greatest congressional backlash against executive dominance in our history. Nixon was followed by two very weak presidents, Ford and Carter, who ceded, or had wrested from them, unprecedented power and privilege in national security. They in turn were followed by two strong presidents in Reagan and Bush, who nevertheless have failed to return to their offices the high prerogatives of the early Cold War.

One would, of course, be going too far to say that a president welcomes a Berlin blockade, a Cuban Missile Crisis, or a Desert Storm, but there is no denying that executive power waxes directly in proportion to the crisis at hand. Without doubt, the great success of President Bush's policy in the Iraq war has set the presidency back on the road to dominance.

———

Until the New Deal, the academic community had traditionally been wary of excessive executive power. But with the New Deal and its support by a large majority of intellectuals, the intellectuals and academics became enamored of the presidency as the new champion of liberalism against conservative and reactionary populism. From the 1930s to the late 1960s the support of the intellectual and academic communities contributed in its way to a steady growth in presidential power. With the World War II victory followed so closely by the onset of the Cold War, the normal swing of the pendulum was interrupted, and presidential dominance, aided by crisis, seemed to last indefinitely. Many observers concluded that the presidency had acquired a permanent monopoly on national security power and that checks and balances in this area were a thing of the past. Democratic intellectuals especially wrote much learned text on how beneficial this powerful presidency was. That is, until the "Tet offensive" in Vietnam in 1968 suddenly curdled the intellectual milk.

With the almost immediate ascendancy of a Republican president in 1969, the academy and the Democratic leadership in Congress turned against presidential power virtually overnight. Sen. J. William Fulbright, the powerful head of the Senate Foreign Relations Committee, had for twenty years been the greatest single advocate of increased presidential power in the history of Congress. By 1971, however, with a Republican president in the White House, he said gravely: "It may not be too much to say that, as far as foreign policy is concerned, our governmental system is no longer one of separated powers but rather one of elected executive dictatorship."[7]

Presidential power over national security policy received its first serious challenge since 1941 during the Ninety-first Congress due to disillusionment with the Vietnam War. The Ninety-second Congress grew far stronger because of Watergate and significantly modified executive policy in virtually every aspect, overriding presidential vetoes of the War Powers Act and of many Indochina restrictions. Later, Congress would add many further restrictions over executive war powers, executive privilege, intelligence activities, and foreign assistance. During the first thirty years of the Cold War, it had been fashionable to ridicule Congress for its parochial ineffectiveness. Watergate brought hoots at the presidency likened by one observer to "catcalls in a vaudeville house." Irreverence directed toward Congress in the media was severely frowned upon.

## The Indochina War

All of the decisions, debates, and struggles over the use of force, and particularly the struggle for dominance between Congress and the executive, have for the past twenty-five years been dominated by the experience of the Indochina War. From the earliest days of the Kennedy administration, opponents of American involvement in Indochina leaned on constitutional arguments, contending that there was no congressional sanction for involvement. As U.S. involvement deepened, the more than twenty annual appropriations bills expressly funding the actions and the nearly unanimous passage of the Tonkin Gulf Resolution were ignored or dismissed as the same meaningless approval given to Theodore Roosevelt to bring back the Great White Fleet he had already sent halfway around the world. But that was rhetoric. The reality was stated by Sen. Barry Goldwater:

> ... the fact is that, Congress is and has been involved up to its ears in the war in Southeast Asia. It has known what has been going on from the start and has given its approval in advance to almost everything that has occurred there. Far from being the innocent dupes of a conspiring executive, Congress has been wholly involved in the policy decisions concerning Vietnam during the entire span of the American commitment there.[8]

Appropriations for Southeast Asia actually began in 1949, with the $75 million emergency fund to be expended in the general

81

vicinity of China, according to that year's Mutual Defense Assistance Act. In 1954, Congress appropriated $400 million for military assistance to Indochinese forces and the next year approved a 1955 SEATO (Southeast Asia Treaty Organization) Treaty by an 82–1 margin. Even at this early stage in U.S.–Indochina relations, the partnership of Congress and the executive was recognized by President Eisenhower, who vowed, "There is going to be no involvement in war unless it is a result of the Constitutional process that is placed upon Congress."

Yet the year 1964 represented a major threshold. The U.S. presence in South Vietnam had swelled to 18,000 with Congress's full knowledge and support. In the summer of 1964 it had become evident that a quantum increase in the U.S. effort would be needed in Vietnam to avoid a Communist takeover. Yet, like Eisenhower before him, President Johnson believed that he should have "the advance support of Congress for anything that should be proved to be necessary"; accordingly, following the Tonkin Gulf incident, he met with congressional leaders and "told them that I believe a congressional resolution of support for our entire position in Southeast Asia was necessary and would strengthen our hand. I said that we might be forced to further action, and that I did not want to go in unless Congress goes in with me."[9] Elsewhere, he expressed the belief that "the resolution was not necessary to do what we did."[10]

Naval officers who have taken part in the Tonkin Gulf incident and members of the National Security Council (NSC) staff at the time have all expressed to me their belief that the Tonkin Gulf incident was ambiguous. The North Vietnamese response to a provocative destroyer foray and aircraft deployments was not unexpected and could have easily been dismissed or ignored as routine. But contrary to the interpretation of many LBJ critics, the incident was seized on not as a method to trick Congress into supporting more vigorous action but was used knowingly by both Congress and the president as a symbolic turning point that would end the enormous frustration of the previous years' actions and send more capable U.S. forces with more aggressive orders. LBJ's floor manager for the resolution, Sen. J. William Fulbright, who since has seemed to suffer a case of extreme amnesia, said at the time that he believed the legislation merely approved the use of existing presidential powers and was used as a show of unity between Congress and the executive.[11]

The resolution itself, drafted in the White House, provided, in Section 2, that the United States was prepared, as the president determined, to take all necessary steps, including the use of armed force, to assist any member or protocol state of the SEATO Treaty that requested assistance in defense of its freedom.

Those who suggest that Congress was somehow misled and unaware that the resolution was in fact a real authorization for a major escalation of the war simply have not read the debate. Certainly the Democratic and Republican leaders in the Senate were fully aware of the possibility of the president's "using such force as could lead to war . . . by this resolution." With its gravity at the forefront of discussion, the resolution passed by the margin of 88–2 in the Senate and 416–0 in the House.

In a series of court cases brought against Secretary of Defense Melvin Laird in 1971, *Orlando v. Laird, Mitchell v. Laird, Burke v. Laird*, and *Massachusetts v. Laird*, the First Federal Circuit Court held that congressional action had legitimized the course pursued by the executive under Presidents Johnson and Nixon and that Congress had failed to assert a conflicting claim of authority.

The real turning point in the Vietnam debate came when President Nixon ordered U.S. forces into Cambodian sanctuaries across the border from southern South Vietnam. Support for the war had begun to drain rapidly away after the Tet offensive in 1968, and this series of battles, which military historians have seen as a decisive military defeat of the Communists, was a media catastrophe for the United States. Portrayed in the media as a major defeat for the United States, it politically devastated Lyndon Johnson and led him to withdraw from the 1968 presidential compaign. No longer constrained by party discipline to support a Democratic president, the Democratic-controlled Congress turned forcefully against the war.

Neutral Cambodia had been used by the North Vietnamese as a sanctuary and supply route and logistics rear area throughout the Indochina war. The American intelligence community had determined that the Ho Chi Minh Trail through Cambodia was the principal supply route for the Communists in the South. In an instructive lesson on the quirks and shortcomings of the American intelligence community, I participated in briefings in 1969 and 1970 in which the American intelligence community insisted there were no North Vietnamese supplies coming in by sea through the Cambodian ports, only over land. The navy alone dissented, believing that far more supplies were brought into South Vietnam by sea along the extensive coastline of South Vietnam and especially through the port of Sihanoukville. The Cambodian ruler Prince Sihanouk accepted this extensive use by the North Vietnamese of supply routes and bases, including bases along the South Vietnamese border featuring supply depots, hospitals, logistical networks, etc., in return for substantial payments. These were known as the "sanctuaries." But he also had a policy of turning a blind eye to U.S. air strikes against those sanctuaries, making it clear that he was not entirely unhappy with such strikes so long as they were in areas devoid of Cambodian population.

Early in 1970, however, Sihanouk was overthrown by the military led by Lon Nol. There had been increasing friction between the Cambodian army and the North Vietnamese and a growing dissatisfaction with Sihanouk's willingness to allow the North Vietnamese to steadily increase their presence and activities in the country. With Sihanouk out of the way, the Cambodian army imposed new restrictions and obstacles against North Vietnamese activities. By early April the North Vietnamese found that their supply routes to the south were completely cut off. At this time I accompanied Henry Kissinger to Capitol Hill, where he briefed congressional leaders on the deteriorating situation, making it clear that he saw no benefit from these Cambodian actions against the sanctuaries because it would merely provoke North Vietnam into taking full control of the areas. The leaders expressed support and urged Kissinger to ask the administration to take every action to urge Cambodian neutrality upon the North Vietnamese.

By the second week in April, the North Vietnamese launched attacks against Cambodian forces in eastern Cambodia, which were extended by mid-month into central Cambodia and led to

North Vietnamese control of the key towns of Saang, Takeo, Snoul, and Mimot.

By this time we had been given access by the new Cambodian regime to the government's records of Cambodian cooperation with the North Vietnamese. To our amazement, these records showed that contrary to the intelligence community's estimates, the North Vietnamese were actually shipping much more of their war supplies by sea through the port of Sihanoukville, where they were transshipped by the Cambodian army for a fee. In a quick about-face, the intelligence community now concluded that this new North Vietnamese offensive was an attempt to secure their sanctuaries in eastern Cambodia and open a secure corridor to the Gulf of Siam in order to reestablish the supply by sea lost when Sihanoukville was closed to them.

Bryce Harlow, the president's chief lobbyist, arranged a series of secret meetings at the White House with congressional leaders to consult with them about these developments and seek their recommendations. President Nixon has told me that he talked to many other members of Congress by telephone during this period. By April 29 he had made the decision to commit U.S. forces against North Vietnamese troops in the Cambodian sanctuaries, and on April 30 he informed the American people of his decision to launch a joint operation with the South Vietnamese. With an eye to constitutional arguments, President Nixon concluded that "the action of the enemy over the last 10 days clearly endangered the lives of Americans who are in Vietnam." He pointed out that the purpose of the operation was not to occupy the areas but to drive the enemy forces from the sanctuaries, destroy military supplies, and then withdraw. Henry Kissinger, in a briefing to the White House press corps prior to the announcements, stressed the limited nature of the operation (extending only twenty miles into Cambodia) and stated that its intent was to concentrate on disrupting the command control and communications network and destroying supply depots. Furthermore, he stated that he did not expect the length of the operation to extend beyond six to eight weeks, thus trying to allay fears among the press that the operation represented an escalation of the war. It was to be an effort to shorten the war and diminish the threat to South Vietnam after the American departure. (On April 20, the president announced his intention of withdrawing another 150,000 troops from the area in the coming year.)

The issue of prior consultation with Congress heated up in the following months. When asked point-blank why he had not gone to the Senate or the House for approval of the operation, the president pointed out that it had not been an attempt to expand the war into Cambodia or to launch a war against Cambodia but to clean out enemy sanctuaries used to attack American forces in Vietnam, which he could do based on his inherent power as commander in chief. If it had been otherwise, he said, he would have gone to the Senate. He also emphasized the importance of the element of surprise and said that without it the losses would have numbered 3,000–4,000 men rather than the 330 actual casualties. He also recalled that President Kennedy had notified congressional leaders only two and one-quarter hours before giving orders to establish the Cuban blockade in 1962. Nevertheless, the incursion had the effect of turning fence sitters in Congress against the administration and began a string of inhibiting legislation that resulted in substantial restrictions on the conduct of American forces and heavier shackles upon the president himself.

---

The Cambodian incursion marked the start of a steady onslaught of congressional restrictions on presidential war powers, an era that has yet to end. It would, of course, be a mistake to view the incursion purely in constitutional terms. It cannot be understood without a feel for the emotions and passions of the times. The announcement created an unprecedented stir among student antiwar groups; demonstrations broke out on every major campus. And then, only days after the incursion began, there was the tragic shooting of four students by panicky National Guardsmen at Kent State University. The justifiably horrified public reaction quickly turned against the president, and a national crisis ensued. Washington was invaded by demonstrators from all over the country. During the week that followed, the administration was forced to surround the White House complex and the Treasury Department with buses parked end to end and backed up by thousands of police. All week long my colleagues and I at the NSC had to dress rough, work our way through the surrounding crowds, and crawl under a bus in order to get to work. Going into the Executive Office Building, one had to step over National Guardsmen in full battle gear who were hidden as a reserve shock force in case the crowds broke through the buses. Not quite the atmosphere for enlightened constitutional discourse.

The president immediately emphasized that his legal foundation for the incursion was not the Tonkin Gulf Resolution or the much more relevant string of authorizations and appropriations bills that followed but simply his more narrow powers as the commander in chief. Since he made no reference to the SEATO Treaty or to the years of congressional legislative support and appropriations, President Nixon drew congressional knives to the very power he chose to defend. Congressional critics immediately inferred that he claimed a limitless reservoir of presidential authority as commander in chief, and immediately the debate set about enacting legislation to hamstring those specific powers. Had he based his actions on the Tonkin Gulf Resolution, SEATO, or the broader congressional appropriations, he may very well have dispersed the congressional onslaught into a much wider and less damaging range of targets.

The Senate Foreign Relations Committee became the focus of an all-out political counterattack. Understanding this, we in the administration insisted on giving the House Foreign Affairs Committee treatment exactly equal to the Senate Foreign Relations Committee and its imperial chairman, Senator Fulbright; the administration had much stronger support in the House. Needless to say, this infuriated Fulbright and most of his committee, but it was very successful in thwarting the rapid passage of any resolutions. The next month saw a cascade of antiwar proposals flood into the hopper in the Senate. Following a meeting by the Democratic Caucus called to rally sentiment against the president, the leadership focused on two draft amendments. One, sponsored by Sen. John Cooper and Sen. Frank Church, was appended to the Foreign Military Sales Act, and another was introduced by Sen. Mike Mansfield and Sen. Mark Hatfield.

The Cooper/Church Amendment prohibiting military assistance to Cambodia was intended to "ensure through the denial of funds to the executive branch, that the military operation in Cambodia shall not be extended into a war in support of Cambodia . . . [and] to protect against the danger that the continuing presence of U.S. Forces in Cambodia may expand the Vietnam War into a new theatre . . . Cambodia." As the debate raged, the president announced on the evening of May 8 his intention to begin withdrawal from Cambodia the following week, with total withdrawal of all Americans by the end of June. Haig and Kissinger were furious, blaming the president's chiefs of staff, John Ehrlichman and Bob Haldeman, for bringing about what they described as "presidential collapse." Thus, against the backdrop of just one week of political firestorm, Congress had succeeded in imposing de facto restrictions of both scope and duration on the executive's policy in Cambodia, all before any legislation was even passed. The North Vietnamese, now informed of the date of U.S. withdrawal, immediately pulled back to await that date. When it came, they simply reoccupied the positions as if the incursion had never happened.

Thus, Fulbright and his allies had succeeded in their objective, but tactically the administration continued to fight a successful rearguard action against legislation. They were able to delay a vote on Cooper/Church until after the troops had been withdrawn on June 30 (when it finally passed in the Senate). There it languished through six months of debate in the conference between the House and Senate bills and finally died. The Fulbright faction then reintroduced it as a rider to House Resolution 1991, the Supplemental Appropriations Bill. This version had compromise language but still prohibited the use of any funds for U.S. ground troops or advisers in Cambodia. Since it didn't actually prohibit any actions then being planned, Tom Korologos, the president's Senate lobbyist, and I were authorized to inform the Senate leadership that the administration could accept the amendment. Within the White House we rationalized that this was fine, because there was never any intention to permanently station forces in Cambodia, but the fact remained that the president had accepted a very explicit tactical limitation on his powers as commander in chief.

As Kissinger's legislative strategist, I coordinated a small working group that met daily to quarterback administration tactics in dealing with the Senate and the House. Its members were David Abshire, representing Secretary of State Bill Rogers; Rady Johnson, representing Secretary of Defense Melvin Laird; and Tom Korologos. We had a very sporty time that spring and succeeded in tying the Senate in knots. In mid-June spies on the Foreign Relations Committee told us that Senators Fulbright, Church, and McGovern were hatching a plot to repeal the Tonkin Gulf Resolution, thus, supposedly, removing congressional authorization of the war. One of our chief allies in the Senate, Bob Dole, came up with the clever idea to have the administration beat Fulbright to the punch and introduce a repeal amendment first to underscore the administration's position that its constitutional authority to conduct the war had nothing to do with the Tonkin Gulf Resolution but rested instead on the president's powers as commander in chief and the annual authorizations and appropriations Congress passed for the war.

Senator Fulbright was taken completely by surprise when, on June 22, Dole introduced the repeal amendment. He reacted awkwardly and put himself in the amusing position of actually *opposing* the repeal. He was swamped in a roll-call vote of 80–10, and the Gulf of Tonkin Resolution died, ironically at the hands of Richard Nixon, who signed the repeal into law on January 11, 1971. Passing almost unnoticed was a comical attempt by the Fulbright faction to pass their own repeal bill the next month. It died in committee.

But these were merely tactical victories for the administration, because Cooper/Church stood as the first restriction on presidential military action in wartime. The restrictions continued to mount despite a very successful guerrilla-warfare effort by our working group. Restrictions were added to each supplemental bill for funding of the war and for assistance to Cambodia, the Mansfield Amendment finally passed, and then, as we will see, came the passage of a ban on air support to non-Communists in Cambodia. As these encroachments on the powers of the president as commander in chief accumulated, opponents of the administration decided to develop an omnibus restriction on all executive war powers, and the War Powers Resolution was born.

## The War Powers Act

Immediately following the Cambodian incursion, the House passed a joint resolution defining presidential war powers.[12] This bill would have required the president to report to Congress after placing troops in combat and reaffirmed Congress's right to de-

89

clare war. The resolution encouraged consultation "whenever fea-
sible." This bill, as well as a similar one in 1972, was never
enacted in the Senate because of effective guerrilla warfare from
our working group.

In 1972, however, the Senate did pass a "War Powers Act," the
first Senate attempt to define the president's war powers under
the Constitution.[13] The act was heralded by Sen. Jacob Javits as
"one of the most important pieces of legislation in the national
security field that has come before the Senate in this century."
The intention of the drafters was to assert for the first time that
Congress had an authority over presidential powers as commander in chief that was entirely separate from merely authorizing and appropriating. It was an explicit declaration of the
subordination of one branch to the other. Under the act, the
president could respond to emergencies in any situation justified
by his own judgment, but unauthorized action would have to be
terminated within thirty days. After a weaker version of the bill
passed by the Senate was passed by the House, we succeeded in
strangling it in the House/Senate conference, where it died. As
Congress went home for the election recess of October 1972, we
had a little celebration party in the East Wing of the White House,
where the congressional liaison offices were located. We had been
fighting a guerrilla war against Senator Fulbright and other war
critics in the Senate and to a lesser extent in the House for nearly
four years, and while Cooper/Church and a string of restricting
amendments had succeeded in passing, we had fended off any
serious encroachment on the president's ability to bring the war
to a close on his own terms.

In November 1972, President Nixon was reelected in a land-
slide victory, and those of us who had spent so much of our time
in legislative negotiations were euphoric. Now we assumed we
could move on to more interesting initiatives with the president
so much strengthened by his electoral mandate. Little did we
know what lay ahead.

## The Post-Watergate Onslaught

With Watergate just beginning to break in the spring of 1973,
the Ninety-third Congress fired the opening salvos in the battle

to gain dominance over war powers. Sen. Tom Eagleton, a cosponsor of the 1971 War Powers Act, stated: "The time has come for Congress to reassert its role within our system. The public is not keenly aware that it is wrong to wage war without the full consent of Congress and the people." With public opinion having turned so heavily against the war, Congress was determined to rewrite history and to instruct the American people that Congress was led unknowingly and unwillingly into Indochina by an unlawful executive.

After numerous hearings, the House Foreign Affairs Committee approved House Joint Resolution 542, with much stronger provisions than the version passed the year before. It imposed a 120-day time limit on the president's ability to act without congressional approval but provided that Congress could end a commitment at any time during the 120-day period. On May 17, a similar bill was approved unanimously by the Senate Foreign Relations Committee. The main difference from the House version was that the Senate bill enumerated a number of emergencies in which the president was permitted to commit American forces to acting in a hostile environment without a declaration of war; it mandated a thirty-day time limit during which Congress must grant its explicit approval. Cong. Peter Frelinghuysen expressed what was the most commonsense objection to the bill. He pointed out that the bill assumed that the president and Congress were always in opposing camps when it came to the use of military force. He rightly saw that if indeed they were of the same view with regard to the use of force, the bill, far from restricting the president, would in fact give him virtually unlimited powers and far more freedom than he had enjoyed in the previous two hundred years. Thus, despite the wish of many members to put the origins of the Vietnam War into the memory hole, the reality is that the president almost never acts unless he senses strong political sympathy in Congress. As a result, the actual uses of force by Presidents Reagan and Bush, for example, have actually been facilitated and enabled by the War Powers Act rather than restricted.

The bill passed the House by a vote of 244–170, despite major efforts by the Nixon administration to block it. Minority Leader Gerald Ford read into the record on July 18 a declaration by the president stating that he was "unalterably opposed to and must veto any bill containing the dangerous and unconstitutional restrictions" in the bill. The Senate version passed by a vote of 72–18, with the crucial support of Sen. John Stennis, who remained one of its strongest backers despite the most intense pressure administration officials, including myself, could mobilize, including calls from President Nixon and Henry Kissinger. There were some quite articulate and determined opponents of the bill, notably Sam Ervin, Roman Hruska, and Barry Goldwater, but the tide was against them—and us.

————

The conference report filed on October 4 reflected a great many compromises between the House and Senate versions. Compromise lengthened the Senate thirty-day deadline to sixty days, down from the House's 120-day limit. Conferees agreed also to a thirty-day interval to provide for the safe withdrawal of troops after the sixty days had expired, provided that the president stated a need for the same. The House version had required a concurrent resolution for mandating withdrawal of U.S. forces after executive action was adopted; the Senate version had required enactment of a law to be signed by the president. The very explicit restrictions on troop commitments in the Senate version were dropped because of House arguments that such explicit definitions would in fact expand the president's powers in crisis. The language agreed upon was as follows: executive action in response to "a national emergency created by attack on the United States, its territories or possessions, or its armed forces." The Senate sponsors were upset; Senator Eagleton remarked that the compromise was "in essence no more binding than a 'whereas' clause in a Kiwanis club resolution." Requirements agreed to in the House of seventy-two hours and in the Senate of forty-eight hours, during which time the president must file a report of a commitment of troops, were changed to "promptly," and ongoing reports would be required at least every six months.

Passage of the conference report by overwhelming votes of 75–20 in the Senate and 238–138 in the House was predictable and swift. President Nixon, on October 24, vetoed the bill and stated that such a bill was "unconstitutional and dangerous to the best interest of our nation." He objected most vehemently to the sixty-day time limit and the concurrent resolution, which would take away "by a mere legislative act, authorities which the President has properly exercised under the Constitution for almost two hundred years." He noted that "the responsible and effective exercise of the war powers required the fullest cooperation between the Congress and the executive" and that some provisions of the bill helped this process. But his grounds for veto rested on the constitutional and practical implications of the bill, and he stated that he would welcome a bipartisan study of their separate constitutional roles in order to facilitate further cooperation.

The veto, while not surprising to anyone in Congress, did have an energizing effect on congressional resolve to see the bill become law. Support for the conference bill was strong, and the vote, despite small but vociferous numbers of administration supporters led by Senators Goldwater and Tower and members of the liberal opposition who viewed it as actually enhancing presidential powers, was 75–18 in favor of override.

We in the administration had pinned our hopes for sustaining the veto on the House, where the conference report had been approved by three votes short of a two-thirds majority. However, despite our intense lobbying, 13 Democrats and 5 Republicans reversed their previous vote and voted for the override, making the override at 284–135. The override seemed to have little to do with the merits of the issue; each day we found support falling away from us because of the growing Watergate conflagration. As we were fighting for override votes, Archibald Cox, the Watergate special prosecutor, was fired; and Elliot Richardson, the attorney general, had resigned. The Watergate tapes were becoming an issue, and everyone kept in mind the Yom Kippur War, which had begun the previous month; another entangling commitment of American troops might follow. All these events gave a sense of urgency to Congress and to the media. In fact, the override was far more significant as a benchmark in the collapse of the Nixon presidency than as a vote on any constitutional issues. It was the first veto to be overriden by the Ninety-third Congress. Seven earlier attempts had failed.

The purpose of the War Powers Act is stated in Section 2(a):

> [to] ensure that the collective judgment of both Congress and the President will apply to the introduction of the United States armed forces into hostilities, or in situations where imminent hostilities are clearly indicated by the circumstances, and to the continued use of such forces in hostilities or in such situations.

The resolution also explains the president's powers over the use of armed forces. Section 2(c) states that the president has powers as commander in chief to introduce U.S. troops into hostilities or imminent hostilities only when Congress declares war; when Congress authorizes specific statutes to permit action; or when there is a national emergency fostered by an attack upon the United States, U.S. territories, or U.S. armed forces.

Section 3 mandates that the president consult with Congress "in every possible instance" prior to introducing U.S. troops into "hostilities or into situations where imminent involvement in hostilities is clearly indicated by the circumstance." Furthermore, the president is to continue regular consultations until U.S. troops are no longer engaged in hostilities or have been removed from the hostile or imminently hostile situation.

Section 4 sets out reporting requirements, involving the need for an executive report within forty-eight hours of an introduction of U.S. troops, explaining the circumstances necessitating the troop deployment, the constitutional and legal authority under which the deployment took place, and the estimated scope and duration of hostilities or deployment. Such a report must be made in any of three situations: when U.S. armed forces are introduced into hostilities or into situations where imminent involvement is clearly indicated by the circumstances; when U.S. armed forces equipped for combat are sent into the territory airspace or waters of a foreign nation (except for supply replacement, repair, or training deployment); or when U.S. armed forces are introduced into a foreign nation in numbers substantially enlarging existing U.S. armed forces equipped for combat there.

Additionally, the president is required to provide Congress

with such other information concerning the initial report as Congress requests "in the fulfillment of its constitutional responsibilities with respect to committing the nation to war and to the use of U.S. armed forces abroad."

Section 5 has proved to be the most constitutionally troublesome section of the War Powers Resolution. Section 5(b) provides that no later than sixty days after a report is required under Section (4) "the President shall terminate any use of United States armed forces with respect to which such support was submitted." The action must stop unless Congress specifically authorizes its continuation, declares war, extends the sixty-day period by law, or cannot meet as a result of a direct attack on the United States. The president may also extend the sixty-day period by thirty days if he determines the "unavoidable military necessity respecting the safety of U.S. armed forces requires the continued use of armed forces in the course of bringing about a prompt removal of such forces."

Section 5(c) carries with it the provision that "anytime the United States armed forces are engaged in hostilities outside the territory of the United States, its possessions and territories without a declaration of war or specific statutory authorization such forces shall be removed by the President if the Congress so direct by concurrent resolution." In other words, Section 5(c) validates a legislative veto over any use of U.S. armed forces outside the borders of the United States even during the sixty- or ninety-day period described in Section 5(b).

In Section 6, as in Section 7, priority procedures for Congress are set out for both a joint resolution or bill and a concurrent resolution. These rules allow for preferential scheduling to be given in the legislative calendar for matters concerning the War Powers Resolution. The expedited procedures for both types of legislation are enumerated.

Section 8 stipulates that no authority to deploy troops into hostilities or imminent hostilities is inferred for any law or treaty unless the law shows a specific intent to allow such authority within the meaning of the resolution or unless Congress passes enabling legislation conferring specific authority. Moreover, Section 8(c) defines direct military assistance to foreign forces as an introduction of U.S. armed forces, thus broadening the parameters of congressional control, while Section 8(d) declares that nothing in the resolution is intended to "alter the constitutional authority of the Congress or President, or provisions of existing treaties." It also states that one act should not be understood as conferring any authority upon the president that he would not already have under the resolution. It reflects a nervous concern that the sixty-day period for action not be used as a blank check for the president to act without congressional authority.

Finally, Section (9) states that if any part of the resolution is held by the courts as unconstitutional and invalid, the remainder of the resolution shall not be affected. This clause was, and remains, a congressional insurance policy against a Supreme Court decision against, for instance, the concurrent resolution, which, when it was declared unconstitutional in the subsequent *Chadha* decision, left the remainder of the resolution in effect.

The Constitution, of course, was never really the issue. As Sen. Gaylord Nelson put it during the debate, "I love the Constitution, but I hate Nixon more."

# 4

# From the War Powers Act to Tripoli's Shores

## Presidential Compliance and Defiance: The War Powers Act in Practice

Since 1973, the "pious, nonoperative, non-binding, non-enforcable language" of the War Powers Act described by Senator Eagleton as the bill's heart has led to numerous conflicts between the president and Congress. The vagueness of the resolution has meant, in practice, that the executive has ignored and avoided living up to the requirements of the resolution in times of crisis or hostility. Since the bill's passage, history has shown that Congress behaves just as it did before it was passed, supporting executive action in direct proportion to its success and to the political profit to be derived from such support.

President Nixon's experience living with the act was brief. The only use he made of U.S. troops that even tangentially invoked its provisions was during the July 1974 evacuation of U.S. citizens from Cyprus. The president ignored the act, engaged in no significant consultation, and took the position that his actions did not constitute involvement in hostilities. Congress ignored the rescue operation, and President Nixon resigned three weeks after the action, rendering the issue moot.

President Ford believed that the War Powers Act was unconstitutional. (He called it "hopelessly naive.") Nevertheless, he sought congressional approval under the act for the evacuation of

U.S. citizens from key cities in Indochina when the Communists swept into South Vietnam in 1975. The debate proved so contentious that approval was not forthcoming, and the evacuations of Da Nang on April 3, of Phnom Penh on April 11, and of Saigon on April 28 were undertaken while Congress was still wrangling. Even so, the president submitted three reports to Congress "taking note" of Section 4(a) (2) of the resolution and citing his authority as commander in chief under the Constitution. Those evacuations remained the high-water mark of presidential compliance with the act: President Ford actually called the entire Foreign Relations Committee to the White House to discuss the Saigon evacuation before he ordered the action. However, that Congress was in recess during the Da Nang and Saigon evacuations showed that there are basic flaws in the act; it may be difficult to consult with congressmen when one cannot find even one in Washington, even if you are the president of the United States.

On May 12, 1975, the merchant ship SS *Mayaguez* was seized by Cambodian armed forces, who boarded the ship en route from Hong Kong to Thailand. The ship's thirty-nine American crewmen were believed to have been taken from the ship to KohTang Island, sixty miles from the Cambodian mainland. Efforts to resolve the crisis by diplomatic means through China failed because of Cambodian intransigence, and President Ford indicated that the use of military force would be necessary. President Ford contacted eleven Senate and ten House leaders "regarding the military measures directed by the President," which would include attempts to prevent moving the crew to the Cambodian mainland. Notification of Congress came, however, after the actions had been ordered. The president also informed the leaders that U.S. military forces in the area, including one aircraft carrier and a marine amphibious unit, were on alert.

On May 14, after a briefing by a State Department official to the Foreign Relations Committee, the president ordered a rescue operation, to consist of a landing on KohTang Island to locate the hostages, marine boarding of the abandoned *Mayaguez*, and a tactical air attack against a Cambodian airstrip and other military targets on the mainland. On the evening of May 14, the president was informed that the *Mayaguez* crew had been released and was back aboard the ship. Minutes later the air strikes against Cambodia that had just commenced were concluded. Yet eighteen marines were killed, and fifty were wounded.

The War Powers Act had been given only the most modest nod. Congressional leaders had not been consulted and had been informed only after forces had been introduced into the area and were engaged in hostilities. There had been no prior consultation, as required by the act, and probably could not have been. Largely overlooked was that the president's action also violated the Cooper/Church Amendment, prohibiting the introduction of U.S. armed forces on or off the shores of Cambodia. The president, in the words of Senate Majority Leader Mike Mansfield, "to a slight extent, bent or violated" the law. Many in the Senate were furious and began planning to take on the president. Just at that point, however, polls were published showing overwhelming popular support for the president's action. Trimming rapidly to the prevailing wind of that sentiment, members on both sides of the aisle began praising the president's decisive action. There was almost no criticism except perhaps for some grousing over the need for better consultation in the future. Even the sponsors of the War Powers Act in the House, Congressmen Clement Zablocki and Dante Fascell, while hoping for better "timeliness in consultation," nevertheless termed the action "bold and successful" and "a job well done," respectively. One of the leading Senate sponsors, Sen. Mike Mansfield, said that the action made him proud to be an American. Another, Sen. Robert Byrd, stated his "pride in the American people for the unity of support in regard to this crisis." The trampled War Powers Act was not mentioned in the wave of political support. The president had acted under his authority as commander in chief and entirely outside the framework of the act and in actual violation of its provisions.

———

The election of a Democratic president in 1976 led the sponsors of the War Powers Act to hope that President Carter would follow a stricter interpretation of its provisions. Yet the first major test of how President Carter would act came after the fall of the shah of Iran in 1979, surely one of the fateful events of the postwar period and an eventuality hastened and welcomed by a president greatly distressed by the shah's record on human rights. When it became clear that the shah could not last, the Iranian military leadership, all pro-American, informed the U.S. government that it intended to establish a new government. The Carter administration sent Gen. "Dutch" Huyser to Tehran to warn the military leaders that if they tried to intervene, the U.S. government would take action against them. Shortly after the succession to power of the Ayatollah Khomeini, fifty-four American diplomats and embassy staff were taken hostage after a siege of the American embassy in Tehran. Six months of diplomatic efforts failed to secure their release. The president ordered a rescue attempt.

The operation, a classic bureaucratic bungle planned and executed from the office of Gen. David Jones, the chairman of the Joint Chiefs of Staff (JCS), began on April 24, 1980. Catering to the Washington wisdom that all military operations should be "joint," a role was mandated by the chairman for each of the military services. The eight helicopters to be used were from the navy, despite the fact that they were minesweeping helicopters; yet they would be flown by marines. There were six C-130 transport aircraft flown by the air force and ninety fighting men "equipped for combat" brought from the three services. It was an ill-conceived affair from start to finish. Three of the helicopters developed mechanical problems while in Iranian airspace, and the mission was aborted short of Tehran. But during the withdrawal, a helicopter collided with one of the C-130s on a desert strip, killing eight U.S. servicemen. It was a sad performance, fairly reflecting the shabby state of the post-Vietnam American military.

President Carter gave a television address the next day and met with congressional leaders at the White House that afternoon. He explained that no prior consultation had been undertaken because it was not required. He argued that involvement in hostilities or imminent hostilities was not clearly indicated by the circumstances of the mission, since the landing was conducted (and the accident took place) at a remote Iranian desert strip, far from any possible theater of conflict. The president must have had to bite his tongue hard as he went on to explain that had the first phase been successful, the White House would *then* have asked for permission from Congress to execute the actual rescue operation. Presumably, this would have taken place, then, while the helicopters were in midair.

On April 26, before the forty-eight-hour reporting deadline had expired, the president sent a letter to the congressional leadership explaining his actions and stating that his report was "consistent with the reporting provisions" of the act. While this language appears more compliant with the act's provision than Ford's "taking note" language, President Carter's overall attitude toward the resolution was abundantly clear: He claimed his authority as commander in chief under the Constitution as justification for the action.

Just as had occurred after the *Mayaguez* incident, the fate of the mission and its impact on popular opinion determined the congressional attitude toward the president's obvious violation of the War Powers Act. The congressional leadership was reported to be furious over the lack of consultation; there were open accusations of presidential violation of the law. Lloyd Cutler, an adviser to President Carter, wrote a legal opinion rebutting the congressional attacks, stating that "the President's constitutional power to use the armed forces to rescue Americans illegally detained abroad is clearly established. [The War Powers Act] should not be construed to require prior consultation under the precise circumstances of this case."

The facts of the case in both the *Mayaguez* and the Desert I incidents were very similar, and in both cases the president ignored the War Powers Act. President Ford was praised and his violation of the act overlooked because the rescue was a popular success. President Carter, on the other hand, was venomously criticized and called to account for his violation of the War Powers Act essentially because the rescue was a failure and his popularity was at a very low ebb.

## Lebanon

When the Lebanese Civil War erupted in 1975, the Palestine Liberation Organization (PLO) and its Shiite allies soon acquired the upper hand. As in 1958, an appeal went out from the Christian factions for U.S. help. But in 1975 Washington could not help. The best we were able to do, with Israeli agreement, was to acquiesce when Syria intervened on behalf of the Christians. "Redlines," tacit rules with Israel, regulated not only Syria's penetration south but also its level of armament in Lebanon. In this way the Palestine Liberation Organization (PLO) was checked.

By 1981, however, the security of this stalemate was crumbling. The Syrians, isolated and fearful after the Camp David Accords brought peace between Egypt and Israel, made common cause with the PLO. Israel's government, under Prime Minister Menachem Begin, had conducted extensive armed sweeps into Lebanon, at the same time solidifying an alliance with the Maronite Catholics, led by Bashir Gemayel, the commander of the strongest Christian militia, the Phalange. Border incidents and internal tensions rose. Finally, in May 1981, when the Syrians and the Phalange clashed, Israeli planes shot down Syrian helicopters. The Syrians promptly moved SAM batteries into the Bekaa Valley, threatening Israel's ability to fly air reconnaissance missions over Lebanon. Thereafter followed a year of intensive political maneuvering and increasing military skirmishing while Washington tried in vain to delay the inevitable.

Israeli tanks rolled into Lebanon on June 6, 1982, following the attempted assassination of the Israeli ambassador to the United Kingdom and an exchange of air and artillery blows with the PLO. From the Navy Department, we in the Reagan administration watched two dramas unfold: Israel's expansion of the war and Secretary of State Alexander Haig's battle to preserve a coherent policy while pitted against elements in the State Department, the White House, and the Defense Department outraged by the Israeli attack and anxious to redirect U.S. policy to punish Israel.

Israel's military success had clearly dealt a heavy blow to America's enemies, among them the PLO, Syria, and by implication, the USSR. The Israeli air force's successful application of American technology to destroy the SAMs and more than one hundred Soviet-built MiGs, all without loss, was a harbinger of the one-sided success of Desert Storm; in fact, this success provided quite a few lessons that were applied by U.S. Air Force,

Marine, and Navy aviators in that later battle. But the diplomatic outcome hinged on the removal of the PLO from Beirut, the withdrawal of all forces, and the reestablishment of an authoritative Lebanese government. For a brief moment, this seemed possible. On June 25, 1982, however, the embattled Haig resigned; the administration had thoroughly undercut him by offering mixed signals about its intentions. The PLO stalled for time, and in the ensuing Israeli bombardments, the fragile Lebanese political coalition, pulled together by Haig, collapsed. There was now no force in Beirut that stood for Lebanon.

Into this void the United States, supported by its allies in London, Paris, and Rome, proposed to put into place a multinational peacekeeping force. As originally conceived, it was to be one element in a far-reaching agreement that provided for the withdrawal of all foreign forces, including those of the PLO, Israel, and Syria. But with Haig's departure, the scope of the plan was narrowed. President Reagan's announcement, on July 6, that the United States would participate in such a force only to achieve the temporary supervision of PLO withdrawal caught all of us in the Navy Department completely by surprise.

In the third week of August, 800 U.S. Marines along with 800 French, 400 Italian, and 200 British troops, landed in Beirut to supervise PLO withdrawal. This multinational force was supposed to stay in Beirut for one month, until the inauguration of Bashir Gemayel, the newly elected president of Lebanon. But on September 10, at the urging of Defense Secretary Weinberger, who had the strong support of those of us at the Navy Department, the marines were withdrawn. Four days later, Bashir was blown up by a bomb universally believed to have been planted by the Syrians. Despite its earlier pledge not to do so, the Israeli army now entered West Beirut in the name of "restoring order." Instead, the Phalange militia avenged themselves on the Palestinians, bringing about what became known as the Sabra and Shatilla massacres, on September 16–18. This led the United States, Britain, France, and Italy to return their forces to Lebanon, and on September 29, the Thirty-second Marine Amphibious Unit, 1,200 strong, landed in Beirut to take up positions near Beirut International Airport between the Israeli forces and West Beirut. Then, in early November, the Twenty-fourth Marine Am-

phibious Unit replaced the Thirty-second. Later that month, marine mobile training teams began to instruct the Lebanese army
in the hopes of making it a true fighting force.

By September 1983, our forces at the airport had already been
fired upon by rockets, artillery, and mortars. Two marines were
killed on August 29, and on August 31, marine patrols were
curtailed. Two more of our marines were killed on September 6.
Meanwhile, the Lebanese army was fighting for its life in the
small hill town of Suq al Gharb, on the edge of Beirut.

Hostile fire on the marines and even the ambassador's residence continued to increase until the battleship *New Jersey* arrived off Beirut on September 25. Attacks stopped, and a cease-
fire was agreed upon.

There were those who claimed that these actions cost us the
protection of our status as a neutral, placing the United States
conclusively on the side of the Christians. The marines were now
seen by all factions as combatants and therefore fair game. But
that perception was in fact well developed long before September
everywhere except at the White House and in the State Department; after all, between August 28 and September 26, four marines had been killed and twenty-eight wounded in action. Thus,
the marines were already under attack well before the order was
given to return fire. As for the policy of U.S. neutrality, it was
difficult to understand what our mission could be if it was not to
support the legal Lebanese government, however hopeless the
mission may have been.

Because of what kind of accounting the War Powers Act would
require, the White House insisted on clinging to the illusion of
neutrality. At one point, in a burst of unusual clarity, the White
House issued a statement saying that the forces were there to
"take what steps are necessary in support of the newly constituted government of Lebanon." After opponents in Congress then
pointed out that this was in violation of the War Powers Act, the
administration hastily revised its position and said that the forces
were there solely "in support of the multinational force and protection of U.S. lives." As secretary of the navy, I was personally
unable to keep up with the rapidly changing party line, and at a

breakfast meeting with reporters, I described what was in fact the case, that "we will be providing supporting fire to Lebanese forces and it isn't linked to incoming fire to the marines." The State Department went berserk. The next day, the White House issued a statement contradicting me, stating that "the secretary's assertions were incorrect" and that "whatever we [the United States] do is in support of the marines." I was ordered by Secretary Weinberger to issue a recantation in a formal statement, which I promptly did, silly as it was. The administration was now trapped by the verbal acrobatics it had undertaken to avoid congressional restrictions. Though everyone knew that the marines were never neutral, in attempting to avoid the strictures of the War Powers Act and satisfy the delusions of the State Department, the military chain of command institutionally forgot the *reality* of the marines' true status as combatants, whatever the political rhetoric. Catastrophe was sure to result.

---

It came on Sunday, October 23, when a yellow nineteen-ton Mercedes truck loaded with an explosive the estimated equivalent of six to nine tons of TNT crashed through the perimeter of the U.S. Marine headquarters building, a seemingly secure four-story, concrete-reinforced structure at the marine compound at the airport. The truck passed through the guard post and penetrated into the building, where it detonated. The force of the explosion lifted the entire building off its foundations, and the structure collapsed on the sleeping marines, killing 241 and wounding 100 more. The sentries, faithful to the rules of engagement that had been designed around the "neutrality" required by the War Powers Act, did not have their guns ready. The cause of this tragedy was the administration's genuflection to the War Powers Act.

---

In his statement announcing the initial deployment of marines, President Reagan had stated that he would be willing to employ troops in concert with French and Italian forces and that he would comply with the War Powers Resolution in doing so. Because the invitation to deploy troops came from the Lebanese government—and in light of the fact that no hostilities were imminent—

a report to Congress was probably not necessary under the resolution, although consultation between the branches was pursued. In President Reagan's first report on Lebanon, dated August 24, 1982, he referred to the action as "consistent with the War Powers Resolution" without citing any section under which he was reporting. The agreement with Lebanon, the president said, "ruled out any possibility of combat responsibilities for the U.S. forces," and the objective was a "permanent cessation of hostilities." Although Judge William Clark, the president's national security adviser, said that such reporting was unnecessary, it was pursued mainly to preclude criticism from congressional leaders.

Nearly a month later, on September 20, after the marines had been evacuated and following the assassination of Gemayel, the Lebanese government extended another invitation to France, Italy, and the United States to reconstitute the multinational peacekeeping force in Beirut. In a televised speech the same day, President Reagan accepted Lebanon's invitation to join the multinational force "similar to the one which served so well last month."

Many in Congress voiced concern that "imminent hostilities" were now very likely. Splitting hairs, the administration concluded that such hostilities were not "clearly indicated by the circumstances." This view was used to excuse the fact that there had been no prior consultation, as would have been required under the act, if hostilities were imminent. Yet on September 29, 1,200 marines began landing in Beirut; President Reagan now filed a report stating, as before, that the troops were "equipped for combat [but] will not engage in combat." The commandant of the Marine Corps, P. X. Kelley, agreed with me, however, that there would be hostilities and that the marines were certain to become targets. Soon three marines died in an unexplained explosion. There was continued sniping in Congress over the president's refusal to cite Section 4(a)(1) of the War Powers Act. Sen. Charles Percy of Illinois argued that "the clock began to run when the first marines landed in Lebanon." During the next year, more violence against marines occurred. By August 1983, there were increasing mortar attacks against the marines, and on August 29 the first marines were killed in what could not be described as anything else but combat. The next day, the administration dutifully made its report to Congress but did not cite Section 4(a)(1), denying that these combat deaths indicated in fact the existence of hostilities, characterizing whatever fighting there was as "sporadic" instead. Some days later, under further pressure, the president made a wonderful verbal contortion, stating that the situation constituted a "generalized pattern of violence" rather than true hostilities. Of course, had he called a spade a spade, Section 4(a)(1) of the War Powers Act would have triggered the sixty-day limit on withdrawal if no congressional affirmative action had taken place. Senator Percy, among others in Congress, was apoplectic: "We have people up in helicopters who are shooting rockets and artillery—if that isn't imminent hostilities, I don't know what is."

Invoking the act through a joint resolution was deemed unrealistic, just as any such bill that passed through Congress would surely be vetoed, and since President Reagan was not the weakened president who had been in office in 1973, his veto would almost certainly have been upheld in at least one house. Congress finally decided on a compromise between the branches that would both invoke Section 4(a)(1) and the sixty-day clock but, somewhat contradictorily, granted the president statutory authorization for eighteen months after its passage.

House Joint Resolution 364 recognized that the United States was engaged in hostilities in Lebanon and that this fact made Section 4(a) (1) operative on August 29, 1983, the date of the first U.S. combat-related casualties. Futhermore, it requested periodic reports from the president on the status of the forces and how he planned to extricate them. Additionally, it laid out four instances in which the authorization would terminate before the provided eighteen months, namely, the withdrawal of all foreign forces from Lebanon unless the president certified the troops were necessary to fulfill the original intent of the multinational force; the assumption by the United States or Lebanon itself of the multinational force's responsibilities; the implementation of another effective security arrangement on the areas; or the withdrawal of all other countries from the multinational force.

The president traded invocation of the War Powers Resolution for at least eighteen months' grace from Congress. But, in fact, when he signed the bill, he took the opportunity to argue with the measure, stating, "I would note that the initiation of isolated or infrequent acts of violence against the United States armed forces does not constitute actual or imminent involvement in hostilities, even if casualties to those forces result. I think it unreasonable not to recognize the inherent risk and imprudence of setting any precise formula for making such determinations." Such quibbling was rather beside the point. But he also took the opportunity to attack the legitimacy of the War Powers Act's infringement on the president's constitutional authority, stating that it would have no effect on his authority as president to deploy armed forces if necessary. Nevertheless, he did sign the bill; if he had been true to his rhetoric, he would have vetoed it. The whole episode simply underlines the fact that whatever the theory or the legislation, the struggle between the president and Congress for control of national security always ends up fought on political rather than constitutional or legal terrain.

---

The disastrous and ill-conceived deployment of marines to Beirut provides an excellent example of the use of military forces that have nothing to do with declarations of war. Certainly marines were in combat; in fact, many more were killed during that non-war than during Operation Desert Storm. U.S. naval, air force, and marine artillery undoubtedly also killed a good many combatants of various factions. But with whom were we at "war"?

Seen from the White House, congressional demands for detailed information on troop placement, procedures, rules of engagement, and plans for extrication were viewed as unmitigated intrusions on the president's authority as commander in chief. Yet Congress had every right to question, challenge, and express its extreme discomfort as to what our troops were doing in Lebanon. The discomfiture, in fact, was a symptom of the lack of persuasiveness of the administration's rationale. I have always believed that if a military mission can't be explained in simple declarative sentences, then it should not be undertaken.

There was, however, another disturbing aspect to the influence of the War Powers Act on U.S. actions in Lebanon. One week before the terrorist bombing that killed the 241 marines, a radio message between two Muslim militia units was intercepted that read: "If we kill fifteen Marines, the rest will leave." This analysis was presumably based on enemy awareness of the difficulty of the American position. Robert Turner, a scholar at the University of Virginia, exhaustively analyzed the event and concluded that "by tying the trigger on the War Powers Resolution to such events as a terrorist attack on American servicemen, Congress had inadvertently both surrendered the initiative to anti-American radicals around the world and virtually placed a 'bounty' on the lives of American servicemen abroad."[1]

The attack on the marines had exactly that effect. Within six months of the bombing, the marines were gone, and President Reagan's policy was abandoned in defeat.

## Grenada

When President Reagan was awakened on October 23, 1983, with news of the marine disaster in Beirut, he had already had a bad weekend. In Augusta, Georgia for a short golfing holiday with Secretary of State George Shultz, a would-be assassin crashed the club grounds.

Yet something else was on his mind as well. A few days earlier, the president had ordered the diversion of a marine amphibious group and the USS *Independence* carrier battle group from its mission to relieve the forces standing off Beirut. Instead, the force headed for the southeastern Caribbean island of Grenada. One thousand Americans, most of them medical students, were caught up in the bloody fall of the island's Marxist government. Grenada was soon to become a theater for the successful exercise of American military power.

Grenada was an odd place for these events. Discovered by Columbus in 1498 and settled initially by the French, it ceased to interest statesmen after the British finally took it permanently in 1783. Only one hundred miles from Venezuela, this southernmost of the eastern Caribbean islands eventually became the placid residence of some 110,000 mostly illiterate farmers who exported cacao, nutmeg, and spices for a modest living. In 1967 the British had set Grenada on the road to independence within the commonwealth, and by 1974 independence had been achieved under the leadership of Sir Eric Gairy.

Sir Eric, an eccentric believer in voodoo and UFOs, was replaced in a bloodless coup in March 1979 by Maurice Bishop. On the same day, the United States announced its recognition of Bishop's government, Bishop announced that he would seek arms and economic assistance from Fidel Castro. The Carter administration, confused by the Nicaraguan revolution and perplexed by Castro's aggressive policies in the Caribbean, stood helplessly by.

Over a four-year period, Grenada sank into economic distress accompanied by Communist resurgence. Bishop received more than $33 million in aid from Cuba. Arms sufficient to equip a 10,000-man force were stockpiled on the island, and an airport designed to accommodate the longest-range Soviet bombers was constructed by a Cuban team of military engineers.

Bishop next took to the world stage to proclaim his support for the Soviet invasion of Afghanistan. Huge pictures of Castro, Ortega, and Bishop began to decorate public buildings. On the island itself, the familiar apparatus of a Communist police state was erected, complete with an East German–designed security system.

Concern about these developments in the Caribbean had become an important element in the Reagan foreign and defense policy in 1981. Indeed, as early as March 1980, candidate Reagan had revealed in a major campaign address the "totalitarian Marxist takeover of Grenada, where Cuban advisers are now training guerrillas. . . . Must we let Grenada, Nicaragua, and El Salvador all become additional Cubas [and] new outposts for Soviet combat brigades?"

While various Reagan officials now indicate that President Reagan's global strategy gave rise to decisive action in Grenada, the reality is that the Communists would probably still be there if it were not for their own ineptitude. As part of the congressional onslaught against the Central Intelligence Agency (CIA), the last intelligence sources in Grenada had been removed in 1979, and other than what we could gather from satellite intelligence, we did not have a clear picture of what was happening on the island. That enabled Pollyannas in the CIA and the State Department, always hoping for the best, to argue against interpreting developments in Grenada as hostile to U.S. interest. The British Foreign Office was even worse. Up to the very day of the invasion, British "experts" had adamantly maintained to Prime Minister Margaret Thatcher that there was nothing happening on the island that justified intervention. This led her to bitterly oppose American action when it came.

Ultimately, the intervention, when it came, did not arise from American grand strategy but from the breakout of chaos within the ruling faction: The Grenadan Communists consumed themselves. Upon his return from a trip to visit his friends in Eastern Europe and Cuba in October, Bishop was arrested by a faction of his cohorts led by Bernard and Phyllis Coard. A week later, he was freed by a mob of three thousand; then he led a march on the main military barracks, where a massacre ensued. On October 19, Bishop himself was killed. On October 21, President Reagan ordered the marine amphibious unit and the *Independence* battle group to the area. Castro immediately dispatched one of his most trusted army officers to Grenada to organize the defenses. On October 23, the president ordered "Operation Urgent Fury" to rescue the thousand Americans on Grenada, restore order, and bring democracy back to Grenada.

The task force commander had planned a classic textbook marine amphibious and air assault of the island supported by the *Independence* air wing and naval gunfire. The JCS, under severe pressure from Senator Nunn and the Armed Services Committee to require all military operations to be multiservice and "joint," overruled the task force commander and ordered that additional elements from the army and air force be added to the navy and marines. The result was a force of some 15,000 U.S. troops plus a contingent of 300 soldiers and police from six neighboring Caribbean countries. They were opposed by the Grenadan People's Revolutionary Army of 1,000 men, several thousand ill-trained militia, and the Cubans. There were over 700 Cubans on the island, the largest number, 636, being a military construction crew finishing Point Salinas Airport. Forty Cuban instructors, assigned to the Grenadan army, together with forty-three regular soldiers, forty-four women, and eighteen diplomats, rounded out the Cuban presence.

So many different unrelated U.S. units were used that there were inevitable foul-ups, mistakes, and some unnecessary casualties. But after ten days, all of the U.S. objectives had been

111

achieved, and the island was secured. Eighteen American servicemen lost their lives, some to friendly fire, and 116 were wounded. Twenty-four Cubans had been killed, and 59 were wounded; 45 Grenadans died, and 337 were wounded.

On October 24, the evening the operation was launched and two hours after the orders had been issued, President Reagan met with a number of congressional leaders for "consultations." He explained that the mission was designed to protect "the safety of innocent lives on the island, including those of up to a thousand United States citizens." The operation was justified on the basis of the president's power to conduct foreign relations and his role as commander in chief.

The day after the invasion, House Speaker Tip O'Neill, speaking for the Democratic leadership, condemned the president for his conduct of "gunboat diplomacy," and on the floor of the House many members demanded the enforcement of the War Powers Act. The Democratic leadership promptly pushed through House Joint Resolution 402, which determined that a sixty-day limit on presidential action was triggered by the Grenada action.

Many congressman would suddenly feel the need to change their attitude; the first polls showed a 90 percent approval rating for the president's action. Speaker O'Neill quickly trimmed his sails and announced that the action was "justified." The loud demands for an inquiry into the president's breach of the War Powers Act were quickly dropped. Debate over constitutional principles had once again been overwhelmed by political reality. Had the operation been a fiasco, it would have been otherwise.

## Dealing with Qaddafi

By 1986, Mu'ammar Qaddafi was a living monument to the weakness and the indecision of the West. On more than one occasion this foremost practitioner of state-sponsored terrorism had been vulnerable to overthrow, only to be spared by European or American vacillation. He had ascended to power in 1969. Following the 1967 Arab/Israeli war, which closed the Suez Canal, Libya had become the focus of serious oil exploration brought to success by Marathon, Exxon, and other major U.S. oil companies. Those were hopeful signs for a country that had suffered brutalization and colonial misrule between 1913 and 1943 and was otherwise famous in modern times only because its desert had provided the forum for the epic Montgomery-Rommel tank duels of World War II.

As Libya's economic prospects brightened, its political system disintegrated. The Americans and the British, both of whom retained military bases in Libya, had helped place King Idris I on the throne when Libya gained independence in 1951. As Idris aged, however, he and his heir fell into a bitter quarrel. When Richard Allen and I were sent to Libya by Henry Kissinger in April 1969, Tripoli was filled with rumors of coups that would unseat the king. Apparently both the monarch and the crown prince were preparing to depose each other, but when a coup was launched on September 1, it turned out to be led by the unknown, though British-trained, Qaddafi. With the old king infirm, ineffective, and conveniently out of the country (his son was judged by all to be unfit to rule), the coup succeeded.

Libya's new master lost little time announcing that he was a disciple of Egyptian president Gamal Abdel Nasser. Yet Qaddafi, a devout Muslim and fierce anti-Marxist, was by no means a Soviet puppet. Shortly after the coup he requested military assistance from the United States and sought, specifically, to buy F-5E fighters and to gain the presence of an air force advisory team. While Kissinger strongly favored the initiative, it was killed by the State Department, under pressure from the Senate Foreign Relations Committee, because they saw the move as "fueling an arms race." Perhaps his anti-Western proclivities would have led Qaddafi to the Soviets, anyway, but this turndown drove him immediately to request Soviet assistance, which was promptly supplied. Shortly thereafter, Qaddafi demanded the withdrawal of the United States and the British from their air force training bases in Libya. The Pentagon and the National Security Council (NSC) both argued that the United States had clear rights to maintain those bases and should hold on to them as we had with our base at Guantánamo Bay, Cuba. The State Department, under the goading of Chairman Fulbright, argued that the bases were a needless source of friction and of little military value. This view carried the day, and the bases were evacuated and turned over to Qaddafi in 1970. For him it was a major propaganda victory.

Next, Qaddafi turned against the Occidental Petroleum Company, demanding a large increase of its payments for Libyan oil. Occidental, at that time a maverick in the Middle Eastern oil fields, appealed to big American companies, "the seven sisters," to sell oil to Occidental should Qaddafi shut down its operations. They refused. Armand Hammer, Occidental's chairman, then took his risk. He agreed to Qaddafi's terms, betting on a seller's market in oil. He was right.

Emboldened by Qaddafi's example, the shah of Iran and then the other Gulf state leaders whipsawed the companies into higher prices. The price of oil had thus already accelerated by 40 percent in the years immediately preceding the Yom Kippur War of October 1973. Libya had led the way.

Qaddafi set about seizing leadership of the Arabs through a potent combination of money (his annual oil earnings jumped from $3 billion a year to more than $12 billion a year in only five years), his purchase of Soviet arms far beyond his needs, and his *green book*—an incoherent series of philosophical ruminations that underscored Qaddafi's megalomania rather than his intelligence. He was aware that in challenging the West he could not win a military confrontation. So he sought instead another route. In the early 1970s, helped by the PLO, he discovered the uses of terrorism.

We in the West have a hard time dealing with terrorism, perhaps because we do not really understand the terrorist purpose. The terrorist knows that he cannot win an open test of strength. His objective instead is to paralyze our will to act, to pit our regard for individual life against our instinct for self-defense. So every terrorist action has a political purpose—to force us to change our policies at the price of innocent lives. Leaders of democracies have found it very difficult to resist this pressure, amplified as it is by sensationalist TV coverage, even if it means that other innocent lives might be put at risk later.

Qaddafi first used terrorism as part of an effort to force the United States and Western Europe to reduce their support for Israel—an effort that began with airline hijackings. At one time or another, Algeria and Syria worked with him. Beyond the Arab/Israeli conflict, Qaddafi also sought to make of himself a "world power" through terrorism. By the early 1970s, as Western Europe reeled under the 1972 Munich massacre, airline hijackings, murders, and mayhem, Qaddafi oil money was financing a terrorist internationale: the PLO, the Irish Republican Army (IRA), the Red Brigades, the Japanese Red Army, even the Moro Muslim guerrillas in the Philippines. The Soviet Union and its Eastern European allies were happy to provide arms and training to these various "freedom fighters" in exchange for desperately needed hard cash. The result was a horrifying paradox: In purchasing Libya's oil, the West was financing Qaddafi's attacks on the West.

By the late seventies, the terrorist cycle had ensnared the victims in confusion, caution, and conflicting interests. Individual fanatics and groups increasingly drew on the resources of Libya and other states. But while individuals and groups often could be handled by good police work, once embassies and foreign intelligence agencies entered the picture, it became another matter. "Police action" against a state means war.

The response of the Western powers to this explosion of state-sponsored terrorism can only be described as paralysis. The reasons were numerous. The European governments who depend on Arab-produced oil preferred police work and "diplomacy," which translated into a pro-PLO Middle East policy or pro-Libyan, pro-Iraqi, or pro-Syrian policies, depending on the source of the trouble. It was rumored that France, a traditional haven for exiles and terrorists, had engineered a deal with the PLO and its state sponsors not to interfere with terrorist operations so long as they did not occur on French territory. Italy, which at one point appeared on the verge of succumbing to the Red Brigades, was widely believed to have done the same, hoping thereby to separate the domestic terrorists from their foreign helpers.

The United States itself was largely free of such terrorist incidents, although Americans abroad were often targets. When Iran's Ayatollah Khomeini turned to open terrorism, the issue transformed American politics. America's inability to come to grips with state-sponsored terrorism helped seal the doom of President Carter's bid for reelection. When President Reagan came to power, we who came to power with him were certain we could do better.

Our rhetoric, at least, *was* better. Upon the release of Americans held by Iran, the president had promised retaliation in the future. Libya was an obvious first place to start. Qaddafi had made of himself a target not just because he blatantly supported terrorism but also because he had expanded his operations to outright aggression; Libyan troops had seized a part of Chad and financed guerrillas in the Sudan. Once President Anwar Sadat of Egypt had begun his journey toward peace with Israel, Qaddafi swore to overthrow him; this led Qaddafi and Libya into a still closer relationship with the USSR. Amid these portents, a more dramatic event took place.

Against international law, Libya had laid claim to the entire Gulf of Sidra, a large indentation in the North African coastline that was flanked by Libyan territory but was unquestionably international not territorial water. This of itself would have been of little consequence and normally would have been treated like the dozens of other unlawful claims that the United States does not recognize. The Gulf of Sidra, however, was the only place in the Mediterranean that was free of any major sea lanes or airways, and for decades the U.S. Sixth Fleet had depended on it for its periodic live-fire exercises. Qaddafi's new prohibition gave the Sixth Fleet a training problem. The chief of naval operations, Adm. James Holloway, strongly recommended that the Sixth Fleet continue its exercises and be prepared to defend itself. The Carter administration, however, received firm intelligence that Qaddafi was prepared to fight. They had no desire for such a confrontation, and the navy was prohibited from deploying any of its ships or aircraft below the thirty-two degrees thirty minutes north latitude line—the "line of death," as Qaddafi called it—thus giving de facto recognition to his territorial claims.

With the new Reagan administration, it was not long before we in the navy put forward a new request to resume operations in the Gulf below the "line of death." It was promptly approved by the president, and the Sixth Fleet proceeded with its plans for a major exercise in that area. None of us involved in the decision had any doubt that conflict was very likely. Under the plain meaning of the War Powers Act, therefore, its terms should have been triggered. We ignored it. In August 1981 the fleet crossed the "line of death," and the Libyan air force, now grown to several hundred late-model MiGs, SU-22s, and Mirages, rose to meet it. Qaddafi had bought far more aircraft then he had pilots able to fly them, and there were Syrian, North Korean, North Vietnamese, and East German "volunteers" manning his force. In the first few days of the exercise, Libyan aircraft attempted to get into firing position on the U.S. fighters protecting the fleet but in every case were unsuccessful. The very high tech F-14s, with their two-hundred-mile radars, were able to maneuver into firing position long before the Libyans ever saw them. Very often a Libyan pilot's first sight of them was turning around to see an F-14 just a few feet off his wings.

Finally, two SU-22s were ordered to fire on a flight of two F-14s from Fighter Squadron 41 off the USS *Nimitz*. They did so despite the fact that they were not in effective firing position, given the model of Russian missile they were carrying. The outcome was never in doubt. The F-14 radar had the SU-22s locked up while they were still on the runway and in their takeoff roll sixty miles away. Under the rules of engagement in force, the American aircraft had to be fired upon before they were able to defend themselves. When the SU-22s sighted the F-14, they immediately fired their missiles in a head-on shot. The Tomcats evaded the missiles and immediately rolled in on the tails of the two SU-22s. Despite their desperate evasion, they were each "splashed" with a single Sidewinder heat-seeking missile.

We in the administration were quite optimistic that this was the first step in what should be a collective Western effort to finish Qaddafi's troublemaking everywhere. It was not to be so. Qaddafi, just as he was to do following our actions in 1986, immediately went to ground and signaled his desire for a "dialogue" with the United States. He pulled back from his active adventures in the Sudan and elsewhere. It was purely a tactical move and was a complete success. The U.S. bureaucracy and a coalition of oil companies effectively stymied any further diplomatic or commercial sanctions against him. By the winter of 1982, Secretary of State Haig finally had to abandon his effort to obtain joint sanctions against Libya. Moreover, the Sixth Fleet was allowed no further permission to operate below the "line of death" in the Gulf of Sidra until nearly four years later, when the president approved another Sidra exercise in 1986. The crisis had passed, and Qaddafi resumed his support of terrorism around the world.

Once again, the success of the shootdown squelched any congressional effort to invoke the War Powers Act. The shootdown

117

was so overwhelmingly popular that Congress chose to ignore the constitutional issue, just as we in the administration had in ordering the action.

By this time I had observed the president often enough to make a few judgments. In his dealings with terrorism, as in other matters, he was the victim of his own romantic confidence in the institution of the JCS. Ronald Reagan longed for the restoration of respect for our military and our flag. He personally would do much to bring it about. But he never realized that the convoluted and bureaucratized ways of the vast JCS almost always deprived him of sensible plans. Only when the JCS chairman takes planning out of the hands of the vast Washington bureaucracy and works directly with the operational commander, as Gen. Colin Powell would do with Gen. Norman Schwarzkopf in 1990 and 1991, does sensible strategy emerge.

This weakness overlay a deeper struggle over the use of American power that constantly distorted decision making during President Reagan's first term and often paralyzed the administration. Following the Lebanese fiasco, Secretary of State George Shultz had taken the "tough" rhetorical road on terrorism. On the other hand, Cap Weinberger, speaking for the JCS, specified elaborate conditions for the use of military force that "if taken literally, ruled out every likely application in the modern world." When you combined Pentagon paralysis and State Department bellicosity, the results were stupefying. Loud talk and no action repeatedly followed the taking of American hostages. We remained unwilling to risk the use of our military power.

In President Reagan's second term, this internal contradiction was to lead to the disastrous Iran-Contra affair. But before that happened, a series of terrorist outrages—and public reaction—finally forced the president to use military power against both terrorists and a state supporting them.

On June 14, 1985, TWA flight 847 had been seized, forced to Beirut, then flown to Algeria, and before our antiterrorist units could act, the terrorists were tipped off by the Algerians to return to Beirut. The pattern proved familiar. The terrorists found an American—in this case navy diver Robert Stethem—and murdered him in cold blood. The killers then demanded that the Israelis release Shiite prisoners taken from Lebanon as part of the Israeli withdrawal. There were dramatic scenes of helpless Americans held at gunpoint. Finally, though no overt American pressure was proved, a deal was reached to release the Shiites.

This incident had frightened and angered the Reagan White House. It was followed in October by a similar incident, but this time with a better ending. On October 3, 1985, the *Achille Lauro* cruise ship departed from Genoa, Italy, for the Middle East. Lax security let four Arab gunman board the ship despite their assorted Latin-American passports and their lack of luggage. Their original mission was probably to infiltrate Israel on one of the ship's port calls, but a steward discovered the four oiling their guns while the ship was moored at Alexandria, Egypt. This was October 7, a Monday.

The pirates then seized control of the ship and forced it to sail for Syria. The Syrian government refused to receive them, and the Israeli government rejected the terrorists' demand for the release of fifty Palestinian prisoners. True to form, the terrorists then murdered an American. This time Leon Klinghoffer, a crippled New Yorker confined to a wheelchair, was the victim.

Upon their return to Alexandria, the terrorists, who belonged to a particularly vicious Palestinian faction, were set free under terms negotiated by their leader, Abu Abbas, with the support of the Egyptian government. The Italian and West German ambassadors, but not the United States, agreed formally to these arrangements, which were to send the terrorists to freedom. As it turned out, however, despite Cairo's claims, the culprits were still in Egypt preparing to fly to Tunisia on an Egyptian plane.

When the White House confirmed this information on Thursday, October 10, reportedly with Israeli help, they then issued an order to intercept the terrorists and force them to land at a NATO (North Atlantic Treaty Organization) air base in Italy. Adm. John Poindexter and Lt. Col. Oliver North, working under Bud McFarlane's supervision and with the president's approval, had orchestrated a daring plan to intercept the terrorists using the ready instrument of the U.S. Navy Sixth Fleet and its brilliant commander, Adm. Frank Kelso.

An alert was sent to Kelso, and he ordered his battle group commander, Rear Adm. Dave Jeremiah, aboard the *Saratoga*, heading for a liberty port call in Yugoslavia, immediately to reverse course. Less than forty-five minutes after receiving Kelso's order, Jeremiah launched six F-14 interceptors, two A-6 tankers, and two E-2C radar-controlling aircraft. After they took off, Kelso ordered the interception of the Egyptian aircraft and fed them continual intelligence updates as they came in. They had to fly five hundred miles in pitch darkness to the spot where they hoped to intercept the Egyptian airliner.

The Egypt Air 737 took off from Al Maza air base for Algiers at 10:10 P.M. Cairo time, only ten minutes after the president made his final decision to intercept. While intelligence had provided to the *Saratoga* the type of aircraft and its side number, there were more than sixty airliners in the air over the eastern Mediterranean at the time. Computer radar aboard the E-2Cs and F-14s helped narrow the number of initial targets, but visual inspection had to be made of four different aircraft before the correct side number was found. In each case, pilots of the F-14s had to fly silently right up next to the unsuspecting aircraft and read the side numbers with a flashlight. One of those aircraft inspected turned out to be the American C-141 carrying Gen. Carl W. Stiner and his commandos, who had been ordered to Akrotiri, Cyprus, in hopes of apprehending the pirates in the event of the successful intercept and who were now returning to Sigonella. When the aircraft was in the air, the intelligence community learned that Abbas, the mastermind of the plot, was himself aboard the Egyptian airliner along with the Egyptian commandos.

When the F-14s found the right airliner, there was a problem with communications in that they were equipped only with military UHF radios and the airliner had only a civilian VHF radio. They communicated, therefore, through the E-2C radar plane, more than a hundred miles away. The E-2C had both. One of the controllers aboard the E-2C spoke to the Egyptian pilot, pretending he was one of the F-14 pilots, and after making initial contact, the F-14s suddenly turned on all their lights. To the amazement of the Egyptian crew, they were surrounded by four F-14s. The initial reluctance of the Egyptian air pilot to change course to Sigonella was soon overcome by threats of dire consequences. He changed course and was escorted some four hundred miles to Sigonella by the F-14s. On approach to Sigonella, the Italians denied the Egyptian planes landing permission, and only when he declared an emergency was he given permission to land. The E-2C controllers had ordered him to make a left turn off the runway over to the American side of the base, but at the last minute the Italian tower reversed instructions as to which runway to use, so that when he turned left after landing, it was onto the Italian side of the field rather than the American side. General Stiner and his commandos landed right behind the Egyptian airliner and followed it off the runway. They immediately surrounded the aircraft and sought to take custody of the pirates. The Italian *carabinieri*, however, arrived and surrounded the airliner and the Americans, and a tense standoff resulted until General Stiner agreed to turn the pirates over to the Italians.

In the meantime, once the F-14s saw the aircraft safely on the ground, they returned the five hundred miles back and trapped (landed) aboard the *Saratoga* without incident.

Now came the moment of truth for the Italian government. It flunked. The higher priority of keeping on good terms with both the PLO and its Arab backers prevailed, and the Italian government guaranteed Abbas safe passage to Yugoslavia and then to Algeria. In the ensuing uproar, the Bettino Craxi government of Italy fell. Eventually, of course, even the Italian courts indentified Abbas as the mastermind of the whole affair, and the four gunmen eventually were sentenced to lengthy prison terms.

In Washington it appeared that the evil spell cast by the terrorists had been broken at last. The president proudly said, "We did it all by our little selves." In the White House, Poindexter, only two months away from succeeding McFarlane as the national security adviser, and North were justifiably riding high. How fleeting is the favor of Washington. Little more than a year later they were forced to leave the White House.

———

Throughout the planning and execution of this deft move, there was not so much as a nod toward Congress or the War Powers Act. Neither the president nor his advisers ever doubted for a moment that his authority as commander in chief gave him all the authority he needed. And once again overwhelming success and public delight preempted the possibility of any congressional squeals.

Unfortunately, however, the action did not reach the heart and

121

source of the terrorist onslaught. On November 23 an Egyptian flight was hijacked after leaving Athens; this time a U.S. Air Force civilian was murdered. Sixty passengers were killed when the Egyptians botched the rescue. The next day, a U.S. military shopping mall in Frankfurt was bombed, wounding twenty-three Americans. A month later, on December 27, the Rome airport was struck: Five Americans, including an eleven-year-old girl, were among the dead; over a hundred people were wounded.

Clear evidence of Qaddafi's complicity in these attacks finally persuaded Washington to do what it should have done years before. Economic links were broken; fifteen hundred Americans in Libya were ordered to leave immediately; and Libya was described by executive order as an "unusual and extraordinary threat to the national security and foreign policy of the United States." Libyan assets in the United States were frozen ($2.5 billion worth), and at last the president declared that Qaddafi must end support of terrorism.

In early January, the president approved a plan, drawn up by a very small working group, to challenge Qaddafi. The idea was to reassert our naval rights in the Gulf of Sidra, even if (and perhaps especially if) it meant clobbering the Libyans to do so.

At this point, everyone in Washington knew that we were headed for a shootout with Qaddafi. In such circumstances the rules of engagement were of the utmost importance. During the shootout in August 1981, the rules of engagement required Sixth Fleet sailors and aviators to hold fire unless the Libyans actually fired upon them. For War Powers Act theologians, this gave at least a way to rationalize why the War Powers Act was not invoked. After all, we had not intended to shoot first. After talking over those rules of engagement with Frank Kelso, I met with Cap Weinberger on February 14. I strongly recommended that he give his personal attention to changing the rules of engagement and that he not allow the multilayered bureaucratic chain of command to botch them the way they had in Beirut. I urged him to streamline the reporting chain for the next operation so that Kelso would report directly to Cap or, if necessary, through Gen. Bernard Rodgers to Cap, but cutting out all of the layers in between. One week later, Cap met with Kelso in Europe and approved Kelso's rules of engagement. Those rules would allow

American aviators to shoot first if they judged that the Libyans had "hostile intent." Weinberger left it up to Kelso to interpret and delegate to his pilots the rules of engagement. Kelso was also given authority to run the operation free of micromanagement from the rest of the chain of command and the service bureacracies, and he knew that he would be held accountable. Thus, the streamlined system that proved so successful in 1991 in Operation Desert Storm was tried out first in 1986 in the Libyan operations. Weinberger became the first secretary of defense to delegate operational authority in crisis to the on-scene commander rather than to allow the Pentagon staffs to micromanage from Washington.

Although high sources leaked daily stories to the media about impending U.S. military action, Qaddafi, like Saddam Hussein four years later, chose to believe the accepted wisdom of the European media that the United States was irresolute and militarily inept. He pursued fresh terrorist plans.

Washington would not be put off. In March the Sixth Fleet prepared to cross the "line of death." The exercises began just north of the line but did not cross it; the purpose was to give our F-14s and F-18s a good idea of Libya's air force. Hundreds of their MiGs and Mirages attempted intercepts, but there was no shooting.

Again, in the second week of March, exercises went right up to but did not cross the line. Once again, hundreds of Libyan aircraft attempted intercepts without success.

After once again pulling back, in the third week of March the fleet assembled again for the third time. This was to be the full challenge—crossing the "line of death." Kelso had under his command three aircraft carriers, the *Coral Sea*, the *Saratoga*, and the *America*; two Aegis cruisers; and 122 other American ships. On March 22 the first ships and aircraft crossed below the line. Qaddafi's response was immediate. In the earlier exercises, there had been more then 160 attempts by the Libyan air force, now grown to more than five hundred jets, to intercept American aircraft or ships. Not a single sortie ever got into a firing position on an American aircraft, thanks to the superb coordination of the Aegis cruisers, E-2C radar aircraft, F-14 intercepters, and F-18 strike fighters. This time Qaddafi's air force clearly was intimidated.

They were ordered away from the fleet, and not one took to the air over water. But as soon as the first F-14s were in range of the Soviet-built long-range SA-5 surface-to-air missiles, Qaddafi gave the order to fire, and a pair of SA-5s was launched. The SA-5 is comparable to our Patriot missile and is highly capable. As soon as they were fired, they were tracked by the Aegis cruisers, and warnings were immediately data linked to the target aircraft. They were able to counter these missiles effectively, and they exploded harmlessly at high altitude. Sitting in the command center in Washington, we heard Kelso promptly give the order to attack the SA-5 missile site. We then heard the pilots report Harm missiles away, and within a few minutes Kelso reported that the missile sites suddenly were off the air. They had been hit by the Harm antiradiation missile that had for years been derided by the media as one more example of high-tech weaponry that would not work. (In Desert Storm more than one thousand were fired.)

In the following hours three Libyan fast-missile boats attempted to engage the fleet. These were the ships that armchair strategists in the media had repeatedly declared would easily sink large U.S. aircraft carriers and Aegis cruisers. In each case, the Libyan patrol boats were quickly destroyed by harpoon antiship missiles and rockeye cluster bombs launched by A-6s from the aircraft carriers. By dawn of the following day, not one Libyan ship or aircraft would venture outside the twelve-mile limit, and not one ever did until after Kelso left the Sixth Fleet to become Atlantic fleet commander.

Kelso's plan called for approaching closer to the Libyan coast, staying outside the twelve-mile limit but increasing the pressure to the point where Qaddafi would have to launch his air force. It was Kelso's expectation that a massive "turkey shoot" would follow, perhaps dealing a mortal blow to Qaddafi's prestige and leadership. To our consternation and astonishment, however, the entire exercise was called off early because of squabbling in the NSC, and the fleet withdrew on March 27, with the job undone.

While Kelso had executed the operation flawlessly, its fullest effect was frustrated by premature termination. Qaddafi seized upon the withdrawal to proclaim victory, which he probably believed he had achieved. He then promptly reactivated a new round of terrorism against civilians. Beginning on March 27, the

124

intelligence community received evidence of almost daily orders for the initiation of terrorist attacks on American and other Western targets by Qaddafi's "People's Bureaus." Because of good intelligence, nearly every one was thwarted, but on April 5, the LaBelle disco in West Berlin, favored by American soldiers, was bombed, killing two Americans and wounding more than fifty others. On April 8, a TWA flight from Rome suffered a midair explosion that cost four American lives, including that of one little girl. While the intelligence community concluded it was Qaddafi's work, there was conflicting evidence of Syrian and Iranian involvement.

Following the Berlin bombing, for whatever reason, a flood of leaks from "official sources" in the White House, the State Department, and the Defense Department filled the media with stories that a retaliatory strike against Qaddafi was imminent. It was, as a journalist remarked, the least secret operation in history. The president had in fact made a decision to proceed; Oliver North's working group was busily selecting targets. Five were finally selected. Two were in Benghazi: a commando/terrorist training camp and the military airfield. Three were in Tripoli: a terrorist/commando naval training base; the former U.S. Wheelus Air Force Base; and the prime target, the Al Aziziyah barracks compound in Tripoli, which housed the command center for Libyan intelligence and also contained one of five residences used by Qaddafi. (The attitude in Washington was that if the Libyan leader happened to be a casualty of the raid, so much the better.) These were all difficult targets located in a built-up area where the danger of collateral civilian damage was great.

Kelso's initial plan was to have been executed by twenty-eight A-6 aircraft from the *America* and the *Coral Sea* supported by an additional forty F-18s and A-7 light attack aircraft from the same ships. But that plan was overruled by the Pentagon bureaucracy. Just as in the Grenada plan, the JCS staff insisted that the operation must be "joint" and include other services besides the navy. The plan was therefore modified to include air force F-111 bombers from the United Kingdom. Kelso rewrote the plan to include the eighteen additional F-111s, but he insisted that they not be combined with navy jets over the same target. Nor would he bend on his insistence that the strike be at night and at

125

low level to minimize American casualties. While the decision to insist on the inclusion of the air force came about because of the recurring political need for joint operations, it was a good precursor of the same aircraft and strike tactics used so successfully in operation Desert Storm nearly five years later.

The stream of leaks beginning on April 6 about the imminent raid greatly distressed the fleet. It had the effect of putting the formidable Libyan air defenses on full-alert status. But as days chased days without any raid, the fleet began to see the defenses relax despite the continuing media stories. At 1:30 A.M. on April 15, when the raid was launched, the city lights were still on in Tripoli. Six minutes prior to the first F-111 hitting its target in Tripoli, the navy jamming aircraft and antiradiation missile shooters began their suppression of Libyan defenses. The air defenses around Libya and Benghazi are among the most sophisticated and thickest in the world. After the raids, the air force and navy compared them in studies with target complexes in Russia and the Warsaw Pact countries. Only three targets behind the Iron Curtain were found to have thicker defenses then Libyan cities. Libyan defenses, in addition to the 500-aircraft air force, included a massive network of surveillance and fire-control radars all netted together and controlling integrated SAM (surface-to-air missile) sites consisting of French Crotale missiles and Soviet SA-2, SA-3, SA-4, SA-5, SA-6, SA-7, and SA-9s. It included a large number of mobile ZSU-23 radar-guided antiaircraft guns and 57-millimeter antiaircraft guns. The system was operated under the direction of 3,000 Soviet air defense technicians. Using the navy EA-6 jammers, which could jam ten different bands simultaneously, and air force EF-111 jammers, the early-warning and fire-control radars were rendered inoperable. With direct intelligence poured from the EA-3 aircraft, the FA-18s and A-7s were able to fire Shrike and Harm missiles down the throats of any surface-to-air missile (SAM) sites that came up operational.

Again using the same tactics that proved so successful in Desert Storm, American forces were able utterly to defeat one of the thickest and most sophisticated air defense systems in the world. Well over fifty SAMs were fired, and not a single one hit an American aircraft. The first F-111 hit its target at exactly 2:00 A.M., and the last cleared the beach at 2:11 A.M. One F-111 was seen by a navy A-7 pilot to hit the water and explode just offshore while exiting the target area. Most probably the pilot simply flew into the water.

Simultaneously, 450 miles to the east, the navy began its attack on the Benghazi complex. At 1:54 A.M. Tripoli time, the suppression aircraft, the jammers, and Harm shooters launched their attack on the defenses. At exactly 2:00 A.M. the first section of A-6s crossed the beach at 200 feet and 500 knots. Eight A-6s hit the Benghazi air base and destroyed more than twenty MiGs, utility aircraft, and helicopters, and six A-6s put their bombs precisely on a target that looked on radar exactly like the commando training base but was in fact a civilian building. Thirteen minutes later, the last A-6 was clear of the beach, and all returned safely to the *America* and the *Coral Sea*. The F-111s hit the Al Aziziyah barracks, but Qaddafi was apparently in his underground command center and escaped harm. The F-111s assigned to Wheelus Air Force Base destroyed a great many Russian-built jet transports and helicopters, and the F-111s assigned to the commando training site put their bombs right on the target. One F-111 dropped its bombs long and neatly destroyed the French embassy.

From a military standpoint the Libyan operation became a template for the future success of Desert Storm. The reasons for success were the following:

1. An experienced and audacious commander who was not afraid to assume full personal responsibility was delegated sufficient authority and used it.
2. The exclusion of the vast bureacratic chain of command, with Kelso reporting directly to the secretary of defense through the chairman of the joint chiefs.
3. Clear rules of engagement.
4. An imaginative but simple plan of attack.
5. Air force and navy units that were ready, well trained, and of the highest quality possible, thanks to the Reagan years of full funding of pay, maintenance, spare parts, ammunition, and training.

The huge Libyan air force, supplemented by aviators from Communist-block nations and Syria, were so intimidated by their experiences with the F-14s and F-18s in the earlier fleet exercises that they refused to take off to defend against the American attackers. Not a single Libyan aircraft rose in opposition.

The Libyan strike was an overwhelming success. Although Qaddafi was not brought down, his standing in power was severely diminished. He lost the confidence of his people and of his military due to his inability to prevent such an effective retaliation. The raid began a series of setbacks for the Libyan leader, and he quietly eliminated all but token support to further terrorist activities for a year or so.

Yet again, the War Powers Resolution was irrelevant. Consultation did take place during the weeks prior to attack, but there was certainly no semblance of a request for congressional authorization for what was an act of war. Since the attack was a dazzling success, most congressmen joined in the applause and basked in the reflected glory.

# 5

# Making Treaties
# Instead of War

## The Nine Lives of Tomahawk:
## SALT and the Treaty Process

Very often the struggle for control of military affairs and war powers takes place on the battleground of debate over the negotiation and ratification of executive agreements and treaties with other nations. The Tomahawk cruise missile, for instance, which proved so brilliantly successful in Operation Desert Storm, was fought over by Congress and the executive for twenty years, principally through various proposed clauses and limitations in treaties and agreements with the Soviet Union. But few people really understand what the treaty process is all about. Before reviewing the Tomahawk battles, it is useful to explore a bit of background.

The enormously different roles of Congress and the president in making treaties reflect the diverse nature of international agreements themselves. Customary international law requires no precise rules or settled patterns for establishing agreements between nations. Contractual arrangements between states come in an almost infinite variety and are given many names—multilateral conventions, treaties, pacts, accords, acts, declarations, protocols, etc.—none of which has an absolute, settled meaning. They are consecrated in every degree of solemnity and informality.

As the international version of the law of contracts, the only general requirement for concluding an international agreement seems to be the possession of both consent and authority by all the parties.

By custom there are normally two stages in the formation of international agreements: (1) signature by "plenipotentiaries" of the contracting states and (2) subsequent ratification by the governments of those states. But even this custom is not necessarily followed in all cases. Many agreements are deemed effective upon signature and ordinarily contain a clause to the effect that, either expressly or by implication, they become binding on signature. If such a clause is not present, there is a presumption that ratification is necessary, though there are exceptions to even this. Recent practice, since the United Nations has introduced so many multilateral agreements, has moved away from the formal ratification process, using instead a clause providing that the agreement shall become binding upon "acceptance," which has the effect of allowing each party to choose the particular form in which it indicates its willingness to be bound. That willingness is the essence of any such agreement.

Actual ratification is a matter exclusively of domestic constitutional law. In most democratic states decision-making powers are normally passed to the legislature before ratification of important treaties. Under the U.S. Constitution, it is a legal requirement, while in the United Kingdom and other parliamentary governments, it is a tradition rather than an obligation and has more often been observed in the breach. Under the U.S. Constitution it is usual to regard the process of negotiation and signature as belonging exclusively to the president, while the process of ratification belongs exclusively to the Senate; however, the Constitution makes no such distinction. Article II, Section II, clause 2 provides that the president ". . . shall have power, by and with the advice and consent of the Senate, to make treaties, provided two-thirds of the senators present concur." Thus, the Senate is associated with the entire process of the making of treaties. But in major treaties (such as the Treaty of Versailles and SALT II) members of the Senate and House have often been part of the negotiating process and have even been official delegates to the negotiations.

The original theory of treaty making, of course, was derived

130

from the Founders' early view of the Senate as a small body of counselors available to the president. Hamilton wrote that the intention of the framers on the treaty power "was understood by all" as giving "the most ample latitude" to make every "species of convention usual among nations." But being quite well acquainted with customary international law, the Founding Fathers knew well that international agreements were a source of domestic law and thus not the exclusive domain of the executive. In Hamilton's words, "A treaty is not an execution of laws: it does not pre-suppose the existence of laws. It is, on the contrary, to have itself the force of a law and to be carried into execution like all other laws by the executive magistrate."

The division of these functions came about almost immediately, however, with the president as the negotiator and the Senate ratifier. In fact, the joint "making" of treaties was attempted only once in the nearly two hundred years of practice under the Constitution, when President Washington, in the first year of his administration, attempted to have the whole Senate participate in the negotiation of a treaty, with unfortunate results.

It was from this disunity that the Senate Committee on Foreign Relations was born. It was created as a standing committee in 1816 for the express purpose of carrying out the advice and consent clause of Article II.

Today the actual negotiation and signing of treaties is by the vast weight of practice and opinion the president's role alone. That fact, however, has not prevented repeated challenges from being raised throughout the ensuing 180 years. Moreover, ratification also belongs to the president alone, although the vast weight of both practice and opinion has decreed that he may not ratify a formal treaty unless the Senate, by two-thirds vote of the members present, approves or, in the case of an executive agreement, at least acquiesces.

In granting its consent, the Senate has made liberal use of its right to do so conditionally, stating its conditions in the form of amendments to the treaty itself or in the form of reservations attached to the act of ratification. The difference is that the former, if accepted by the president and the other party, changes the nature of the obligations for all parties, whereas reservations merely limit the obligations of the United States under the proposed convention. Use of the latter form has been the norm for multilateral conventions. In effect, these reservations and amendments very often are major renegotiations of the agreement itself, and on occasion their adoption has resulted in the rejection of the entire agreement by either the president or the other party. Between 1789 and 1929 about nine hundred treaties were negotiated by the president and ratified by the Senate. Another two hundred were either rejected outright by the Senate or so amended or reserved by it that either the president or the other party rejected them.

In the famous *U.S. v. Curtiss-Wright* case the U.S. Supreme Court in 1936 sanctioned the negotiating role as the president's alone. "The President alone has the power to speak or listen as a representative of the nation. He makes treaties with the advice and consent of the Senate; but he alone negotiates. Into the field of negotiation, the Senate cannot intrude; and Congress itself is powerless to invade it." Unfortunately, Justice George Sutherland, whose opinion I quote, was wrong. Congress has indeed intruded and continues to intrude quite directly right up to the present day, as we shall see in the Tomahawk case.

---

Between the end of World War II and 1965, the Senate was represented by observers, advisers, or delegates at twenty-one major international conferences. Since June 1965, senators, and on a number of occasions Senate staff members, have been accredited as representatives, advisers, and observers to at least sixty-eight international conferences, and senators have served at all but four of the meetings of the UN General Assembly. Senators participated in the UN Conference on International Organization in 1945, the Paris Peace Conference in 1946, the Conference on the Peace Treaty with Japan in 1951, the Mutual Defense Treaty with the Philippines in 1951, the Anzus Pact, and the SEATO Treaty. For the last four of these treaties, senators were delegates and actually signed the treaties. In theory, of course, such senators, when acting as delegates, are actually employees of the president (rather than representatives of the legislature) and are supposed to be bound by his instructions.

Direct participation is not, of course, the only or even necessarily the most effective method of Senate involvement in negotiations. While there were persistent requests by Congress to have members put on the SALT delegation, for instance, none ever were. That did not mean, however, that Sen. Henry Jackson and some others did not exert a strong and continuing influence on the lengthy negotiations themselves. In that case, Henry Kissinger would have agreed with Sir Ivor Jennings: "Negotiations with foreign powers are difficult to conduct when Lynx-eyed opposition sits suspiciously on the watch."

But if the Senate has continuously barged into executive negotiations at its pleasure, it is nothing compared with executive circumvention of the Senate's right to advise and consent. The method used has been that of executive agreements, resorted to instead of treaties with ever-increasing frequency since the middle of the nineteenth century. In the year immediately following the Civil War, the Senate, during an era of congressional domination, had exercised its ratification powers with a vengeance, amending and rejecting treaty after treaty negotiated by presidents. In fact, it ratified no important treaty between 1871 and 1898. In 1868, the Senate further expanded its ability to rewrite treaties by revising its rules to permit the amending of treaties by a simple majority.

By 1885, an exasperated Professor Woodrow Wilson, later to become president, lamented in regard to ratifying treaties that the president was made to approach the Senate "as a servant conferring with a master . . . it is almost as distinctly dealing with a foreign power as were the negotiations preceding the proposed treaty." He noted wryly that the treaty-making power had become the "treaty marring power."

Some years later, President McKinley and Secretary of State John Hay, who had had considerable experience as Lincoln's private secretary, seriously doubted, as Hay wrote, that "another important treaty would ever pass the Senate." Hay viewed advice and consent to treaties by the Senate as the Constitution's "irreparable" mistake and that "the attitude of the Senate toward public affairs makes all serious negotiations impossible."[1]

To escape and evade such obstructionism, the president began to seek a way around the two-thirds veto. The device resorted to once again was the power as commander in chief, and modest agreements requiring no ratification began to be signed on the sole authority of the chief executive. This device was resorted to as early as 1817, when the demilitarization of the Great Lakes was formally agreed to by a simple exchange of notes between British minister Charles Bagot and Secretary of State Richard Rush. Similarly, the protocol of 1898 between the United States and Spain in which Spanish territories in the Caribbean were ceded to the United States was a simple executive agreement with no reference to Congress. Such agreements became increasingly numerous after that and included the famous "Open Door" Agreements, the Northwestern Fishery Agreements, the Agreement for Ending the Boxer Rebellion in 1901, the Agreement Ending World War I, the Litvinov Accords of the 1930s, the Yalta and Potsdam Agreements, and the Spanish Base Agreement during the late 1960s. During the first fifty years after independence, of eighty-seven international agreements, sixty, including most of the important ones, were full treaties. In the next fifty years there were 215 treaties and 238 executive agreements.

In 1905, when the Senate declined to ratify a treaty with Santo Domingo, President Roosevelt simply put the agreement into effect for two years until the Senate capitulated, and he did not even bother to tell the Senate of secret agreements he made with Japan regarding the Japanese protectorate in Korea.

By the mid-twentieth century, the ironic situation had developed whereby important matters were handled by informal executive agreements; unimportant matters, by solemn treaties. In 1951, the year when the United States released Italy from military restrictions under the Italian Peace Treaty by simple executive agreement, the Truman administration submitted a treaty on the regulation of sugar. In 1953, the year in which the Eisenhower administration, by executive agreement, gave up its rights over the Amami Islands, the president submitted a solemn treaty with Belgium on double taxation. In 1954 the territory of Trieste was divided between Italy and Yugoslavia by executive agreement, but solemn treaties were submitted disapproving slavery and resolving tax matters with the Netherlands. In 1968, the year in which the Bonin Islands were given back to Japan by executive agreement, President Johnson submitted to the Senate solemn treaties with Mexico regarding radio broadcasting and the safety of life at sea.

An important variation of this device, halfway between a treaty and an executive agreement, was resorted to in the more important matters in which congressional support was deemed necessary but Senate veto feared. This has been the presentation of an executive agreement to both houses of Congress for approval by a joint or concurrent resolution. This device was first attempted successfully when Texas was annexed in 1845 by joint resolution. It was followed one-half century later when Hawaii was annexed by a similar joint resolution; right after a treaty had been rejected by the Senate. Later, the war with the Central Powers was brought to a close in 1921 by joint resolution; the United States accepted membership in the International Labor Organization by joint resolution in 1934.

In 1972, Tom Korologos and I recommended to Henry Kissinger that this device be used for an agreement with the Soviets on offensive weapons; we were certain that Scoop Jackson could muster at least one-third of the Senate against it if it were in treaty form. Kissinger agreed, and that was the way it was submitted; we still did not escape substantial renegotiation by Jackson when it hit the Senate.

The relatively unchallenged success of these two devices, approved repeatedly by the Supreme Court, leads one to conclude that there is essentially no limit to the power of the president, working with a majority of both houses of Congress, to carry out the foreign policy on which they agree, regardless of whether the Senate officially advises or consents.

Serious attempts, nonetheless, have been made in the Senate to curtail this executive latitudinarianism. The routine resort to these devices by Presidents Roosevelt and Truman to get around Republican obstructionists in the Senate set off a conservative counterattack to bridle this power in the successive attempts and variations of the Bricker Amendment. It went through many versions, but the common theme was that both treaties and executive agreements should become effective as internal law only through enabling legislation, as in the British system. In its final attempt at passage, it failed by only one vote to obtain the two-thirds majority necessary to pass a constitutional amendment.

After that failure, the Republicans narrowed the attempt to a bill requiring that all agreements be transmitted to the Senate within sixty days of their execution. That passed the Senate in

135

1956; but since it excluded the House, that body never acted. The same measure, however, sweetened for the House by including a requirement that both houses must receive such agreements, was passed by the Democrats over Nixon administration objections in 1972.

## The Tomahawk Cruise Missile and the SALT Treaties

At 5:30 P.M. Eastern Standard Time on February 16, 1991, the first shots of Operation Desert Storm were fired at Iraq. Those shots were Tomahawk missiles launched from the battleships *Missouri* and *Wisconsin*, and the cruiser *Bunker Hill*. Their targets were key command and control centers and early warning radars for the massive air defense system of Iraq, the Presidential Palace, the Baghdad telephone exchange and power plants, and other key nerve centers.[2] Those missiles each had traveled about six hundred miles and hit within ten feet of a pinpoint on their target, whereupon their thousand-pound warhead detonated. Ninety percent of these cruise missile attacks were bull's-eyes, and along with strikes by the F-117 Stealth, the shock and surprise sufficiently disrupted Iraq's air defense system and enabled the navy and air force precision bombers (A-6s, F-111s, F-15Es, and Tornados) to finish the work of destroying the heart of the surface-to-air (SAM) missile defenses of Iraq. As the war continued, Tomahawks continued to be used against high-value targets in Baghdad and throughout Iraq. In addition to the battleships, each carrying thirty-two reloadable launchers, the Tomahawks were also fired from Aegis cruisers and two submarines. For the first time, the world got a good look at a system that had been banned in four draft treaties and for nearly twenty years had been attacked by the Russians, cut from the budget by congressmen, dismissed by admirals, and ridiculed by a president.

The jet-powered Tomahawk missile has three versions: The first is an antishipping version with a range of 800 miles and a 750-pound conventional warhead. This model operates much like the Exocet missile except that it can fly for hundreds of miles searching for each target before going into its sea-skimming attack, whereas Exocet can fly only twenty miles with a 450-pound warhead. The second is a conventional land-attack version with

136

a range of 800 miles. This was the one used in Desert Storm. It has two types of warheads for different targets. One is a thousand-pound bomb, and the other scatters small bomblets for attacking airfields and land forces. After launch from a ship, it can travel 800 miles very close to the ground, following the terrain and using mountains and valleys to avoid detection. It navigates by mapping the ground it flies over with a radar altimeter, matching it to a digitized map stored in its computer. The third version is equipped with a nuclear warhead for land attack and has a range of 1,500 miles. This missile was deployed briefly in Europe in a ground-launch version with the U.S. Air Force, until it was banned by the INF (intermediate-range nuclear forces) treaty, signed in 1988.

All three of the sea-launch versions are interchangeably launched from torpedo tubes of submarines and launchers on surface ships. The successful deployment of the Tomahawk has enormously broadened the capabilities of the U.S. Navy for striking inland targets with precision from the sea. One could not help noting with irony that at the very time NATO (North Atlantic Treaty Organization) was paralyzed with debate over deployment of the ground-launch Tomahawk to England, the Netherlands, and Italy, the battleship *New Jersey* came right into the Mediterranean and stayed for many months loaded with the very same missile, generating not a single comment. Today the United States has submarines cruising all over the world with Tomahawks, creating absolutely no political problem. We have destroyers and cruisers deployed globally in their routine pattern, with the Tomahawk aboard without any political fuss.

The incredible saga of how this cost-effective new dimension to deterrence came into being well illustrates the interplay between Congress and the executive in the negotiation of arms control treaties.

----

The idea for the Tomahawk came out of an air force concept for a cheap armed decoy that would help B-52s penetrate defenses in the Soviet Union. The successful development of two basic technologies made the concept possible. One was a disposable jet engine that could fly reliably for a long one-way trip and would be very cheap to produce. The other was "Tercom," a system for navigation enabling an on-board computer to record the terrain features under the missile flight path with a radar altimeter and match it with a stored digital map of the route to the target. Both of these technologies were proved achievable in the early 1970s. The common wisdom in Washington holds that the uniformed military is the great engine of new weapons starts. The Tomahawk was different. Thanks to the foresight of Dr. John Foster; the Pentagon research and development chief, David Packard; the deputy secretary of defense; and Melvin Laird, the secretary of defense, the concept was transformed into a system for an air-, sea-, and land-launch cruise missile with both nuclear and conventional capabilities.

The program received no high-level attention until the SALT I agreements were nearing completion in 1972. There was in the government at the time widespread skepticism about the deal that Henry Kissinger had negotiated. Laird, Foster, and most of the military chiefs did not like the package. Opposition in Congress, led by Sen. Henry M. Jackson, was very strong, and some of Kissinger's advisers, including me, were telling him he had got a bad deal. The SALT I agreements essentially gave up a huge U.S. lead in antiballistic missile (ABM) capability in return for a freeze on the very large numerical lead that the Soviet Union had achieved in offensive missile systems. The ABM treaty effectively killed the American ABM systems, while the agreement freezing levels of offensive weapons locked in a three-to-two Soviet advantage. The Soviets were allowed 1,618 intercontinental ballistic missiles (ICBMs); the United States was limited to 1,054. The Soviets were allowed 62 ballistic submarines and 748 submarine-launched ballistic missiles (SLBMs), while the United States was limited to 44 and 656, respectively.

The terms of the interim agreement (discussed in detail below) were controversial, but the 40 percent advantage yielded to the Soviets in ICBMs and SLBMs was explained at the time by Henry Kissinger in the following way:

By 1969, therefore, we had no active or planned program for deploying additional ICBMs, submarine launch ballistic missiles, or bombers. . . . In other words, as a result of the decisions made in the 1960s, not reversible within the time frame of the projected agreement, there would be a numerical gap in the two categories of land and sea base missile systems whether or not there was an agreement.[3]

In a masterful performance of bureaucratic skill, Kissinger negotiated the acceptance of this bad deal first with the Joint Chiefs of Staff (JCS) and Secretary Laird and, second but simultaneously, with Scoop Jackson and the conservatives in Congress.

In dealing with the Pentagon, Kissinger astutely fastened on two programs to buy them off. One was the Trident submarine and missile; the other was the Tomahawk cruise missile. Kissinger became an enthusiastic booster of both systems and pledged his undying support of them to the chairman of the JCS, Adm. Thomas Moorer, and Melvin Laird.

Thus, beginning in 1972, the Tomahawk program was funded by the Defense Department as a high priority. The program was taken out of the air force and the navy, and a joint cruise missile program office was set up in the defense research office.

By 1976 the Tomahawk was very far along, including specific plans for integration into submarines, destroyers, and cruisers. Henry Kissinger was equally far along in negotiating yet another SALT agreement, SALT II. At the time, I was deputy director of the Arms Control and Disarmament Agency (ACDA) and very much involved in SALT policy. When, in early 1976, Kissinger cabled back from Moscow what the outlines of the new treaty were, I was amazed to find that his enthusiam for the Tomahawk seemed suddenly to have disappeared. He had agreed to a ban on deployment of the Tomahawk in submarines and the limitation of deployment on surface ships to only ten cruisers with ten Tomahawks each (about one-third the number eventually launched in Desert Storm). While apparently keeping the Tomahawk alive, he well knew that Congress would never fund such a tiny number, too small to have any real military utility.

At the time, of course, Gerald Ford was running hard for reelection, facing a very strong challenge from Ronald Reagan and the conservatives and expecting an uphill fight against the Democrats in the first post-Watergate presidential election. President Ford was determined to have a SALT II agreement to run on in his reelection bid.

Kissinger knew he must act fast, and he sent outlines of the agreement to Secretary of Defense Donald H. Rumsfeld and Gen.

George Brown, who had succeeded Moorer as chairman of the JCS. They were attending a NATO ministerial meeting in Oslo, Norway. Based on what Kissinger sent to them, both Rumsfeld and Brown approved his initialing of an agreement. A hurried meeting of the National Security Council (NSC) was called by the president to get everybody aboard. At the time, Bill Clements, Rumsfeld's deputy, was the acting secretary of defense, and Adm. Jim Holloway, the chief of naval operations, was the acting chairman of the JCS. Prior to the meeting, I had several meetings with Holloway at the Pentagon, and Fred Iklé, the director of the ADCA, talked extensively with Clements. We were concerned not only that Kissinger was giving up the Tomahawk but also that he had caved in to the Russian's insistence that their new "swing wing" Backfire bomber be excluded from any limitations. In addition, we feared that there probably were other disadvantageous clauses in the agreement and that it would be far more prudent for the president to withhold approval until Kissinger returned and there was a chance to have a thorough internal debate over the concessions that had been made.

Admiral Holloway was under tremendous pressure from the Joint Staff to follow General Brown's lead and approve the agreement. He refused. He saw the advantages that the Tomahawk held for the U.S. Navy, particularly for a conventional, that is, nonnuclear, strike. He was adamantly opposed to giving it up for the sake of an agreement that allowed the Soviets missile numbers higher than they actually possessed. At the first NSC meeting with President Ford, Iklé and Holloway were alone in opposing approval of the agreement. In the second meeting, Clements joined in opposition; President Ford was very upset. He could not afford to proceed against the recommendations of the acting secretary of defense, the acting chairman of the JCS, and the director of the ACDA. Reluctantly, he witheld approval with the intention of knocking the dissidents into line when Kissinger returned. After Kissinger did return, he and the president, with Gen. Brent Scowcroft, Ford's national security adviser, and Scowcroft's deputy, Col. Bud McFarlane, spent the rest of the spring trying to bludgeon Iklé and Holloway into line to approve the deal. Instead, Holloway used the time to convert General Brown to opposition. Don Rumsfeld also came around to join the opponents.

There was one final NSC meeting in which the president attempted to bring the Pentagon and the ACDA into line. As it happened, Iklé was traveling in Europe, and I was the ACDA's acting director; on this occasion, I got to sit at the cabinet table rather than in the back chairs lining the room. I saw this as my big chance to persuade the president to save the Tomahawk. The scales were sure to fall from his eyes. What I got instead was a most unpleasant tongue-lashing from President Ford. After the initial briefings that started the NSC meeting, the president went around the table and asked each member to state his agency's views on the draft agreement. Ford sat passively as each recited his position. When my turn came, he frowned as I started to speak. As I recited our concerns over the cruise missile limits and the exclusion of Backfire, the president's expression grew darker. When I finished, the president said in a most unfriendly manner: "What I'd like to know is why the Arms Control and Disarmament Agency is here supporting the Pentagon against an arms control agreement." Realizing that I had failed utterly to impress the president with either my charm or my logic, I figured I wouldn't soon be invited back, so I pressed on: "Mr. President, because a bad agreement is worse for arms control than no agreement and giving up the Tomahawk and leaving out Backfire is a bad deal." The president just glowered at me and moved on to the next person. And, indeed, I never was invited back. At the conclusion of the meeting, it was clear that the president and Kissinger were losing rather than gaining ground. The issue was sent back to the interagency group and basically languished there, amid bickering, until the election.

---

The Carter administration came into office determined to push through a SALT II agreement. On June 18, 1979, they achieved their wish, and it was worse than the deal Kissinger had approved. The Tomahawk was once again effectively killed in a protocol attached to the main agreement.

After a protracted battle, in the Senate (which I recount below) during which the Tomahawk was a major issue, the treaty died. It had become clear there was a majority of votes to kill it. It was dead when the Reagan administration took office in 1981.

Thus, when we organized the Reagan transition team and sat down in 1981 to our defense-budget meetings, we had in hand a weapon system in the Tomahawk that had survived a decade of political turmoil and attempted assassination. While the Tomahawk still presented engineering problems, it was essentially ready for introduction to the fleet. There was no opposition to the program in the Reagan administration. Yet the Tomahawk saga was not over. Within the navy itself, the weapon had no constituency.

The Tomahawk had originally been assigned to a joint program office because the navy would not find a place for it. The professional submariners did not want it because their professional focus was on Soviet submarines, not on surface ships, and certainly not on land battles. Therefore, the mission of the Tomahawk for precision strike of land targets was a distraction from the submariner's primary responsibilities. Moreover, every Tomahawk aboard a submarine left it with one less torpedo to do the primary job; and if it was a nuclear Tomahawk, it was greatly feared that the submarine would be tied to a specific firing position during alert periods, frustrating their basic pelagic instincts.

The aviators certainly had no love of a system that did not carry a pilot and yet could do some things that carrier aircraft could do.

The destroyermen, the surface-warfare officers, saw no great benefit from the Tomahawk in complementing their primary mission of antisubmarine warfare and anti–air warfare. After all that the poor orphan Tomahawk had been through, I was not about to let it be heaved over the side by the sailors. Luckily, in Adm. James Lyons, Tom Hayward, the chief of naval operations, and his successor, Jim Watkins, I found three naval officers who had the common sense to see the future value of this system to the navy. Together we simply crammed it down the throats of the reluctant submariners and destroyermen.

The Tomahawk was ready for its first mission in 1983. When the terrorist attack on the U.S. Marine barracks in Beirut killed 241 marines, the Tomahawk had just become fully operational aboard the battleship *New Jersey* off the Lebanon coast. The navy immediately recommended retaliation against Syrian and Iranian targets using the battleship's sixteen-inch guns together with a Tomahawk missile strike on the Syrian Defense Ministry in downtown Damascus. The proposal was turned down by the deputy secretary of defense and the chairman of the JCS. In frustration, I took the planning materials, including pictures of the window in the ministry in Damascus that the Tomahawk would fly through, to Bud McFarlane at the White House. He could not overcome Pentagon opposition to using the Tomahawk. Thus, the Tomahawk had to wait eight more years to humiliate its critics—in Baghdad rather than Damascus.

## Salt and the Treaty Process

The story of SALT begins in the Johnson administration. Strategic nuclear policy under Johnson had settled firmly around the theory of "mutually assured destruction." Under this peculiar but broadly held consensus in the administration, nuclear weapons were only useful for targeting against cities and population centers; therefore, once the destruction of the majority of the Soviet population was assured by sufficient numbers of strategic nuclear weapons, there was no need to deploy any more. Prior to the Johnson administration, the United States had built and deployed quite a few thousand nuclear warheads in some thirteen hundred manned bombers, forty-one Polaris and Poseidon submarines, and more than a thousand ICBMs. The administration held that there were already too many and quietly and unilaterally began to dismantle and reduce their number. The leading administration proponent of this view, Robert S. McNamara, the secretary of defense, believed without a doubt that the Soviets would follow our unilateral reductions and accept his theory of mutual assured destruction. In 1965 he announced that "the Soviets . . . are not seeking to engage us in . . . the quantitative race. . . . There is no indication that the Soviets are seeking to develop a strategic nuclear force as large as ours."[4]

Unfortunately, however, the Soviets apparently failed to understand Secretary McNamara's new theories, and by 1967 the administration felt the need to establish negotiations with the Soviets for treaty limitations on the numbers of strategic weapons. The Central Intelligence Agency (CIA) survey of the policy of the period describes it as follows:

The U.S. approach under Secretary of Defense McNamara was one of unilateral restraints. . . . In 1963, McNamara ordered the start of the deactivation of 185 Atlas and Titan ICBMs, most of which had only recently been completed. He ordered the phasing out of the entire force of U.S. B-47s and B-58 medium bombers.[5]

By the time negotiations were actually convened in 1969 at the beginning of the Nixon administration, the Soviets had success-fully built up their forces well beyond the reduced levels of Ameri-can strategic forces. Since no new strategic programs had been started in the Johnson administration, it was already too late to unilaterally do anything about the loss of numerical superiority in the nuclear balance. But the new administration specifically rejected the doctrine of mutual assured destruction and adopted instead a policy of achieving "parity."

As President Nixon described this problem in his foreign policy message of February 25, 1971:

I must not be—and my successors must not be—limited to the indiscriminate mass destruction of enemy civilians as the sole possible response to challenges.

It would be inconsistent with the political meaning of sufficiency to base our force planning solely on some finite—and theoretical—capacity to inflict casualties presumed to be unacceptable to the other side.

In May 1972, the SALT I agreements were signed: a treaty limiting both countries to a maximum of two sites for ABM de-fenses (later reduced to one by protocol), to run indefinitely; and an interim executive agreement limiting offensive weapons for a period of five years. The terms of the interim agreement on offen-sive weapons were controversial.

When the terms of the SALT I agreements were made public, there was an outcry about the significant 30 percent advantage in numbers conceded to the Soviet Union. Kissinger's argument that he had to accept inequalities because the Soviets were build-ing new programs and we had no new ones found little favor in the Senate.

As the negotiations had proceeded, many had advised Kis-singer that the issue of equality could not be sidestepped in the offensive agreement. While equality was a minimum requirement in the U.S. position at the beginning of negotiations, Kissinger had backed off in a series of concessions and had finally agreed to Soviet superiority in offensive weapons. But in order to get even that limitation, the United States had to accept a tight limit on the technology that worried the Soviets, the ABM system, in which we had a huge technological lead. Kissinger knew that an unequal treaty would run into a buzz saw in the Senate lead by Senators Jackson and Tower. Knowing this, Kissinger decided to make separate agreements on ballistic missile defenses and offensive weapons. With regard to the ABM system, he had negotiated limits of two sites for each, which in effect killed the system, but at least the terms were equally applicable to the Soviet Union, so that was made a full treaty. But with regard to offensive weapons, having conceded Soviet superiority, he decided prudently on an executive agreement rather than a treaty in order to avoid the possibility of a Senate veto.

This tactical maneuver, which I and others had recommended, proved in practice to be insufficient to succeed. Jackson and Tower were far too effective parliamentarians to be outmaneuvered. Jackson coraled sufficient votes to hold the ABM treaty hostage, and then, through his powerful influence among committee chairmen in the House of Representatives, he succeeded in gaining a commitment from the administration to seek a joint resolution of approval for the executive agreement on offensive weapons. It soon became clear that he had sufficient votes in both houses to either kill the agreements or heavily modify them.

Kissinger knew he had to try to make a deal. He chose me to negotiate with Jackson, Tower, and the congressional skeptics because it was well known that I was very critical of the agreements and because my stock was very high with Jackson and the conservative Democrats and Republicans who were coalescing into a strong anti-SALT block. Kissinger assumed that if I was able to negotiate an agreement for their support of this SALT deal, he could then step in and seal it with Jackson. If I was unable, then his hands were free to get President Nixon to commit his prestige to defeating the conservatives in the Hill battle.

In my negotiations with Senator Jackson and his staff (led by

Richard Perle and Dorothy Fosdick), we hit on the solution of amending the agreements in the Senate with new language offered by Senator Jackson and drafted by Perle that would require any permanent agreement limiting offensive weapons in the future to be based on equality.

After much gnashing of teeth, the administration bowed to the inevitable and endorsed the amendment, which was swiftly adopted. The treaty then passed the Senate easily; the joint resolution then passed by the Senate and the House in strong votes. In addition to the language of the Jackson amendment, commitments were extracted from the administration for the full-scale funding of the B-1 bomber, the Trident missile and submarine, the MX missile, and, of course, the Tomahawk, as I have outlined. Thus, the irony of this first strategic arms control measure was that it gave the Pentagon far more than if there were no agreements.

After the administration's battering at the hands of Senators Jackson and Tower in the Senate and the subsequent modification of the amendment of the executive agreement, Kissinger had a sour assessment:

> I am convinced that . . . SALT became the whipping boy in a more fundamental philosophical contest over East-West relations. For its votaries, SALT turned into an end unto itself; for its opponents, it was a danger to be combated at all costs. SALT was no longer a part of a broader coherent strategic policy or an overall strategy. Thrust upon itself, it became an orphan and a victim, ground down between a liberal idealism and a conservative dogmatism unleavened by a sense of proportion or strategy. And it was doomed above all by the inability of the President to supply consistent leadership during his Watergate travail.[6]

Negotiations for a permanent treaty on offensive weapons, SALT II, began early in 1973. The objective of the Nixon administration was to redress the inequalities that had been accepted by necessity in SALT I and particularly to obtain limits on the massive four to one throw-weight advantage that had been allowed to the Soviets. The underlying concern over this issue was that as the Soviets improved the accuracy of their ICBM force, it was a mathematical certainty that within a decade the Soviets would have the military capability to make a disarming first strike against the United States' ICBMs that could destroy over 90 percent of that force. In such a situation, the United States would have no response available other than the suicidal option of attacking Soviet cities with a less accurate submarine missile force and the few surviving B-52s.

During the ensuing year of negotiations, when faced with the categorical refusal of the Soviets to consider any limitation of throw weight or any reasonable low level of warheads on ICBMs, the United States gave up and shifted to the less ambitious goal of negotiating equal aggregate numbers of launchers. Thus, the one way in which SALT might have actually stemmed the arms race in a meaningful way shrank as the Nixon administration grew ever weaker during the burgeoning Watergate scandal. The Soviets refused to make any concessions as they watched the decline and fall of the Nixon presidency.

By the time President Ford took office, in August 1974, it was clear that the Soviets would not accept any limitations on their programs for achieving a first-strike capability against our Minutemen force. In October 1974, agreement was reached in principle on the shape of the SALT II agreements. The accords signed at the summit meeting in Vladivostok City provided for the following:

• Main limit: 2,400 offensive delivery vehicles (freedom to mix ICBMs, SLBMs, and heavy bombers).
• Sublimit: 1,320 MIRV (multiple independently targetable reentry vehicle) equipped missiles.
• No limits on throw weight, cruise missiles, Backfire, or strategic air defense.

It was generally expected by both sides that signing a formal treaty embodying those three principles was a mere question of drafting it. This did not prove to be the case, however, because two issues outpaced the drafters. The first was the handling of the Backfire bomber. This Soviet weapon, about 80 percent the size and range of the American B-1 bomber, was just becoming operational. While there was no disagreement that the Backfire could reach the United States on a one-way unrefueled mission, there was considerable disagreement over whether the Soviets intended ever to use it as a strategic nuclear system.

The second major issue was the growing Soviet concern about the Tomahawk. As successful testing of this unique American technology proceeded, the Soviets soon regretted leaving out any reference to it in the Vladivostok accord.

As a result of Soviet demands that the Backfire be excluded from consideration and that U.S. cruise missile programs be included, the negotiations settled into a stalemate that endured through a change of American administrations despite the Ford administration's offer of four separate proposals to find a way around the impasse.

The Carter administration came to office in 1977 with a strong commitment to arms control. There was, however, to be no honeymoon on the issue. In the first weeks of the administration, President Carter sent to the Senate for confirmation the nomination of Paul Warnke as director of the ACDA and the chief U.S. SALT negotiator. Warnke was an old Washington hand who had been an architect of Robert McNamara's unilateral arms reductions. He had written extensively on the theme that the arms race was principally caused by American arms buildups, which the Soviets responded to in his view like "two apes on a treadmill." Senator Jackson immediately took on the Warnke nomination as a warning shot across the president's bows. After a bitter debate, Warnke's confirmation as director of the ACDA passed the Senate by a vote of 58–40 after Carter made a concession to Jackson and removed Warnke as the chief SALT negotiator.

The Carter administration began its approach to the SALT II negotiations in March 1977, putting forward a proposal that had been drafted with the assistance of Senator Jackson. It included a return to the original SALT II emphasis on obtaining limits and reductions to throw weight and warheads, seeking to prevent achievement by the Soviets of a first-strike capability. This proposal had strong bipartisan support in the Senate but was strongly opposed by the principal policymakers in the administration, who felt that the terms were too stringent for the Soviets to accept.

Faced with immediate, strong Soviet resistance in the first

148

negotiating sessions, the Carter administration abandoned the proposal with surprising swiftness. The administration then made important concessions to the Soviet demands on cruise missiles and on Backfire. These concessions led to the defection of both Senators Jackson and Tower from support of the administration's position. Their opposition should have raised important storm signals to the Carter administration. With a treaty all but negotiated, the Carter administration, in late 1977, began major slowdowns in all strategic programs. The administration had already announced the cancellation of the B-1 bomber, and to this was added the cancellation of the Minutemen III production line, the reduction and slowdown of the MX missile program, and the dropping of all funding and planning for the production of the Tomahawk cruise missile as well as an indefinite hiatus for the Trident missile program. Not surprisingly, these far-reaching concessions by the Carter administration elicited no reciprocal concessions or slowdowns by the Soviets.

With Senator Jackson now openly in opposition to the administration's draft treaty, the president fell back on the tactic of threatening to submit the text of the final document as an executive agreement instead of a treaty over which Jackson might have a veto. Expecting this ploy, Richard Perle had begun drafting dozens of possible amendments to any such agreement that might be submitted, and it soon became evident that Jackson could marshal the simple majority to pass his amendments. President Carter had no alternative but to submit the treaty to the tender mercies of the Senate. As President Carter was about to leave for Vienna to sign the treaty, the air was filled with evil portents. Jackson drew parallels to Neville Chamberlain: "To enter a treaty which favors the Soviets as this one does on the ground that we would be in a worse position without it, is appeasement in its purest form."[7]

On June 18, 1979, the treaty was presented to the Senate for consideration and referred to the Foreign Relations Committee, where extensive hearings were scheduled.

At the time, I was chairman of the Republican National Committee Advisory Council on Defense, made up of former Nixon administration officials and academics who couldn't wait to get their teeth into the Carter treaty.

We worked closely with the Committee on the Present Danger,

a bipartisan group of former officials led by Democrat Paul Nitze. Nitze was and is one of the most experienced and effective members of the Washington establishment. His opposition to the Carter SALT concessions carried enormous weight with moderate Democrats.

Members of both groups met every Wednesday during 1978 and 1979 and became the ad hoc steering group for opponents of the treaty on both sides of the aisle. Senators Jackson and Tower were our chief strategists and floor leaders. By the time hearings began, we had already persuaded many key senators, including Minority Leader Howard Baker, to oppose the treaty.

At the time, I was also meeting with and advising George Bush, who was seeking the Republican presidential nomination. As a former CIA director and cabinet member, he needed no tutoring in the complexities of strategic policy or in the technicalities of the treaty. He was strongly against it because he believed that it conferred "substantial superiority" to the Soviets.

Shortly after the SALT II treaties were signed, George Bush was called in by the Carter White House for a briefing on the treaty; President Carter hoped that Bush might be persuaded to support SALT II because Ronald Reagan, his principal rival for the 1980 Republican nomination, was so opposed to it. Bush asked me to come with him to the White House briefing. We were ushered into the Roosevelt conference room, across the corridor from the Oval Office. It was my first return to the room since that last NSC meeting with Ford. I could not help noting that seven years before, I had sat in this same room with Kissinger attempting to persuade reluctant Democrats to *support* SALT I. I was amused to note that the portrait of Theodore Roosevelt, which had always graced the room, was gone, as were other bits of Republican Roosevelt memorabilia. The briefing was given not by the president or Zbigniew Brzezinski, his national security adviser, but by Brzezinski's deputy, David Aaron. Bush listened carefully. Aaron's briefing indicated that Aaron himself had not been informed accurately on what the treaty had actually conceded to the Russians. He made a most unconvincing case. Bush had been a participant in the SALT process since 1969 and knew the issues in detail. He knew a bad deal when he saw one.

Bush had already formulated his thoughts on what was wrong

with the SALT II agreement, and he opposed it vigorously during the rest of the campaign. He objected to the total number of warheads and vehicles allowed by the treaty as being too high; and he opposed leaving Backfire outside the agreement. He was also a strong supporter of the Tomahawk and thought it was foolish to ban it just because the Russians demanded we do so.

Having lost the battle on the merits of the treaty before it had begun, when hearings opened on July 9, administration officials decided on a totally different tack. Cyrus Vance, the secretary of state, pointed out that twenty-seven senators has been present at various times at Geneva and participated in negotiations and that hundreds of congressmen had participated in briefings without dissenting during the negotiating process. They were, he implied, already obligated to support it.

The administration also emphasized "linkage." Whatever the flaws of the treaty, it must be seen as part of engaging the Soviets in patterns of cooperative behavior. They argued that the treaty must be approved in order to create a dynamic of cooperation and trust.

This strategy of linkage blew up in the administration's face one month later when a Soviet combat brigade that had actually been based in Cuba for many years was "rediscovered" in Cuba by, of all people, Democratic senator Frank Church, chairman of the Foreign Relations Committee, who was beating a path rightward, chased, as he was, by the first serious reelection threat he had ever faced. Church blew the meaning of the brigade all out of proportion to its actual importance and, in so doing, hoisted the SALT II treaty on the administration's own petard.

---

In another desperate effort, the administration put its politically loyal chairman of the JCS, Gen. David Jones, prominently out front to argue the merits of the treaty, calling it "modest but useful" and dismissing the concessions made to the Russians as unimportant. The four service chiefs were also made to march to the hill in support, though they looked decidedly uncomfortable on camera. The cause received a jolt when Lt. Gen. Ed Rowny, who had been a member of the SALT negotiating team until its signing, resigned in protest because he felt that too many concessions had been made to the Soviets. He testified that a better agreement could be negotiated if the treaty were not ratified. Of the outside witnesses, Paul Nitze delivered a devastating critique, and Henry Kissinger, while not specifically opposing the treaty, picked its terms apart and suggested a postponement until better terms were negotiated.

On the other side of the ideological spectrum, Jeremy Stone, of the Federation of American Scientists, urged that Senate reservations be added to the ratification resolutions to obtain reductions in offensive systems. It soon became evident that at the very minimum the treaty would have to be heavily modified with amendments in the Senate in order to have any hope of ratification.

In their growing fear, administration officials announced that any amendment would be considered a "killer amendment," and the Soviet embassy underlined this view. The Senate was in effect given an ultimatum to either ratify the treaty as it stood or kill it. This had the opposite effect intended. John Glenn rose to withdraw his support until means of verification were improved. Sam Nunn concentrated on how the treaty would affect our NATO commitments, most notably the cruise missile's potential in Europe. In desperation, the administration announced that it intended to change course and build two hundred MX missiles. Again the move backfired by winning no new advocates for SALT II and provoking liberals George McGovern and Mark Hatfield to withdraw support. The administration was making too many concessions to the hawks.

On November 9 the treaty was reported out of the Foreign Relations Committee by a 9–6 vote, much closer than the administration had hoped. The committee chairman had been successful, however, in voting down numerous amendments. But neither Senators Jackson nor Tower were members of the committee; they were waiting hungrily for the treaty to reach the Senate floor in January. But the great floor debate and expected massacre of the treaty never took place. Instead, it died a quiet death.

The SALT II treaty was set aside for good in January 1980 immediately following the Soviet invasion of Afghanistan. By this time the Carter administration had reversed course on its linkage arguments, but the move came too late. Our steering committee had coordinated a very broad lobbying and public relations effort against the treaty involving such organizations as the Committee on the Present Danger and the Heritage Foundation. We provided a range of speakers to meet any request to appear on all television talk shows. The presidential primaries were now in full swing, and Republican candidates George Bush and Ronald Reagan were vying with each other to vilify the appeasement policies, defense cuts, and the unacceptable SALT treaty of President Carter.

In January 1980 the treaty was finally taken off the Senate agenda at the administration's request. Their vote count showed that it would have been rejected by an almost four to one majority, and they had no stomach for such a humiliation.

———

The story of SALT ends with the election of President Reagan. He had campaigned vigorously not only against the SALT II treaty but against the entire SALT process and the assumptions underlying it. The Reagan administration put the most promi-nent SALT critics in the most important policy-making positions. Richard Perle became the assistant secretary of defense in charge of strategic nuclear policy; Ed Rowny and Paul Nitze became the principal negotiators and strategists. The administration dropped the SALT approach entirely and instead began a comprehensive rebuilding of both theater and strategic nuclear forces. Simulta-neously, new negotiations were begun with the Soviets for much deeper reductions in strategic arms reduction talks (START), a separate negotiation for deep reductions in intermediate-range nuclear force (INF) negotiations, and an entirely new approach to the long-standing conventional forces in Europe (CFE) negotia-tions, which had begun in Vienna in 1973 (to which I had been a delegate in 1974). An INF treaty was signed on December 8, 1987, and ratified by the Senate with little controversy on May 27, 1988. A CFE treaty was signed after the end of the Cold War, on July 8, 1991, and ratified, along with five reservations added by the Senate, on November 25, 1991.

While there were many internal struggles and debates during the ensuing eight years of the Reagan administration, the consen-sus was far stronger than in any previous administration: The vigorous building program would—and did—give the Soviets entirely new incentives to make concessions as their attempt to compete brought them to economic collapse.

The power of Congress to stop major weapons programs has had a considerable effect on the negotiation and outcome of American arms control efforts. The START negotiations, for instance, were set back considerably when the MX missile deployment was delayed by Congress to persuade the administration to negotiate more seriously during the first Reagan administration. Moreover, the strategic defense initiative (SDI) was slowly pared away as the negotiations proceeded. John Tower, chief START negotiator in 1986, later remembered that he was

> naturally disturbed when I was told by Ambassador Glitman that a member of a delegation of congressional observers had taken Karpov aside at a reception in Geneva and told him not to worry about SDI. Glitman had heard this Senator say, "Congress is going to take care of" the program. I could only imagine how much comfort that might have given the Soviets.[8]

Congress also had played a substantial role in shaping long-term negotiating positions. In relation to the START negotiations, the aftermath of the 1983 Scowcroft Commission's report brought several key congressmen (most notably Sen. Albert Gore and Cong. Les Aspin) to force the administration to commit to the report's goals of reducing warheads on U.S. land-based ICBMs. This congressional pressure led to the administration's commitment to the single-warhead "Midgetman" ICBM and the proposed negotiating positions of trading U.S. bomber superiority for Soviet land-based ICBM superiority. This direct congressional influence continued throughout the negotiations until a treaty was finally signed on July 31, 1991. By then, however, it was already irrelevant because of the collapse of the Soviet Union.

Finally, the development of the Senate's bipartisan Arms Control Observer Group has involved the Senate in arms control in a manner that speaks reasonably well for future executive-senatorial relations on these matters. Founded in 1984, one year after the Soviet walkout of the START negotiations, the group's functions include visiting Geneva at plenary sessions and receiving regular briefings from the U.S. negotiating team in Washington. In all, the group has made over fifteen trips to Geneva since 1985.

## Conclusion

The ten-year saga of the SALT process and the various agreements it produced has certainly confirmed the wisdom of the power over treaties vested in the Senate by the Founding Fathers. They saw that the adoption of treaties as part of the enforceable laws of the nation was too grave a responsibility to leave in the hands of executive officials charged by their duties with too close a focus on immediate events. The requirement for a two-thirds majority was also quite rightly intended to ensure that commitments of such importance command not just a bare majority but a strong consensus. Yet the evasion of this difficult obstacle course through the ploy of executive agreement has also proved to be a useful process. Such agreements are relatively easy to modify and amend and do not have the sanctity of a treaty. They nevertheless provide the executive with tactical flexibility that promotes effective dealings in international relations. The treaty process has evolved over the last two-hundred years, and given my experience in the Reagan administration, I tend to think that we have got it about right.

# 6

## The Power of Inquisition

### Background

The power of Congress to investigate is nowhere to be found in the Constitution. Like so many other powers, it is a derived power flowing from the principle that each branch of the government has granted to it those powers that are not explicitly prohibited and are necessary to carry out the duties and functions explicitly granted in the Constitution.

Almost certainly the Founding Fathers contemplated an inherent investigative power for the new Congress. The House of Commons has exercised investigative power since the sixteenth century, and the experience of most of the drafters in their colonial legislatures and the Continental Congress, where the parliamentary practice of investigation was prevalent, disposed them to accept this as a necessary concomitant of the legislative function.[1]

The first use of this implied power was not long in coming. In 1792, the House of Representatives decided to look into the defeat of Gen. Arthur St. Clair's disastrous expedition against the Indians of the Northwest Territory and set up a committee to do so. President Washington's cooperation with this committee helped provide the important congressional power of investigation with its present unquestioned legitimacy. With this case Congress established the precedent that the investigative power would be exercised through committees. A special or select committee was established for the purpose of the St. Clair investigation, and a majority of all investigations from then until the Reorganization Act of 1946 were carried out by such ad hoc committees, which expired with the conclusion of the particular investigation.[2] Another enduring precedent set by this investigation was the heavy role of party politics in the creation of the committee and in the supression of its final report.[3]

In 1828, the investigative power was further broadened by the granting of subpoena power for the first time to a standing committee—the House Committee on Manufactures. Heretofore the limiting of the investigative power to ad hoc committees acting in a judicial capacity had kept the scope of the investigative power quite narrow.[4]

At first, the House of Representatives dominated congressional investigations. It conducted twenty-seven of the thirty investigations between 1789 and 1814. As time passed, however, the Senate took the dominant position: Between 1900 and 1925 it conducted forty of the sixty congressional investigations.[5]

Since that first investigation in 1792, the exercise of this power has made many important contributions. In the words of Martin N. McGeary, "They have illuminated many a dark problem, lighted scores of shadowy corners, and sometimes disclosed carefully hidden skeletons."[6] A proclivity established by this very first inquiry was the congressional fondness for the investigation of military operations. It is in this field, most observers agree, that the investigative power has made its least admirable contributions. Every conflict in which the United States has been involved, except the Spanish-American War, has been the subject of later or even simultaneous congressional investigation. Undoubtedly the most infamous of such inquiries was that conducted by the Joint Committee on the Conduct of the War, authorized in December 1861. It was mandated to investigate "past, present, and future defeats, the orders of executive departments, the action of generals in the field, and the questions, of war policies."[7] It had been set up in the aftermath of the defeat at the first battle of Bull Run and immediately became a political vehicle for the Radical Republicans opposed to Lincoln.

As some later committees have attempted to do, it took over a partial control of military operations, investigating strategy, interrogating subordinate officers to gain evidence against particular generals, and demanding particular resignations or reassignments by President Lincoln. Setting yet another hallowed precedent, the proceedings of these sessions, while supposed to be highly secret, were usually leaked to the press without delay.[8] As a result of the committee's activities, the Confederate commander in chief, Robert E. Lee, observed that what he learned from its investigations was ultimately worth about two divisions of Confederate troops.[9]

President Lincoln, in exasperation, echoed almost exactly by his twentieth-century successors, cried, "This impoverished vigilante committee to watch my movements and to keep me straight . . . is a marplot, and its greatest purpose seems to be to hamper my action and obstruct military operations."[10]

Another exercise of the investigative powers that reflects no credit on this congressional role was the notorious Senate Special Committee Investigating the Munitions Industry, established in 1934. Despite Democratic control of the Senate, a progressive Republican, Gerald P. Nye of North Dakota, was appointed its chairman; and he set out to use what became the Nye Committee as a vehicle to ride to the vice-presidential nomination in 1936 as the leader of an increasingly popular isolationism. Nye believed that the public was convinced that the "merchants of death" had dragged the country repeatedly into war, and he set out to prove his case. The committee ran off in many different directions. It was able to disclose instances of bribery and corruption, and expose the enormous influence of the Morgan Bank, which earned 1 percent commission on all British arms purchases, in bringing the United States into World War I on the side of the bank's major debtor, Great Britain. Its overall impact was to fan the flames of isolationism in the pre–World War II period.[11]

Performances such as these led some observers to denounce the "senatorial debauch of investigations—poking into political intrigue . . . the level of professional searchers of municipal dunghills."[12]

The reputation of the congressional investigative powers was somewhat refurbished during World War II. Created in March 1941, nine months before the attack on Pearl Harbor, the Truman Committee sought to uncover and halt wasteful practices in war preparation. When the war broke out, it greatly expanded its authority "to make a full and complete study and investigation of the operation of the program for the procurement and construction of supplies, materials, vessels, plants, camps, and other articles and facilities in connection with the national defense."[13]

Although many executive-branch officials were less sanguine in their assessment of the committee, most observers believed in retrospect that the Truman Committee was very effective in bringing about needed improvements in the administration and in rationalizing the enormous expenditures for industrial production during the war.

The investigative power was greatly strengthened immediately following World War II. Passage of the Legislative Reorganization Act of 1946 (Public Law 79–601) cut the number of standing committees in the House from forty-eight to nineteen and in the Senate from thirty-three to fifteen. It authorized standing committees of both chambers to "exercise continuous watchfulness of the execution by the administration agencies concerned of any laws, the subject matters of which is within the jurisdiction" of the respective committees. It also provided a permanent budget for investigation and for the hiring of professional staff members for all standing committees. The effect of this act, together with the vast expansion of the federal bureaucracy during the 1930s and 1940s, resulted in a tremendous growth in the number of investigations in the postwar years. Compared with approximately five hundred investigations from 1792 until 1946, the Ninetieth Congress of 1946–47 alone authorized 496 investigations.[14]

Many observers now view the investigating and informing function of Congress as more important than even its legislative function. As Woodrow Wilson put it:

Unless Congress have and use every means of acquainting itself with the acts and the disposition of administrative agents of the government, the country must remain in the embarrassing, crippling ignorance of the very affairs which it is most important that it should understand and direct.[15]

The shift of congressional investigations to intelligence affairs in the mid-1970s had several causes. First, bitterness over the defeat in Vietnam served as a foundation on which a sweeping criticism of military administration could be established. The divisive nature of the war and its shattering of a Cold War consensus on foreign policy led to far-reaching questioning within and outside the government of the proper role for the CIA outside our borders. Second, the surfacing of reports of CIA covert operations in Chile to overthrow the incipient Allende regime and of CIA assistance to non-Marxist Angolan factions in 1974 (leading to the Clark Amendment, to be discussed later) provided critics with strong ammunition. This allowed Congress, in light of the political climate, to seek control of all intelligence activities and thus to "root out Cold War adventurism so as to weed out those actions less politically desirable at its source," as Sen. Frank Church put it. Finally, the revelations of the Ervin Committee, showing involvement of former Central Intelligence Agency (CIA) officials early on in the Watergate cover-up (though not actually implicating the CIA), further prepared the intelligence community for targeting by the hostile Congress. The weapon chosen was the use of select committees in both the Senate and the House. The Ford administration attempted to head off this ambush of its proprietary activities by starting highly visible investigations of its own. The Rockefeller Commission (the commission on CIA activities within the United States), under the direction of the vice-president, was the initial attempt to investigate charges of CIA surveillance of U.S. citizens in violation of the law prohibiting the agency from involving itself in law enforcement or internal security. Established by Executive Order 11828 (January 4, 1975), it issued its report on June 6, 1975 and recommended restrictions and a new form of joint legislative-executive organ to oversee intelligence activities.

The Murphy Commission, whose report was issued three weeks later (June 27, 1975), was formed to study not the legal aspects of intelligence gathering but the possibilities for a more coherent system of foreign policy formulation. Although established in 1972 before Watergate, the timing of the report was such that it had an impact on the development of restrictions regarding intelligence; it made proposals for covert-action restrictions and better oversight provisions.

In contrast to the executive commissions, which strove for

meaningful and sober bipartisan solution (the Murphy Commission was actually appointed in part by Congress and started in the Nixon administration), the Senate Select Committee to Study Government Operations with Respect to Intelligence (the Church Committee) and its House counterpart, the House Select Committee on Intelligence (the Pike Committee), took on the partisan character of the contemporary Congress, and their recommendations reflect that stridency.

The Church Committee and the Pike Committee, both founded in 1975, were the direct precursors of the modern intelligence committees. The Church Committee endowed itself with the mission of finding "the extent, if any, to which illegal, improper, or unethical activities were engaged in by any agency of the Federal Government,"[16] and its seventeen-volume report, containing 183 recommendations, left even the National Security Act in question (it was suggested that it be replaced by other legislation), as well as charters for each organ of the intelligence community. More noteworthy was the committee's treatment of the crisis in Chile, presumably fostered by the CIA with President Nixon's (and other administration officials') full knowledge and support. The committee's findings led to the persecution and fining of CIA director Richard Helms for denying to a Senate committee the existence of such activities.

The Pike Committee was created to "investigate the intelligence-gathering activities of the U.S. government,"[17] presumably to determine the desirability of such actions. Although the final report was never released to the public (even so, the *Village Voice* published key parts of the report before its scheduled release), the findings were in favor of tight controls over covert action, increased oversight methods, and budgetary procedures designed to curb what was perceived as an unmanageable intelligence force.

The Ford administration continued to try to preempt the issue. Executive Order 11905, signed in February 1976, limited many areas of intelligence gathering and vested cabinet-level advisory status in the director of Central Intelligence, then George Bush. Also, each intelligence organ was given parameters and concrete responsibilities, much as the Church Committee suggested, and an Intelligence Oversight Board, consisting of three members, to constantly review intelligence pursuits in relation to their legality, was created. Finally, the executive order dealt with restrictions on intelligence activities in general. It went far to institutionalize the recommendations of the two commissions and two select committees.

Congressional critics, of course, forged ahead, ignoring the executive measures. They wanted their own congressional reorganizations of American intelligence gathering. The December 1974 Hughes-Ryan Amendment to the Foreign Assistance Act of 1961 provided a major congressional oversight of intelligence activities in covert operations. Meant as a reaction to U.S. actions in Chile, it mandated that a presidential finding be reported in a "timely" fashion following any covert action. Additionally, it stipulated that congressional committees involved, namely, the House and Senate Foreign Affairs/Relations, Appropriations, and Armed Services committees, be informed of any covert operation. While the amendment did not necessitate prior congressional consent, it nonetheless greatly reduced secrecy by increasing the number of congressmen and staff aware of an action. As broad as Hughes-Ryan was, its passage fed the appetite for even stronger, more controlling measures and oversight powers. Hence, a more permanent, forceful instrument of control could be fashioned in the form of two powerful committees with control not only over sensitive information but authorization of virtually the entire CIA and intelligence-community budget.

Taking the recommendations of the Church and Pike committees, Congress created a Senate Select Committee on Intelligence in 1976 and the House Permanent Select Committee on Intelligence in 1977, in contrast to earlier proposals that the two houses create a single joint committee on intelligence affairs. Both Senate Resolution 400 and House Resolution 658 had similar membership structures (overlapping with the Foreign Relations/Affairs, Armed Services, Appropriations, and Judiciary committees), and both were empowered to control budgetary authorization and legislative authority over the CIA, with these powers to be shared with the Judiciary and Armed Services Committee in the cases of the Federal Bureau of Investigation (FBI) and the Department of Defense. Membership was to rotate. The Senate committee was given authority to declassify sensitive intelligence information unilaterally, with disputes with the executive to be resolved by the entire Senate; the House, while not allowed to act on its own, could still recommend declassification. In both committees, service is limited (eight years in the Senate and six years in the House) to avoid favorable treatment of intelligence groups by the legislative overseers. The committees were endowed by Congress with broad authorization powers that provide enormous influence over intelligence activities.

———

The special prosecutor (independent counsel) provisions of the Ethics in Government Act of 1978 took full advantage of the Watergate scandal as justification for its existence. When the cover-up was shown to include members of the Department of Justice, President Nixon was forced by the congressional and public outcry to appoint a special prosecutor, Archibald Cox, to investigate the case. However, the president's dissatisfaction with the lack of control he was able to exert over Cox's investigation and Cox's subpoenaing of Nixon's White House tapes caused Nixon to call for the special prosecutor's replacement. This was done, but not before the attorney general, Elliot Richardson, resigned and the solicitor general, Robert Bork, replaced Richardson and removed Cox, installing Leon Jaworski as the new special prosecutor.

Jaworski came to office amid executive promise of his nonremovability, a promise that was used by the Supreme Court to uphold Jaworski's subpoena of the same tapes in the *United States v. Nixon* case.[18]

The Cox affair guaranteed that the Senate Select Committee on Presidential Campaign Activities (the Watergate Committee) and the Senate Judiciary Committee would take up the issue of inherent conflict of interest when the attorney general controls U.S. Attorneys in the prosecution of appointees with political ties to the attorney general and his superior, the president; in effect, the special prosecutor is investigating his boss, who is the president. Inevitably, a number of proposals over the next four years aimed at establishing a permanent mechanism for the independent appointment of special prosecutors. These proposals endowed the courts rather than the executive with appointment responsibility and did away with the power of the president and attorney general to remove a special prosecutor. Congress passed a provision for court appointment of special prosecutors in the Ethics in Government Act of 1978.[19] The drafters were careful to exempt members of Congress and staff from the act, a pattern that has been followed in all subsequent legislation.

The act provided for court appointment of a special prosecutor (later changed to "independent counsel" by amendment in 1982) to investigate and, if necessary, prosecute alleged wrongdoings of executive-branch officials. In accordance with the act, the process of appointment of an independent counsel is begun when the attorney general is made aware that a certain high official (defined as the president, vice-president, White House staff, cabinet members, and high Justice Department officials as well as close advisers and family members of the president) may have violated federal criminal statutes. After a maximum of ninety days, during which the attorney general is to conduct a preliminary investigation, he must, unless no reasonable grounds to prosecute are found, apply for the appointment of an independent counsel. A panel of three District of Columbia Court of Appeals judges, whose selection is designated by the chief justice to last for two years, selects the independent counsel, who is vested with full investigative and prosecutory powers and a scope to be defined (or enlarged) at the discretion of the three-judge panel.

The special prosecutor has a broad spectrum of investigative powers under the act, ranging from conducting grand jury proceedings, applying warrants, subpoenas, and immunities to using the resources and personnel of the Department of Justice. Furthermore, he or she is required to adhere to a detailed set of prerequisites pertaining to reporting to and directing Congress, including contact with oversight committees and recommending impeachment. He is also responsible for drafting indictments and overseeing prosecutions. In short, the independent counsel handles all facets of the federal case assigned to him in a fashion previously allowed only to U.S. Attorneys. Yet the attorney general can remove independent counsels only for "good cause."

To date, eight independent counsels have been appointed. On November 29, 1979, Arthur Christy was appointed to investigate allegations of cocaine use by Hamilton Jordan, then President Carter's chief of staff. Using terms that unjustly imply guilt, this first independent counsel found "insufficient grounds to prosecute" in May 1980, and charges were dropped.[20]

An accusation against Carter's national campaign manager, Tim Kraft, prompted Gerald Gallinghouse to be named on September 9, 1980, also to investigate possible cocaine use. These charges were dropped in January 1982.[21]

Charges against President Reagan's secretary of labor, Raymond Donovan, involving connections to organized crime and alleged bribery of labor union officials led to the appointment of Leon Silverman on December 29, 1981. Thus began a complex series of investigations leading to indictment and trial. After years of ordeal, Donovan was acquitted on all counts. Then, reflecting the sentiments of previous and subsequent innocent targets of these new inquisitors, he asked "to which office do I go to get my reputation back?"

On April 2, 1984, Jacob Stein was chosen to investigate Edwin Meese, President Reagan's attorney general designate, and charges concerning his financial disclosure and other public improprieties. No criminal charges were brought, and the investigation closed on September 20, 1984.[22]

Alexia Morrison was appointed in May 1986 to investigate Theodore Olson, former assistant attorney general, suspected of giving false testimony to Congress during the Environmental Protection Agency (EPA) scandals. No criminal charges were ever brought, although the investigation precipitated a landmark Supreme Court decision (to be discussed later).[23]

The allegations against Michael Deaver, a former Reagan aide, brought Whitney North Seymour to the post of independent counsel to investigate purported postexecutive employment conflict-of-interest violations in May 1986. Seymour prosecuted and obtained a conviction of perjury on three counts in December 1987.[24]

Lawrence Walsh, appointed on December 19, 1986, was chosen to investigate illegal arms sales to Iran and the direction of profits to the Contra resistance in Nicaragua.[25] Walsh succeeded in indicting Lt. Col. Oliver North, Air Force Maj. Gen. (Ret.) Richard Secord, Rear Adm. John Poindexter, and Albert Hakim on March 16, 1988. But eventually most charges would be dropped and the convictions of North and Poindexter were reversed by the court of appeals.

166

James McKay was appointed on February 2, 1987, to investigate Franklyn C. (Lyn) Nofziger, a former White House staff member, in connection with possible violations of postemployment conflicts of interest surrounding his lobbying for the Wedtech Corporation.[26] He proceeded to indictment and obtained a conviction on February 11, 1988, which was overturned on appeal.

In these eight matters, which led to three convictions, all subsequently overturned by appeals courts, the legitimacy of the independent counsel was seriously questioned. It was, however, upheld by the Supreme Court. The case of *Morrison v. Olson*, because of its direct contradiction of an earlier Supreme Court decision, deserves a more complete study, since it had an impact not only on the continuing existence of the independent counsel but also on the constitutionality of nonexecutive bodies performing tasks of a distinctly executive nature.

Questions about the independent counsel's constitutionality tend to crystallize into three separate groups of argument: separation of powers, the appointment organ for the independent counsel, and the removal provisions. The realities of the independent counsel's stature, impact, and powers suggest a considerably more persuasive argument against the office's constitutionality, regardless of the outcome of the most recent judicial affirmation to the contrary, *Morrison v. Olson*.

The separation-of-powers argument rests principally on the exclusive power of the president under Article II, Section I of the Constitution to alone handle all executive tasks. Furthermore, the Constitution is unambiguous and implies no sharing of power with any other branch. Vesting all executive power in the president would seem to rule out the exercise of such power by any entity created by Congress outside the executive branch.

The legislation provides that an independent three-judge panel has responsibility for appointing, terminating, and defining the scope and reviewing the actions of an officer with prosecutory (executive) powers. That seems clearly to breach the idea of separation of powers. The independent-counsel provisions can't be reconciled with the idea that the courts "are not to interfere with the free exercise of the discretionary powers of the attorneys of the United States in their control over criminal prosecution."[27]

167

Proponents of the independent counsel cite the fact that only the attorney general can order a counsel to be appointed as a sufficient indication of its being under executive control. They cite the case of the *Nixon v. Administrator of General Services* decision, which said, among other things, that it is an "archaic view of the separation of powers as requiring three airtight departments of government."[28]

Another constitutional shortcoming of the independent counsel is its clear violation of the appointments clause in Article II, Section II of the Constitution, whereby "officers of the United States" are to be appointed by the president, subject to senatorial advice and consent. *Buckley v. Valeo* clarified this point further while stating that one who exercised a marked authority under the laws of the United States is an "officer" of the United States and, as such, should be appointed in accordance with Article II, Section II.[29] And since *U.S. v. Nixon* found that the prosecution of federal offenses is a core executive function, this officer should be chosen and controlled by the executive.[30] Finally, the decision in *Myers v. United States* held that the president has the authority to appoint and remove any official exercising an executive function.[31] Hence, since the independent counsel is an executive officer performing a core executive function, he should be appointed by, and removed by, the president.

---

The main argument for the constitutionality of the appointment process of the independent counsel comes from the implications of the *ex parte Siebold* decision, which allowed the courts, by an act of Congress, to appoint election overseers.[32] This decision was based on the Article II, Section II clause that allows congressional action to give the courts the power to appoint "such inferior officers, as they think proper." But it is a long stretch to equate a quasi-judicial election commissioner with the undoubted executive powers of a special prosecutor.

The 1982 amendment to the independent-counsel provisions inserted removal for "good cause" instead of "extraordinary impropriety," presumably to stifle as much as possible any doubts about the constitutionality of the removal mechanism. Regardless of the phrasing, the *Myers* decision, which described the president as having and needing "unrestricted power to remove the most important subordinates in their most important duties,"[33] seems, in light of the theoretically limitless powers and executive nature of the independent counsel, to be inconsistent. If, as supporters of the mechanism contend, the independent counsel is constitutional and hence under the jurisdiction of the executive, then the president should enjoy unlimited appointment and removal power.

## Morrison v. Olson

In a 7–1 vote, the independent-counsel provisions were supported by the Supreme Court in *Morrison v. Olson* in 1988. In this case, the constitutionality of the independent-counsel law was challenged by Theodore Olson, an assistant attorney general in the Reagan administration who was investigated for five years by special prosecutor Alexia Morrison at the request of Chairman John Dingell's committee after the Environmental Protection Agency (EPA) declined to turn over internal documents to the Dingell Committee. After five years of agony, Olson was exonerated of all charges, but the Court upheld the legitimacy of the legislation.

One aspect of the provisions that is addressed is the removal clause, as the act is seen merely to "reduce the amount of control"[34] that the president or attorney general can exert. This characterization contrasts sharply with the fact that the judicial council—not the president—has effective control over the independent counsel and that the "good cause" mechanism is asserted to be a symptom of executive control, not a legislative check on his removal authority, as it is usually characterized. That the Court needed to stretch the reality of the independent counsel's nature this far does not bode well for the durability of its verdict.

The crux of the Court's argument was whether the "removal restrictions are of such a nature that they impede the President's ability to perform his constitutional duty."[35] The judgment that the provisions did not, and thus were constitutional, leads to a rather curious view of the executive branch, since, in the Court's view, the president's main power over his subordinates is not his power to control all executive power, as Article II and *Myers* says, but because his duty is to "take care that the laws are faithfully executed." In this view, the president's role is something that Congress has no real need to harness, since the president's main task is the carrying out of successive legislative fiats. It seems to imply an executive that is subordinate to Congress, with his control over subordinates reduced to relieving from duty only those executive officials who refuse to comply with and implement the orders of Congress.

Although it is true, as the *Morrison* decision stated, that "the Constitution does not give the President illimitable power of removal over the officers of independent agencies,"[36] it is also true that the Constitution hardly addresses the issue of independent agencies at all, nor does it suggest that any new offshoots of *any* branch can be independent of that branch. Otherwise Congress could create de facto new branches at will, thus in effect dismantling and dismembering the executive and judicial branches.

## The Inspector General Act

As constitutionally troublesome but not as fiercely contested by the executive are the numerous inspector general (IG) offices set up by the Inspector General Act of 1978. Intended to curb fraud and abuse of power in major executive departments, the act, amended almost annually since its inception to include more departments and currently encompassing dozens of departments, administrations, commissions, and agencies, has taken on a dynamic of its own. That the act has not been challenged on constitutional grounds is the fault of the executive, for the separation-of-powers question raised is similar to that of the independent-counsel provisions. That IGs are very popular with the media, having fed it a steady diet of stories regarding $700 toilet seats and faulty missiles, has made it difficult to confront. Who in the executive cares to take on the hunters of "waste, fraud, abuse," and risk becoming themselves a target of investigation?

The Inspector General Act actually was a modification of a 1976 establishment of an Office of Inspector General in the Department of Health, Education, and Welfare (HEW; now the Department of Health and Human Services).[37] A 1977 Organization Act for the Department of Energy created a similar office in that department, with the mandate to "provide such additional information or documents as may be requested by either House of Congress or . . . by any committee or subcommittee thereof."[38] The allegations of fraud in the General Services Administration in 1977 and 1978, coupled with news stories from the HEW IG revealing Medicare waste and corruption, led Congress to consider more sweeping IG programs in 1978. Not surprisingly, the committee report's arguments for the proposed act's constitutionality bore a strong resemblance to the arguments for the special-prosecutor provisions, passed the same year.

The Senate report states that in his reports to the head of the agency, the IG "acts *in part* [emphasis mine] as an executive official in aid of the agency head's duty to execute the laws enacted by the Congress."[39] However, since the IG can also find incriminating evidence regarding agency officials at high levels, the act provides for unaltered transmission of this information directly to Congress rather than to the executive. This, it was said, was "fundamental" to the bill, allowing the IG a high degree of independence from the executive branch. Like the special prosecutor, a quasi-executive official would be responsible for reporting to Congress on an executive agency or official without any possibility of removal by his "superior," either the agency head or the president. Creating such a direct-reporting requirement is incompatible with the separation of powers, but President Carter signed the bill without dissent in October 1978.[40]

The law created, in addition to the IGs in HEW and Energy, statutory IG offices in Agriculture, Commerce, Housing and Urban Development (HUD), Interior, Labor, Transportation, the Community Services Administration, the National Aeronautics and Space Administration (NASA), the Small Business Administration, and the Veterans Administration (VA). By later amendments, IG offices were created in the departments of Education (1979), Synthetic Fuels Corporation (1980), State (1981), the Agency for International Development (AID) (1981), Defense (1982), the Railroad Retirement Board (1983), the United States Information Agency (USIA) (1986), the Arms Control and Disarmament Agency (ACDA) (1987), and in 1988, Justice, Treasury, the Federal Emergency Management Administration, the Nuclear Regulatory Commission, and the Office of Personnel Management (OPM). While many in the executive branch were appalled at the prospect of swarms of new police working in effect for the Democrats in the most aggressively political congressional committees, President Reagan feared being portrayed as favoring waste, fraud, and abuse and so signed all the bills.

The final version of the act requires an IG to report any findings to its agency heads and to Congress. Removal of an IG must be for "good cause," and the president must cite his reasons to Congress in a formal report. The IGs of the individual departments and agencies listed are nominated by the president and confirmed by the Senate. Thirty-three other IGs are appointed by agency or commission heads, including IGs for the National Endowment for the Arts and the Smithsonian Institution.

The presidentially appointed, statutory, IGs are permitted to conduct investigations, issue subpoenas at their own discretion, protect the identities of lower-level "whistle-blowers," conduct audits, hire personnel, have access to all agency information and the head of the agency, and provide recommendations to the agency head or Congress or, in the case of extreme impropriety, the attorney general. The IGs were to become "independent and objective units"[41] within their agency and were to ensure the ability of Congress to monitor virtually all executive activity; these IGs were to be chosen on their merit as accountants and administrators.

The result of the proliferation of IGs among executive agencies, aside from increasing the ablility of Congress to manage even the most minute details of executive activities, has been the almost endless flow of information, classified and not, to Congress from executive agencies. This had led not only to revelations of fraud and abuse but to the disclosure of a wide variety of executive information. In fact, IGs have become mighty engines of inquisition, providing their delighted creators in Congress with a steady bounty of "scandal" to fuel hearings and press conferences. This in turn has produced more pressure on the IGs to produce more dramatic "revelations" and bag some real trophies among the "higher-ups." Constitutional problems aside, the IG provides such a steady flow of accurate information regarding executive vulnerabilities that it may be useful to view the IG as a congressional "mole" planted by Democrats in Congress to operate against the Republicans at the White House. One nasty side effect of this zealous search for evil is the invention by the IGs of the "waste, fraud, abuse anonymous hot-line." Under this gestapolike system every office must have the 800 number posted, and all are encouraged to inform anonymously regarding any suspicious behavior. "Your boss didn't recommend you for promotion? Call the 800 number and blow him away during coffee break," as Steven Coontz put it.

The Defense Department IG now has nearly twenty-five thousand investigators and auditors under its control. The IG legislation ignores the Myers-affirmed right of the president to remove any of his high officials (which holds for every other executive appointee) without cause. Other than filling vacancies among the IGs, the president has very little influence over these officers and cannot force, request, or influence them in any effective way to resign or, for that matter, comply with his wishes. Although some might argue that the president has control over the IGs, it is only true insofar as he controls new appointments and not their actions. What Congress created, then, was a mechanism *for* Congress, accountable to virtually no one after appointment but the committee chairman. That an executive-appointed official has no responsibility to the executive presents the key constitutional problem.

*INS v. Chadha* stated that "the hydraulic pressure inherent within each of the separate Branches to exceed the outer limits of its power, even to accomplish a desirable objective, must be resisted."[42] In no case is this more true than in that of the IGs. Their aims are no doubt noble; but the existence of the IG infringes on the executive even more than the specter of the independent counsel does. To oppose the IG would seem, to the public, either an affirmation of executive malfeasance or an intention to commit same, as no politician finds it easy (or politically profitable) to oppose a bill aimed at uncovering fraud and waste in the government.

Unless we adopt a system of government that assumes that cabinet offices and presidents are venal and corrupt and therefore only the congressional chairman can be trusted to expose malfeasance, the president must demand a return to constitutional integrity: his authority over the IGs must be asserted, regardless of congressional outcry.

173

## The Iran-Contra Hearing Process

In October 1986, information became available that certain secret activities involving the sale of arms to Iran (possibly in contravention of the Arms Export Control Act), in exchange for the possible release of U.S. hostages held in Lebanon by pro-Iranian parties had been taking place since August 1985. It was also apparent that to outmaneuver Boland Amendment prohibitions against funding the Nicaraguan resistance, the Reagan administration had solicited private citizens and foreign governments for contributions for the "Contras." Furthermore, part of the profits from the arms sales was alleged to have been diverted to the Contras by means of an intricately conceived system of Swiss bank accounts. The affair prompted not one but five separate investigations; one by the executive, three by the legislature, and one by an independent counsel.

The first investigation was started by Attorney General Edwin Meese, who, in a short period of time, determined that there was a diversion of funds to the Contras. The president then formed a three-member Special Review Board consisting of John Tower, Brent Scowcroft, and Edmund Muskie, empowered to determine whether the structure of the NSC system was sound or had actually facilitated the affair. The executive's willingness to appoint a special prosecutor, in addition to its appointment of the bipartisan Tower Board (both moves, incidentally, were intended to preempt Congress), had no chance of appeasing the Democratic majority in Congress. The Democrats smelled blood. Here at last was a major scandal, one that, if handled well, could decide the upcoming presidential election.

The first congressional probe into the affair convened in early December 1986, when the Senate Intelligence Committee and the House Foreign Affairs Committee each held hearings. But as a result of the inconsistency of some witnesses' testimony and the refusal to testify of others, including Oliver North and Vice Adm. John Poindexter, on Fifth Amendment grounds, the Democratic leadership decided to schedule joint hearings of the Select Intelligence Committees of the Senate (formed January 6, 1987) and House (formed January 7, 1987).

As Congress was completing its preparations for joint hearings, the Tower Board presented its findings on February 26, 1987, in the form of a lengthy report on the nature and implications of the Iran-Contra affair. The findings of the Tower Report were as follows:

1. The Iran-Contra affair was managed and directed by the NSC staff, mainly by Vice Adm. John Poindexter, the national security adviser, and Lt. Col. Oliver North, a NSC staff member.
2. Certain CIA and State Department officials were tangentially involved, including CIA director William Casey.
3. A CIA finding, mandated by the Hughes-Ryan Amendment to precede any covert action, was signed by the president after the arms sale took place.
4. A "timely" report to Congress on any covert action, also mandated by Hughes-Ryan, not only did not take place but was explicitly forbidden in said finding.
5. Vice Adm. John Poindexter "on one or more occasions" deceived Secretary of State Shultz on the matter, in the face of Department of Defense and Department of State objections to a prospective sale.

However, the Tower Report found that any congressional or executive restructuring of the NSC system was inappropriate and superfluous, noting that the affair was a result of poor judgment on the part of a few staff members. Additionally, the Tower Report broached the subject of the lack of secrecy within Congress as a possible motivation for the lack of executive notification, stating that the number of members (and staff) that are supposed to be notified "provided cause for concern and a convenient excuse for Presidents to avoid Congressional consultation"[43] regarding covert activities. The issue of the inability of Congress to safeguard sensitive information was to become a major one in light of Congress's dissemination of crucial operational information during its own investigation in the weeks to come. In 1991, however, it was revealed that throughout the period of the various Boland Amendments, the CIA had been providing the White House with transcripts of intercepted communications between Sandinista officials and certain congressmen and their staffs opposed to Contra aid, reported by the *New York Times* to include House Speaker Jim Wright and fellow Democrats Barnes of Maryland and Bonior of Michigan. "At one point some administration officials proposed that members of Congress or their aides be prosecuted . . . intelligence officers who supported the administration's policies considered conversations with the Sandinistas to be damaging breaches of national security, if not treasonous. . . . The officials said they became seriously concerned that lawmakers or their staff members were advising the Sandinistas to adopt specific diplomatic and military tactics to help the congressmen defeat administration proposals to provide the Contras with military aid. . . . At one point in late 1987 and early 1988, there were discussions within the National Security Council over whether to prosecute Mr. Wright or his aides under the Logan Act of 1799. . . . These officials said, '. . . they simply could not trust the Congress to keep details of the Iran arms sales and Contra support program secret.' "[44]

Nevertheless, the Tower conclusion that the affair was not a result of a flawed policy-making process was not a view well received by Congress, and the Democratic strong negative response to the inadequacies of the Tower Report helped bolster the idea that the forthcoming congressional investigation was necessary and legitimate.

On March 18, 1986, it was decided that the two houses of Congress would hold joint hearings, for reasons involving the inconvenience, redundancy, possible public resentment, and prospective length of separate hearings. The joint hearings structure presented opportunities and limitations of major proportion. The Senate majority leader, Robert Byrd, and the minority leader, Robert Dole, announced that they were to appoint a select committee on the Iran-Contra affair. This committee and its counterpart in the House were formed on January 6, 1987, and January 7, 1987, respectively.

The posture adopted by Congress—like the proverbial piano player in the bawdy house, they had no idea what was going on upstairs—was faintly absurd. Everyone in Washington knew there were off-books efforts to help the Contras. In 1985, McFarlane "offered the chairman of the House subcommittee the opportunity to read Colonel North's files provided he did not bring along staff members."[45] This offer was rejected, as McFarlane expected, simply because no staff members were allowed to participate. In 1985 and 1986, when reports continued to surface in the press that the White House was secretly assisting the Contras, only cursory examination of the allegations was pursued. No one wanted to know.

The Senate Select Committee on Secret Military Assistance to Iran and the House Select Committee to Investigate Covert Arms Transactions with Iran first met on the day that the Tower Report was released, February 26, 1987. The committees, and especially their Democratic chairmen, proceeded from the premise that by exposing the details of the Iran-Contra affair, the broader national interest would best be served. They were urgently warned by the newly appointed independent counsel, Lawrence Walsh, that their show trials would seriously damage his ability to gain criminal conviction. He was ignored.

A congressional select committee, with the power to subpoena witnesses, grant immunity, and take testimony under oath, has in principle, far more resources than the Tower Board, which had none of these powers. The granting of even limited immunity to persuade witnesses, such as Oliver North, to testify horrified the independent counsel; the twenty-six witnesses granted this immunity would all use it as a defense against being brought to trial. Ultimately, Walsh would be unable to prove that information gathered at these hearings had not influenced him. Because of this, all charges against Oliver North would be dropped in September 1991.

The congressional hearings rotated from House to Senate chambers with each session, with Rep. Lee Hamilton, chairman of the House committee, and Sen. Daniel Inouye, chairman of the Senate committee, rotating chairmanship of the joint committee. The questioning was done in the House by Arthur Liman and in the Senate by John Nields, both private lawyers hired as "quasi-prosecutors." The questioning was highly combative and was, in addition, televised internationally, leading John Norton Moore to conclude that the hearings resembled "a televised star chamber."[46] The proceedings were conducted as if they were a made-for-television movie (or made for constituents), with long arguments by witnesses' attorneys and obvious points reexplained throughout the investigation, as if slurs against the witnesses and the Reagan administration were asides to the viewing, that is, voting audience.

Poindexter and North were by far the most important witnesses in the investigation, and each presented his own view as to why notification to Congress should be avoided during covert operations. North blamed Congress for having a "fickle . . . policy toward the Contras,"[47] thus making a concerted policy action necessary until Congress made up its mind.(This aspect is explored further in chapter 8.) Poindexter took an even stronger stand against Congress, asserting that if it had been aware of the NSC's actions, it would have tried to stop both the arms sale and the subsequent diversion of funds. Hence, his goal was to protect an executive policy from legislative tampering.

The final report of the committee (supported by all of the committee Democrats plus Republican senators Rudman, Trible, and Cohen) characterized the findings of the joint committee as "based on a record marred by inconsistent testimony."[48] The failure of some witnesses to remember important events, the shredding of NSC documents in 1986, and the death of William Casey, said by North to have been involved, added to public doubts about the conclusiveness of the body of evidence included in thirty-three volumes of testimony and depositions. The final report by the Democratic majority found that there was a substantial departure from legal process once the administration adopted covert "policies." The report also cited "pervasive dishonesty" in North's and Poindexter's dealings with Congress relating to the arms sale, noting the lack of congressional notification about the president's finding. The report recommended consideration of twenty-seven points, including stricter reporting requirements of covert actions and maintainance of the separation of the congressional intelligence committees despite CIA urging to make one joint committee to stop leaks from Capitol Hill. Also, the committee concluded that the actions taken by the NSC staff were "in violation . . . of the Boland Amendment"[49] and recommended steps to ensure that future covert actions, when taken, were legal.

In this case, the joint report consisted of both a criminal investigation (an executive function, complete with defense lawyers) and a legal finding (a judicial function). Put another way, Congress succumbed to the overwhelming temptation to make public political hay, even at the cost of hindering its own creation, the independent counsel. In such circumstances, it is hardly surprising that quite apart from the properly exposed foolishness and malfeasance, details regarding many covert intelligence operations were made common knowledge during the hearings, further eroding the willingness of allies to share intelligence or cooperate in legitimate covert operations and, of course, further strengthening the intelligence community's dearly held view that nothing sensitive can be shared with Congress without certainty of exposure. But among all the legal persiflage surrounding the hearings, the reality was once again that simple political motives were carried out by quasi-judicial prosecution. The Democratic majority in Congress opposed the Republican policy in Central America; since only one of the twenty-seven majority recommendations has since been implemented (involving more explicit reporting requirements), it is clear that Congress was in no rush to reform the intelligence oversight system but that their goal was to block executive policy in Latin America through their investigative powers and through criminal prosecution by their independent counsel. Since the two were in obvious conflict, the prime-time TV opportunity afforded by the committee hearing took precedence.

## The Kroll Affair

The House Committee on Energy and Commerce, a 1980 modification of the earlier Interstate and Foreign Commerce Committee, has had a strong impact on a wide range of issues. Of particular interest is its Subcommittee on Investigations and Oversight, chaired by Rep. John Dingell, who also chairs the committee. The mandate of the subcommittee seems to be infinitely broad, including issues such as contract fraud in the Department of Energy, bank mergers, corporate takeovers, televised college football, and the threat from substandard metal fasteners. The notoriety of Dingell's investigations of the Environmental Protection Agency (EPA) in 1983, leading to the resignation of the EPA administrator Anne Burford and the conviction of Michael Deaver for lying to the Subcommittee under oath, has caused

179

some journalists to accuse Dingell of a "new McCarthyism." In short, the sweeping jurisdiction of the subcommittee is best characterized by the satellite photo of Earth that occupies a wall in the anteroom of the subcommittee's hearing chambers as a sign of the chairman's ideas on the scope of his committee. The increasing aggressiveness of congressional investigation in the House, with its permanent Democratic majority, is well illustrated in the so-called Kroll Incident.

In 1989 the subcommittee began an investigation of Drexel Burnham Lambert, an undertaking based on the committee's supervision of the Securities and Exchange Commission (SEC) (itself a constitutional encroachment, as the Congress once again finds itself enforcing the law). The problem arose when a member of Dingell's staff asked William Bertain (a previous witness for the Committee on Drexel Burnham) to secretly tape-record a conversation with private investigator John Gibbons in January 1989. Gibbons was suspected of working for Drexel Burnham and misrepresenting himself as a congressional staff member, neither of which is legal. The staff member, Brian McTighe, authorized taping of the conversation, which is illegal in California without permission of the other party. Instead of expressing immediate distaste for this action, Dingell subpoenaed Gibbons to testify; portions of the tape were played in an attempt to discredit him.[50] Moreover, Dingell and Rep. Dennis Eckhart threatened Gibbons with contempt of Congress should he not testify, although he had not been entitled to counsel. Then Dingell's staff concocted a legal jurisdiction for his actions (two months after the fact) concerning the taping, based on the Speech or Debate clause in the Constitution, permitting exemption from liability or members' actions or words on the House or Senate floor. Only when the head of Gibbon's firm, Jules Kroll, threw his full support behind Gibbons, hired high-visibility legal counsel, and promised a donnybrook did Dingell back off, but without a hint of apology or admission of impropriety.

Taken together, these new directions in Congress's investigative powers—the independent counsel, the IGs, the intelligence oversight committees, the Brooks and Dingell committees—have had the effect of usurping the power of the executive in seeing that the laws are faithfully executed and placing these powers either in independent bodies or in Congress itself. Taken together, they cut deeply into the areas of criminal prosecution, agency control, and foreign policy. But far more destructive of our political health has been the effect of criminalizing policy differences that these recent congressional initiatives have brought about.

# 7

# Keeping Secrets

## Executive Secrecy

There is, needless to say, a fundamental, inherent conflict between the congressional powers of investigation and the executive need for secrecy. Like the congressional power to investigate, the executive's right to secrecy is nowhere mentioned in the Consitition; it derives from the executive powers granted under Article II. That the Founding Fathers assumed this was the case is indisputable. The Constitutional Convention was closed by a bond of secrecy. Benjamin Franklin admonished his colleagues to maintain that secrecy after the convention when, noting some of the doubts he had expressed about the Constitution during the Convention, he said, "Within these halls they were born and here they shall die."

While nowhere explicitly granted to the executive, paragraph 3, Section V, Article I of the Constitution states: "Each house shall keep a journal of its proceedings, and from time to time publish the same, excepting such part as may in their judgment require secrecy."

The Federalists explicitly discussed the need for secrecy in the executive in the area of diplomacy, where "perfect secrecy and immediate dispatch are sometimes requisite," and in the area of intelligence, where "the most useful intelligence may be obtained if the persons possessing it can be relieved of the apprehensions of discovery."

183

Over the years the kinds of information that the executive branch has, with limited success, attempted to keep secret have fallen into five categories.

The first category, the protection of diplomatic negotiations, was perhaps most succinctly defended by, of all sources, the Senate Foreign Relations Committee in 1816, which stated: "The nature of transactions with foreign nations, moreover, requires caution and unity of design, and their success frequently depends upon secrecy and dispatch."

Justice Potter Stewart most recently gave the court's stamp of legitimacy to that first category; to a second category, the protection of defense matters; and to a third category, the protection of the integrity of internal discussions within the executive branch, when he said:

> It is elementary that the successful conduct of international diplomacy and the maintenance of an effective national defense require both confidentiality and secrecy. Other nations can hardly deal with this nation in an atmosphere of mutual trust unless they can be assured that their confidences will be kept. And within our own executive departments, the developments of considered and intelligent international policies would be impossible if those charged with their formulation could not communicate with each other freely, frankly, and in confidence. In the area of basic national defense the frequent need for absolute secrecy is, of course, self-evident.[1]

A fourth category of protection is that mentioned in *The Federalist*: the protection of intelligence sources and methods. The National Security Act of 1947 specifically requires the director of Central Intelligence to be responsible for such protection; and in connection with the U-2 incident the Senate Foreign Relations Committee explicitly recognized that, with regard to intelligence operations, "the administration had the legal right to refuse the information."

The executive branch has exercised its right to secrecy through two means. To protect against public disclosure, it has evolved a system of security classification of information. To deny disclosure to Congress, a system of executive privilege has evolved.

Executive classification of material as "confidential" and "secret" can be traced back to the War of 1812. The present system of classification, however, appears to have begun during World War I. Through a series of general orders of the War Department and presidential executive orders, some supported by statute and others not, an elaborate network of regulations and restrictions accumulated.

By 1970 this rambling accretion of regulations had reached a ridiculous and unmanageable proportion. In 1962 the House Committee on Government Operations found there were "more than a million government employees permitted to stamp permanent security designations on all kinds of documents." The General Accounting Office (GAO) has estimated that this chaotic system costs the taxpayers between $60 and $80 million a year. And a retired Pentagon security officer, testifying before the House Government Operations Committee, stated that in the Pentagon alone there were over 20 million classified documents and that only 1–5 percent of these legitimately required protection.

On March 8, 1972, after a thorough study within the executive branch, President Nixon issued Executive Order 11652 in an attempt to begin to rationalize the system and reduce the amount of material classified. Signing the document, the president said, "We have reversed the burden of proof. For the first time, we are placing that burden—and even the threat of administrative sanctions—upon those who wish to preserve the secrecy of documents rather than upon those who wish to declassify them after a reasonable time."

Executive privilege, or the prerogative of the executive to withhold sensitive or exclusively executive documents or information from the Congress, stands naturally at odds with the congressional power to investigate. However, the combination of the post-Watergate presidency's lack of will to press claims of privilege and the ascendancy of the more ambitious congressional investigative chairmen, with their willingness to seek criminal indictments (and its recent counterpart, the contempt power), have had the consequence of nearly eradicating the privilege altogether. The implications of this phenomenon on an effective and healthy executive is the focus of this chapter.

From the very first investigation it undertook in 1792, Congress has found itself in conflict with the executive branch over access to information that the Congress believes is needed for its inquiry and the executive believes requires protection from disclosure. In that first instance, the Select House Committee requested all documents relating to the St. Clair Expedition. President Washington very carefully considered the question at a cabinet meeting and, according to Thomas Jefferson, decided that "the Executive ought to communicate such papers as the public good would permit and ought to refuse those the disclosure of which would endanger the public." In that case the president decided that none of the requested papers should be regarded as confidential; consequently, they were turned over.[2] In 1796, however, President Washington claimed executive privilege for the first time when he refused a House request for correspondence relating to the controversial Jay Treaty with Great Britain.

The Constitution nowhere confers executive privilege on the executive branch, any more than it confers on Congress the right to compel disclosure by the executive. The former is implicit in the powers of the chief executive; the latter, in the legislative powers. Both are firmly rooted in history and precedent.[3]

The Supreme Court explicitly recognized the doctrine of executive privilege as early as 1803 in *Marbury v. Madison*, where it was held that the president is not bound to produce papers or disclose information when *in his judgment* the disclosure would, on public consideration, be inexpedient.[4] In *United States v. Reynolds*, the Court ruled that when there is a strong showing of necessity, the claim of privilege should not be lightly accepted, but even the most compelling necessity cannot overcome the claim of privilege if the Court is ultimately satisfied that military secrets are at stake.[5] Moreover, the decision in *Barenblatt v. U.S.* stated that the congressional power of inquiry "is not without limitations ... that it cannot inquire into matters which are within the exclusive province of one of the other branches of government ... neither can it supplant the Executive in what exclusively belongs to the Executive."[6] In short, the overwhelming body of Court decisions prior to Richard Nixon's presidency undoubtedly supports a strong basis for the doctrine of executive privilege, a doctrine thoroughly reinforced by precedent.

Congress itself explicitly and implicitly recognized the existence of the privilege on many occasions. One such evidence was the time-honored formula for resolutions of inquiry. This was the normal way for Congress to obtain information from the executive until the tremendous expansion of investigative activity in the period immediately following World War II and the period after Watergate. Resolutions of inquiry directed to the Department of State in matters of foreign relations always contained the caveat "if not incompatible with the public interest."[7]

In 1807, Thomas Jefferson stated what seemed to be the accepted view of what the public interest should be made: "He, of course, the President from the nature of the case, must be the sole judge of which of them the public interest will permit publication. Hence under our Constitution, in requests of papers, from the legislative to the executive branch, an exception is carefully expressed, as to those which he may deem the public welfare may require not to be disclosed."[8]

The boundaries of these conflicting powers have been the source of continuous conflict. As Senator Fulbright aptly quoted *The Federalist*: "Neither the Executive nor the Legislative can pretend to an exclusive or superior right settling the boundaries between their respective powers."[9]

The issue has often been quite confused because executive privilege has been invoked by the executive not because it desired to keep the information from Congress but because it knew that the purpose of the investigation being pursued was not to inform the Congress but to make public the material in order to buttress the *a priori* conclusions of the investigation under way. In military matters this is of real concern to the executive. Just as Robert E. Lee believed that the Committee on the Conduct of the (Civil) War was worth two combat divisions to him, the executive has feared in recent times that investigations, while pursuing legitimate purposes, can, through disclosure, furnish the enemy with extremely valuable strategic and tactical combat information. The investigators have, on occasion, admitted this. Chairman J. William Fulbright, for instance, had declared that this is a price that must be paid for an open society.[10] It is to be expected, then, that the executive can, on occasion, be unwilling to pay that price, which is readily translatable in its mind not only to military and political advantage but also to the lives of American soldiers.

187

This kind of problem suggests what more often than not is at the heart of the conflict. Traditionally, Congress had been most interested in investigating those subjects that executive departments would just as soon forget, for if they are brought to light, they might cause embarrassment to the administration or to executive officials.[11] It is through this aspect of investigation into executive and administrative activities, methods, mistakes, and inefficiencies that the greatest contribution can be made; as Clinton Rossiter had described it, such investigation serves the purpose of keeping the chief executive and his helpers in touch with democratic realities.

The temptation of the executive to resort early to claims of executive privilege is not surprising in such circumstances. In the face of such frustration there used to be little Congress could do. As Woodrow Wilson commented:

> Congress stands almost helplessly outside the departments. Even the special irksome, ungracious investigations which it from time to time institutes . . . do not afford it more than a glimpse of the inside of a small province of federal administration. It can violently disturb, but it cannot often fathom the waters of the sea in which the bigger fish of the civil service swim and feed. Its dragnet stirs without cleansing the bottom.[12]

Nixon's experiences with executive privilege were broad and significant. However, as his influence weakened along with the presidency, so did the strength of the privilege, finally leading to a string of judicial rulings on executive privilege, the rise of the contempt power, and the development of executive disinclination to enforce claims of privilege altogether.

## The Nixon Test

Richard Nixon's first administration contended with the issue of executive privilege at length during his dealings with the Senate Foreign Relations Committee's Subcommittee on United States Security agreements and Commitments Abroad. It was chaired by Sen. Stuart Symington and established immediately after Nixon's inauguration on February 3, 1969, with the intent to undertake "a detailed review of the international military commitments of the United States and their relations to foreign policy."[13] The subcommittee held two years of investigations and hearings on American defense policy and foreign basing arrangements.

Although initially the executive had promised full cooperation with the subcommittee as far as access to information was concerned, the successive leaks of classified information, most of which were attributable to the subcommittee, including the Wood-McClintock Study on overseas bases, security arrangements with Indochina and the Philippines, and nuclear basing agreements, turned the free-access policy into a two-year battle over each new request for documents by the subcommittee. Moreover, as it was Nixon's perception that the subcommittee was formed not as much for information but to subvert the administration's policies, especially in Indochina, his openness of information shut rapidly upon assessment of the damage to U.S. policy in Asia done by the subcommittee's vigorous activities. Even though the subcommittee was excluded (by its own charter) from examining the U.S. commitment in Vietnam, its study of the Philippines resulted in U.S. charges of Filipino "mercernaries" being paid to keep forces in Vietnam, which in turn prompted a furor in Manila resulting in withdrawal of their forces from Vietnam and a doubling of the rent they demanded for U.S. bases in the Philippines. Additionally, the revelations of the subcommittee concerning American military policy in Vietnam (including air force rules of engagement) served to harm the war effort, as the North Vietnamese were watching every word of the hearings with great interest. The indiscretions of the subcommittee turned the remarkably open initial policy of the president on information to one of acute restriction. By 1971, President Nixon had developed a strong distrust of Congress's ability to keep sensitive material secret, a fact that led to establishment of the infamous "plumbers," established to plug leaks.

With growing distrust of Congress within the Nixon White House, executive-privilege claims proliferated and spread well beyond military policy. In November 1972, for instance, it was invoked on behalf of the Securities and Exchange Commission's (SEC) refusal to provide information to the House Interstate and

189

Foreign Commerce Subcommittee on Oversight and Investigation about ITT. The next month, the Department of Defense refused to provide documents pertaining to relieving General Lavelle of duty following charges of his ordering unsanctioned air strikes over North Vietnam.

Executive privilege's greatest test, however, came with Nixon's out-of-hand refusal to surrender various types of information to the Watergate Committee. When, in 1973, the president was subpoenaed to provide information to the grand jury investigating possible administration wrongdoings during the 1972 election (most notably, the Watergate break-in), the president refused to do so on the ground of executive privilege.

A Washington, D.C., District Court case, *Nixon v. Sirica*, resulted from Nixon's assertion of privilege over the information.[14] The court's decision held that the importance of executive privilege should be tempered with a sense of the public interest. In other words, a claim of executive privilege is to be balanced against the good that can be derived from the investigation's use of the document. In this case, it was judged that the public was served more fully by the document's release, although the caveat that presidential discourse was "presumptively privileged" was added, an indication that the balance of forces on privilege were at this point still in the executive's favor.[15]

With the *Sirica* decision firmly in hand, the Senate Watergate Committee proceeded to subpoena from Nixon similar documents and tapes to support a congressional investigation. When Nixon refused again to supply the items requested, the Senate took the case to D.C. District Court, where it was found that the court did not have appropriate jurisdiction to rule on the case. The Senate, after passing a special law conferring such jurisdiction,[16] then took their case to the appellate court. The case of *Senate Select Committee v. Nixon*, using the framework set by *Sirica*, found that there were insufficient grounds of need to overcome Nixon's "presumptive privilege."[17] The needs of a congressional inquiry, then, did not have the same weight, in the view of the court, as a criminal proceeding, when executive privilege was in the balance. The court found that the need of the committee for such information "is too attenuated and too tangential to its functions to permit a judicial judgment that the President is required to comply with the Committee's subpoena."[18]

In the aftermath of this victory, it is clear that Nixon did not see the ruling in *Select Committee* as the last on executive privilege, and he went to work on bolstering his case for an absolute privilege by insisting that all government employees were under his executive privilege to withhold information and ordering his staff not to give any information, even after leaving office.[19]

The Nixon assertion of an absolute privilege led to the first explicit recognition by the Supreme Court that such a privilege exists. Unfortunately for President Nixon, however, they said it didn't apply in this situation. Using the decisional framework of *Sirica*, the Court, in *U.S. v. Nixon*, spoke to the relation of executive privilege to the adequate dispensing of criminal justice. Although noting that certain aspects of presidential confidentiality have greater merit than does the public interest in that information's disclosure, the Supreme Court reserved for itself the responsibility "to say what the law is" in this and, it is implied, any claim of executive decision as to what is privileged information should *any* substantial conflict arise from the chief executive's decision.[20] The Court further stated that to the degree that the president's interest in confidentiality "related to the effective discharge of the president's powers, it is constitutionally based,"[21] showing that some claims of privilege are legitimate and other may not be. The Court claimed the right to decide the issue in a dispute. *Sirica* also was used to underline the assertion that confidentiality of military secrets was necesssary and that presidential communications were presumptively privileged.

The *Nixon* case forced the president to forgo executive privilege when subpoenaed for information by a criminal court, specifically the grand jury investigation to examine the Watergate break-in.

The decision was not only a blow to Nixon, who resigned just days after turning over the subpoenaed information, but also the presidency, since an unlimited privilege was considered and rebuked for the first time by the Supreme Court, eliminating the historical precedent of allowing the president to decide what is privileged. The advent of judicial review for the presidential claim of privilege was the major shift of power over information that has affected each president since Nixon in their ability to deal with the growing power of Congress to penetrate ever further into the president's domain. There is no judicial review of congressional subpoenas or contempt citations.

191

## The Rise of Congressional Contempt Power

The Ford, Carter, and Reagan administrations not only had to deal with a diminished ability to control access to executive secrets but also the growth of Congress's ability and disposition to use contempt citation in subcommittee to enforce its demands for information, whether protected by statutory confidentiality clause or conventional executive privilege.

The congressional contempt power is derived from two sources: so-called inherent contempt, based on Congress's constitutional need to enforce testimony or document discovery, and statutory contempt, derived from specific legal authorization. As the inherent type involves trial by Congress (and possible imprisonment in the Capitol jail), it is almost never used, mostly because Congress is not willing to carry on its involved procedural requirements alongside an already large work load. However, Congress can empower itself and the federal courts to prosecute in civil litigations contempt charges emanating from Capitol Hill. Moreover, the 1975 decision of *Eastland v. United States Serviceman's Fund*,[22] whereby the Supreme Court found the congressional investigation and subpoenaing power within the "legitimate legislative sphere" of Congress, further emboldened Congress to seek criminal enforcement of its subpoenas if violated. It is the threat of this type of contempt that Congress has used, one might say excessively, to compel information from executive officials, including cabinet members.

In 1975, Secretary of State Henry Kissinger was cited for contempt for his refusal to supply documents concerning his advice to the NSC on numerous covert operations. The newly formed House Select Committee on Intelligence did this in the face of President Ford's certification that executive privilege exempted these items from publicity.[23] Ford, forced to negotiate to keep his secretary of state from civil prosecution, agreed to a classified oral briefing on the topic of Kissinger's advice in return for the lifting of contempt proceedings.[24]

Also in 1975, the Subcommittee on Oversight and Investigation of the House Interstate and Foreign Commerce Committee, seeking documents to support noncompliance charges against American oil companies during the Arab boycott, cited Secretary of

Commerce Rogers Morton on November 11, 1975, for failing to disclose them. In this case, Secretary Morton based his actions on confidentiality provisions of the Export Administration Act, which ostensibly protected the information from disclosure, according to a brief prepared for the attorney general.[25] Morton later agreed to supply the information after interbranch negotiations, and he did so before the full committee voted on his contempt.

President Carter's experiences with executive control over administration secrets were no less compliant, although the constitutional line of privilege became better defined by two court decisions during his watch. The first, *Nixon v. Administrator of General Services*, saw former President Nixon seeking enforcement of a contract allowing him control over his presidential tapes and documents. The Supreme Court, in an unusual decision, denied his request in the name of the populations' right of access to them while at the same time reaffirming the existence of executive privilege even for former presidents.[26]

The second case, *United States v. AT&T*, arose from a congressional subpoena by the House Interstate and Foreign Commerce Committee's Oversight and Investigations Subcommittee of AT&T for documents (specifically, national security requests) revealing wiretapping by the FBI. The House subcommittee was investigating the extent to which warrantless wiretapping was taking place and whether this practice was being conducted lawfully. When negotiations between the executive and congress broke down over exactly how the letters were to be edited and their general accessibility by noncommittee members, the Department of Justice filed suit to force AT&T not to comply with the subpoena. The executive's actions were supported by the D.C. District Court decision, which enjoined the subpoena.[27]

However, in the court of appeals, the district court ruling was overturned, citing its "nerve-center constitutional questions."[28] Instead of a strong reprimand of the executive, however, the parties were urged to negotiate further, yet these negotiations did not satisfy the parties either, and, in a second appeals decision, the court decided not to rule in favor of either party, instead suggesting means to resolve the dispute and highlighting the shared role of the president and Congress in informational disputes.[29] The matter eventually was solved through a renegotiation of the documents' availability, and the Justice Department dropped its suit.

In *AT&T*, a balancing test, independent of the courts, was encouraged by the courts in an effort to get the branches to work out their own problems. However, the assumption here that a decidedly political question does not belong in court is in contrast to the unfortunate reality that executive officials can find themselves in jail for contempt of Congress if they act as the court recommends.

When, in 1978, Secretary of Health, Education, and Welfare (HEW) Joseph Califano was cited for contempt of the House Interstate and Foreign Commerce Committee's Subcommittee on Oversight and Investigations for refusing to supply documents concerning drug processing by pharmaceutical manufacturers on the basis of the administration's interpretation of a provision of confidentiality,[30] the administration directed him to provide the information prior to the full committee vote on contempt. Also, President Carter's energy secretary, Charles W. Duncan, invoked executive privilege in 1980 when subpoenaed for documents concerning the president's oil import tax by the Subcommittee on Environment, Energy, and Natural Resources of the House Committee on Government Operations, but Carter furnished the documents before the full committee had voted.[31]

By the time President Reagan came to office, the precedent for congressional contempt and executive compliance had been firmly established, and the new president soon found himself in a compromising situation similar to his predecessors. In July 1981, Reagan's secretary of energy, James B. Edwards, was cited for contempt by the Environment, Energy and Natural Resources Subcommittee for failing to turn over documents on the estimated cost of federal subsidy of synthetic fuels projects on the grounds of executive privilege, only to have the subpoena and citation lifted after the executive agreed to furnish the information.[32]

In February 1982, Secretary of the Interior James Watt was cited for contempt by the full House Energy and Commerce Committee for refusing, on the grounds of executive privilege, to produce documents to its Oversight and Investigations Subcommittee. At issue was the leasing of mineral rights on government-owned land to Canada, in the context of Canada's privilege of reciprocal status under the law, and the advice given Reagan by his attorney general, William French Smith, was to refer to the documents as "fundamental to the decision-making process" so as to avoid having to turn the papers over.[33] Under threat of a full House contempt vote, the president lifted his claim to privilege and allowed only the subcommittee members to examine the documents in a secure Capitol Hill room. The contempt citation was removed in exchange.

A completely new development in the decline of executive privilege struck the Reagan administration when the Environmental Protection Agency (EPA) administrator, Anne Gorsuch Burford, was subpoenaed to appear before the House Committee on Public Works and Transportation's Subcommittee on Investigation and Oversight in relation to charges of the EPA's preferential enforcement of statutes under the Superfund hazardous waste site cleanup legislation. The subcommittee called her to supply "all books, records, correspondence, memoranda, papers, notes, and documents drawn or received by the Administrator or other EPA officials since December 11, 1980."[34] President Reagan originally had agreed to allow the documents to be supplied as long as strict confidentiality could be ensured, but when the Dingell Subcommittee of the House Energy and Commerce Committee also subpoenaed virtually identical documents, the president instructed Administrator Burford that sensitive documents in active law enforcement files should not be disclosed on the basis of executive privilege. When Administrator Burford related these orders verbatim to Congress, the subcommittee drafted and passed a contempt resolution that was brought before the entire House on December 16, 1982.[35] The resolution was passed 259–105 that same day by the entire House and marked the first time that a high executive official was found in contempt of the entire House.[36]

Although the matter was presumably to be prosecuted by the U.S. Attorney's office, it took no action; instead, it sued the House on the ground of lawful executive privilege having been invoked. This 1983 case was not adjudicated because all avenues toward negotiation had not been exhausted. In February 1983, both the suit and the contempt charges were dropped, as the president and the House worked out a "deal" whereby, in exchange for the edited documents being made public (and unedited versions of all the documents requested being made available to the subcommittee throughout executive briefings and papers), the president's EPA administrator would not be prosecuted. The extent to which the president's privilege had been emasculated was seen when the president viewed this particularly nefarious form of congressional extortion as "consistent" with the doctrine of executive privilege.[37]

After the Burford case, the executive found itself in an even deeper crisis of will. Reagan's attorney general, William French Smith, was cited in 1984 for contempt as a result of his failure to produce Department of Justice records involving an ongoing criminal investigation of false defense-contractor overrun claims in the navy. The president on the advice of his public relations advisers moved quickly to furnish the documents to the Senate Judiciary Committee in order to extricate his attorney general from a difficult confrontation in an election year.[38] This case also showed the fear of the executive to stand behind even the most legitimate claims of privilege concerning the protection of files of active criminal investigations for judicial action.

The erosion had gone so far that executive privilege did not even surface during the most ambitious congressional subpoenaing effort—the Iran-Contra hearings. In an unprecedented move, President Reagan agreed to make documents as well as his aides fully accessible not only to the courts but also to Congress. He did this without even a legal explanation of his actions in the long-term interest of executive privilege. Although Secretary of Defense Weinberger called the move a "one-time exception"[39] to the rules of executive privilege, the Reagan record on privilege does not support the claim. The Iran-Contra hearings in the joint committee included testimony by cabinet-level officials and high-level advisers, such as former chief of staff Donald Regan and former national security advisers John Poindexter and Robert McFarlane. These advisers were questioned entirely on their personal advice to the president, and not one refused to answer on the grounds of its bearing on national security. In addition, tens of thousands of documents were provided the joint committee, completely unedited, though some were protected by closed hearings. Even with closed hearings, however, the final report was based on all of the hearings, posing another de facto leaking problem along the same lines (and with the same deleterious effects) as the Symington Committee leaks. The main difference between the two was that executive privilege still existed as a viable option to the Nixon administration after the Symington hearings, while the Reagan administration had all but abandoned the claim, quailing before the threat of contempt citations.

## Bush and Beyond

The Bush administration, within weeks of taking office, continued the flaccid policies of the Reagan administration. The early test of the Bush White House came with the nomination of John Tower for secretary of defense, where raw, unedited FBI files on Senator Tower were turned over to the hostile chairman of the Senate Armed Services Committee, Senator Nunn, and used extensively and with great effect against Tower's nomination. These FBI files were forwarded by the White House, upon request, to the Senate Armed Services Committee without any hesitation, leading Tower himself to believe that at least some around the president wanted to do him in. That the FBI reports, in Sen. James Exon's own words, "were 90 percent . . . garbage" apparently did not affect the decision. Instead, at least for Senator Exon, "the remaining 10 percent were major enough to give me concern."[40]

This refusal by Bush even to consider claiming executive privilege not only sank Tower but of course also weakened the future ability of the executive to resist similar requests for raw investigatory files, laying the groundwork for the obscene spectacle of the Clarence Thomas confirmation circus.

A temporary respite from this assault on privilege came in March 1990, during the trial of John Poindexter, former national security adviser. Here the principle of privilege was bolstered as Federal Judge Harold Greene ruled that former President Reagan did not need to turn over about thirty excerpts from his private diary to Poindexter's attorney, citing the discretionary executive privilege of Reagan and the Bush administration in their attempts to deny the documents' publicity. In a preliminary ruling one month earlier, Judge Greene ordered Reagan to produce the diaries. However, when the incumbent Bush administration and the former president protested, the court found that "the claims of executive privilege filed on behalf of the former President and of the incumbent President are sufficient . . . to defeat the Defendant's demand.[41] In his explanation of the grounds for privilege, Reagan's attorney, Theodore Olson (of *Morrison v. Olson* note), stated that the private reflections of the president were of the utmost secrecy and actually touched a core aspect of the presidency.

This case and the *Nixon v. Administrator* case involved mainly matters of former presidents. In both cases, the right of the incumbent president to certify the withholding of documents from Congress, the judiciary, or semiautonomous agencies was never addressed. But the cases seemed to inject the administration with a dose of courage. In July 1991, the paladin of congressional incursions, Cong. Jack Brooks of the House Judiciary Committee, issued a subpoena to the attorney general that said, "You are hereby commanded to produce the things identified on the attached schedule." They involved the president's power to send FBI agents to apprehend fugitives in foreign countries. President Bush asserted executive privilege and ordered the attorney general to ignore the subpoena. Uncharacteristically, Brooks backed down.[42]

The future of executive privilege does not lie in the hands of Congress but in the hands of the executive. Just as *Nixon v. United States* showed the constitutional legitimacy of executive privilege, should the president decide to assert it, so *Eastland v. United States Serviceman's Fund*, which allowed the contempt process to enjoy Court sanction, provided for enforcement of congressional subpoenas, should the Congress decide to press them. Now the only alternative is the option that the AT&T court decision fostered, that of compromise, which, after all, was how the privilege remained intact until tested by Nixon on a bad case.

By compromise I do not mean the Ford through early Bush executive's capitulation on executive privilege every time some committee charges contempt and threatens prison time for cabinet members. The president should defy congressional threats when and only when there is a solid case on the underlying policy merits of a claim. Until July 1991, the White House had become unable to protect its internal confidential advice and national-security-related formulations and data. I have been told by several foreign officials that they can no longer deal in confidence with the United States since they must assume that their personal advice will someday be printed in a congressional hearing. Most friendly nations now refuse to share sensitive human intelligence with us because it cannot be protected. And since raw FBI files on everyone, even on Mother Teresa (if they exist), always contain unsubstantiated hearsay gossip of the worst kind, if they fall into politically or personally hostile hands, as they did in John Tower's and Clarence Thomas's case, they can devastate a reputation. As former Attorney General and later Justice Robert Jackson said: "Disclosure of information contained in the reports (would) be the grossest kind of injustice to innocent individuals. Investigative reports include leads and suspicions, and sometimes even the statements of malicious or misinformed people. Even though later and more complete reports exonerate individuals, the use of particular or selected reports might constitute the grossest injustice, and we all know that a correction never catches up with an accusation."[43] After the Thomas fiasco, President Bush boldly announced that he would no longer provide FBI files on nominees to congressional committees. In February 1992, however, he meekly agreed to resume providing them after the Senate Judiciary Committee held up further confirmations.

Finding quality nominees for presidential appointment has become extremely difficult after the Tower and Thomas precedents and the dozens of lesser nominations that have been garroted beyond the cameras by the same sleazy practices. To accept a presidential appointment today requires a reckless disregard for family and reputation.

Finally, the notion that, through executive privilege's clash with the contempt power, political differences should be solved through criminal litigation is deeply corrosive. Yet, ironically, until the executive shows its willingness to suffer a test of its resolve by the Congress in a contempt proceeding, the matter of executive privilege will remain highly uncertain. It is but one more example of the evils flowing from the modern trend of criminalization of political disagreement.

# 8

# Covert Action and the Invasions of Panama

The Panama story, convoluted, still half-hidden and shrouded in the demimonde of covert action, is a cautionary tale about executive-congressional and judicial interaction in making war and foreign policy.

Foreign policy by covert action has always had a seductive attraction to American governments. As Justice Brandeis has noted, the dispersing of war powers among the branches was done to prevent tyranny, not promote efficiency. Strong executives with bold objectives have always been exasperated by the gross inefficiency of having to share power with unenlightened parochialists of Congress. Since Ben Franklin covertly arranged the fitting out of the *Bonhomme Richard* in France to evade the strictures of the Continental Congress, the executive branch has frequently resorted to this tempting expedient. With some notable exceptions, the results of covert action have not been impressive.

In World War II covert action became an institutionalized part of the intelligence-gathering function. In Britain the Special Operations Executive (SOE) and in the United States the Office of Strategic Services (OSS) combined sabotage, commando operations, and assassination with intelligence gathering. They have been bureaucratically intertwined ever since. There were highly publicized successes in the war, for example, destruction of the heavy water plants in Norway by OSS commandos and organizing the French underground by colorful commandos like the famous Douglas Bazata. These events boosted Allied morale, but it is difficult to make the case that they actually hastened the war's end.

After the war, the OSS and its covert activities became institutionalized in the Central Intelligence Agency (CIA). It had some famous victories in undoing the leftist Mossadegh in Iran and installing the shah and ousting the leftist government in Guatemala. There were many lesser accomplishments as yet unchronicled. There were, of course, also such immense failures as the Bay of Pigs and the Indochina war.

With its legacy of "Terry and the Pirates" romanticism and the tempting escape from congressional restrictions, the seduction of covert operations has often been used as an expedient substitute for a disciplined, coherent foreign policy. One cannot escape the conclusion, upon reviewing 215 years of American covert operations, that we haven't conducted them very well and that we might have been better off not to have tried.

The American system creates so many constraints and obstacles to real secrecy—necessary safeguards to our free institutions—that security has never been reliable, with compromise and failure as common as success.

But perhaps more fundamentally important, covert operations require the professional practice of lying, falsehood, deception, and betrayal. Persons skilled and comfortable at such arts in peacetime are often courageous and colorful, but they usually are also chancers, eccentrics, and bunco artists undevoted to ethics or morality. It is a demimonde peopled also with some intensely unpleasant characters who are neither gentlemen nor democrats. Wholesome bureaucrats and oversight committees staffed with bright young strivers do not succeed in attempts to control this nether world. Nathan Hale was the first of many idealistic Ivy Leaguers to dabble unsuccessfully at espionage.

Thus, U.S. covert operations, from the very beginning, have often been blighted by amateurism, fiasco, and chicanery interrupted by some notable, if rare, successes. Certainly necessary and valuable in wartime, when peace returns, such actions are fundamentally at odds with our government principles and institutions, and quite simply, they usually fail, often fabulously. Manuel Noriega's Panama was to be a cameo demonstration of that point.

On a pleasant January evening in 1986, a man arrived at a posh address in Coral Gables, Florida. He was there to celebrate several years of huge business success that had made him and his partners very wealthy men. Amid the lobsters and champagne, however, the man was surprised by his partners. After one final deal, they were turning over the business to him, free. But he had a surprise for them. He was not their buddy Danny Martelli but instead a federal narcotics agent, Daniel E. Moritz, a fact they were to discover when several weeks later their last planeload of cocaine was seized and the arrests began.[1]

Two years and a long legal trail later, these surprises gave birth to a third: an indictment of Gen. Manuel Antonio Noriega, chief of the Panamanian Defense Forces (PDF), the real ruler of Panama and an American ally who, as it turned out, had often worked for the CIA. That Noriega was involved in the drug trade was in itself not a new story. But the indictment at the hands of a Florida grand jury at the request of a Republican U.S. Attorney was surprising indeed. And this in turn set off another chain of events leading to the American invasion of Panama on the night of December 20, 1989.

When the blow came, General Noriega was about to enjoy the favors of a mistress in a Panamanian military recreation center. By all accounts, Noriega simply disregarded ample warning of the impending American assault. He had bluffed the Americans for so long and they had bluffed him for so long that an actual invasion seemed beyond his imagination. When the shooting started, Noriega pulled on his pants, fled into the night, and spent the next four days driving aimlessly about Panama City incognito in a small Korean car instead of the big armored Mercedes he used as a decoy. It worked. The Americans could not find him. Finally, he slipped into the papal nuncio's house with a group of cronies.

Excruciating negotiations followed. The marines applied bizarre psychological warfare—hard-rock music played at maximum volume in the belief that Noriega, who detested rock, would lose his nerve. After pleas from the nuncio that Noriega was sleeping through it all while he, the nuncio, was in danger of losing his mind, the marines desisted. Eventually, on January 3, 1990, Noriega surrendered to the mercies of the American justice system. As of this writing, he remains incarcerated in a comfortable, if lonely, three-room suite in a Florida jail, traveling regularly to Miami to the federal courthouse for his trial.

When the invasion was all over, 23 Americans and more than 500 Panamanians had lost their lives; 312 Americans had been wounded. Over a billion and a half dollars had been lost to Panama through the yearlong economic sanctions that preceded the American intervention. Two coups had failed, with fatal reprisals for the would-be coup makers. Of all that could be said of this saga, one conclusion would merit universal agreement: It was *not* a famous victory.

The indictment, search, and seizure of Noriega exposed an America in the throes of a classic and self-inflicted dilemma: the struggle for constitutional balance in the conduct of foreign affairs. Idealism and realism, the Congress and the executive, all pulled against each other, stretching the national interest in getting rid of Noriega to the near breaking point. This Gothic tale of semiparalytic overt and covert action had a surprise ending: The third branch of government, the domestic legal system, forced the hand of both the executive and Congress. Massive use of American military power eventually resolved a problem largely the making of covert intelligence activity. In theory it is supposed to work exactly the other way around.

## Panama and the American Ethos

That the United States should enter the final decade of the twentieth century intervening in Panama was an event rich in historical associations. For it was there, at the beginning of the century, that the United States had taken a large step away from its traditional isolation.

Then president Theodore Roosevelt had understood that America's "coming of age"—its growing industrial power and military strength—enabled the United States to shape events overseas rather more actively than we had in the past. He dispensed with the pretense that the doings of other powers didn't matter or that the oceans protected us from them. This approach, of course, enabled the vigorous "Teddy" to depart as well from what Professor Woodrow Wilson had described as "Congressional Government" in the conduct of virtually all of the nation's business.

204

Roosevelt has often been depicted as the prototypical American imperialist, with his "speak softly, carry a big stick" doctrine. In fact, he did speak loudly and often about the virtue and glory of conflict. After experiencing the Rooseveltian ebullience on the subject, Mark Twain declared that the president was ". . . clearly insane . . . and insanest upon war and its supreme glories."[2] Roosevelt also carried a big stick in the form of a hyperactive "Great White Fleet." But his Spanish-American wartime exploits and big talk notwithstanding, Roosevelt's own presidential terms were peaceful from the first day until the last. No American lives were lost in wars, for there were none. He became the first and only American president to receive a Nobel Prize for his peacemaking at the end of the Russo-Japanese War of 1905.

The Panama Canal was Theodore Roosevelt's glory and a great legacy. It was acquired without war, and yet it offered huge military and economic advantages to the United States. As most Americans know (or used to know), the Canal was begun by Ferdinand de Lesseps, the French visionary whose earlier project, the Suez Canal, had eventually come under British control. The Isthmus of Panama was then part of Colombia, and de Lesseps had been allowed to sink vast sums of borrowed money in digging it up because it was considered the wrong spot. Two U.S. commissions had concluded that Nicaragua was far preferable, being both technically easier and not subject to the yellow fever plague that turned Panama regularly into a death trap for visitor and resident alike. The American interest in a canal connecting the Pacific and the Caribbean had taken a more urgent turn in 1898, when our most powerful warship, the USS *Oregon*, was caught in Puget Sound, nearly missing the war with Spain over Cuba because it had to steam around South America.

In 1888 a huge financial scandal, which rocked France to its foundations, sank de Lesseps's Compagnie Universale. With de Lesseps in jail, his enterprise was succeeded by a Compagnie Nouvelle, controlled by a former partner, Philippe Bunau-Varilla. That worthy decided that only American money could rescue the great canal project. Bunau-Varilla found that then as now a modest amount of money buys a good deal of influence in the United States Congress. In fact, his success in lobbying Congress has probably never been surpassed. Aided by the timely eruption of the volcanic Mount Monotombo in Nicaragua, Congress shifted in favor of a canal on the Isthmus—if it could be secured "within a reasonable time." Bunau-Varilla was ready to sell, but Colombia was not. The January 1903 treaty negotiated by Secretary of State Hay with the Colombian government was rejected by the Colombian senate because it granted U.S. control of the land for $10 million, while the United States would pay $40 million to Bunau-Varilla's French company for its rights.

The somewhat sordid details of why the United States and Colombia could not come to an agreement need not detain us here. Suffice to say that on September 15, 1903, Roosevelt noted to Hay that there was an alternative. "In some way and shape to interfere when it becomes necessary so as to secure the Panama route without further dealing with the foolish and homicidal corruptionists in Bogota."[3]

The Panamanians were now themselves affronted by the Bogota "corruptionists." Their union with Colombia in the 1820s had been an emergency resort after declaring independence from Spain. Three times they had revolted thereafter, only to be crushed. Now an opportunity to be politically independent and economically advantaged was at hand. A revolution was duly concocted, and on November 4 independence was declared. There was a semiserious attempt by the Colombians to put it down, brought to a sudden close by the appearance of ten American warships and stout Panamanian resistance. Meanwhile, in New York and Washington, Bunau-Varilla, as the new nation of Panama's first minister plenipotentiary, helped the State Department redraft Secretary Hay's document in a way no U.S. senator could reject. Rather than risk the loss of their new independence, the Panamanians decided to accept it, and the Isthmian Canal Convention was signed on November 18, 1903. It gave the United States absolute control over the future Panama Canal.

In Washington, there was a sense of constitutional harmony. "Uncle" Joe Cannon, Speaker of the House, had once described Roosevelt this way: "Roosevelt is all right but he's got no more use for the Constitution than a tom cat has for a marriage license."[4] Yet on this occasion, Theodore Roosevelt had considered the legalities very carefully. So had John Hay, the secretary of state, who had once publicly detested the entire ratification power of the Senate, saying that like a bull entering the ring, no treaty could emerge alive from the process. Having been in his youth a personal secretary to Abraham Lincoln, Hay made it his business to sign the treaty using an inkwell once owned by the great man himself, perhaps thereby adding a veneer of morality to the document that he suspected it lacked. A sticky editorial in the *New York Times* greatly offended Mr. Roosevelt, and he rebutted its points with vigor, but in so doing, he flaunted his disregard of Colombian claims. The secretary of war, the eminent Elihu Root, was amused by the exchange. "You have shown," he said to the president, "that you were accused of seduction and you have conclusively proved that you were guilty of rape."[5]

When all was said and done, Bunau-Varilla resigned and got his $40 million; the new Republic of Panama got its independence and its lifelong American patron. The United States got its canal, Colombia was bereft of its most strategic territory, and a huge bust of Count Ferdinand de Lesseps was raised in Panama City's Plaza de Francia.

## The Time of Trouble

U.S.-Panamanian relations thereafter had both the advantages and disadvantages of their birth. Compared to most Central or South American states, Panama had higher living standards, a larger middle class, and until the late sixties, a more or less civilian-run democracy. But the country also suffered the traditional extremes of wealth and poverty—a glistening Panama City versus a hopelessly decayed Colón. Its citizens bristled under a relationship that seemed to consign Panama's principal assets— bananas and Canal tolls—in near perpetuity (United Fruit and the ninety-nine year Canal lease) to the "Colossus of the North"— the yanquis. Moreover, the Zonians, as the American "colony" running the Canal were known, looked upon the Panamanians as bumptious incompetents. Skillfully playing upon these feelings, various demagogues in Panama, some friendly to Fidel Castro, agitated for change. Arrogance and accident touched off a disastrous riot in 1964, and late that year both the United States and Panama resolved to rewrite the treaty to symbolize a new relationship.

As formulated by a generation of State Department diplomats

and various "experts" in Latin psychology, this new relationship meant the dissolution of the American colony and turning over the Canal to Panamanian control. In return, U.S. security was to be safeguarded by formal treaty. Such an arrangement had to assure that the Panamanians were capable of running the Canal (and their own affairs!) and that the U.S. Southern Command, headquartered in Panama, would continue to function undisturbed—a considerable military presence, even without civilians. Thirteen years were to pass before these ideas became reality and a new treaty was declared.

During the early seventies, when I worked for Henry Kissinger, we noted a diminishing of the Canal's importance because neither supertankers nor supercarriers could fit through. And the enormous growth of the Soviet Pacific fleet meant that we could no longer "swing" the fleet from the Pacific to the Atlantic in time of war. Nevertheless, it remained a valuable military asset. A vast quantity of supply and commerce would have to pass through the Canal, and indeed the entire Caribbean Gulf, in the event of war. The Soviets and their Cuban allies had therefore not ceased their efforts to build up a strategic position in the region, even within the limits set by the settlement of the Cuban Missile Crisis. Panama itself was obviously a considerable prize in such a contest.

In the wake of the 1964 riots, as the United States began the slow process that would eventually yield the Canal treaties, Panama was in the throes of change. Just before the beginning of the Nixon administration, the Panamanian National Guard had overthrown the civilian government. This in itself was odd, because Panama, unlike many other Latin countries, had never had a real army—or needed one—making do instead with a well-trained and smartly uniformed police force and occasional American intervention. In the fifties, personal ambition, anti-American sentiments, and (paradoxically) the availability of U.S. military aid and a special police training academy in Washington run by the Agency for International Development, had propelled the guard upward in its ascent to control. By 1968, 5,000 men, 65 officers, and a $3 million a year U.S. grant made it very formidable for a small mercantile, ethnically mixed population of only 1.5 million people in the shadow of American military power.

Then, in October of that year, the guard overthrew the elected President, Anulfo Arias, a demagogue who had made clear in the past his resentment of the guard's monopoly on police power. Arias had so frightened a sufficient number of respectable people that after the coup, the military was able to attract front men. The United States was frightened, too; it recognized the junta just a week after President Nixon's election. Then a guerrilla war broke out, and Panama was unsettled continuously with plots, counterplots, and abuses. Eventually, the coup makers themselves fell out, and from the scramble emerged Omar Torrijos. One of his principal deputies was Manuel Noriega, who had put down the insurrection in the Province of Chiriqui with sadistic efficiency.

The record of the Torrijos regime, even though aided by the United States, was such as to give great pause to the proponents of a new treaty that would turn the Canal over to Panama. This was the catch-22 that caught the United States throughout the Vietnam period and beyond. We wanted good, clean, honest, democratic government, responsible enough to be a partner in safeguarding our mutual interests. But out of respect for national sovereignty we could never impose such a government, nor was it prudent to take the side of the bad government's enemies—especially if those enemies were allied to Castro or in Soviet pay. The only practical way out was to follow FDR's famous quip about the elder Somoza: "He's an SOB but at least he's our SOB."

Torrijos eventually became our SOB, though a mild one, lacking Somoza's greed or Noriega's cruelty. He was enough of one, however, to arouse opposition in the United States, and his choice of Noriega as subordinate was disturbing. After years of CIA stipends, President Carter's CIA director, Stansfield Turner, cut off Noriega's. President Carter himself, however, pushed through with all of his authority, over strong opposition, a new treaty that would eventually turn over the Canal to Torrijos and Noriega.

Sen. Jesse Helms, the scourge of the liberals, charged hypocrisy: a regime that no self-respecting liberal could tolerate but a regime that no one who favored the liberal terms of the Canal treaty could denounce. After heated debate and desperate measures by the new president, the treaty passed the Senate by one vote.[6] It provided for a turnover of the Canal and its operations to Panama in stages subject to security provisions and Senate confirmation of the first Panamanian director of the Canal administration.

## The Reagan Administration's Policy

We must now pass from the incoherent U.S.-Panama relationship bequeathed by the Carter era to the difficult but eventually equal incoherencies of the Reagan era. The Canal and Panama were still a vital interest, as they had been when I served in government a decade earlier. But the American position in Central America, as in much of the rest of the world, was in deepening trouble. A year after the Canal treaties had been reached, the Sandinistas took over in Nicaragua. The Communist subversion of El Salvador was well under way. Cuban troops were fighting in Africa, the Soviets had invaded Afghanistan, and our diplomats were hostages in Tehran. There was, as President Carter put it, a sense of national "malaise," a loss of national confidence.

This gloomy atmosphere had contributed to the victory of Ronald Reagan in 1980. President Reagan's self-confidence, sunny disposition, and simplistic assumption of America's infallibility dispelled Americans' unease about the country's rectitude and its future. But, as the Germans like to say, the "devil is in the details."

American policy toward Central and South America had often run in cycles, active and interested, then passive and neglectful, then active all over again. During the campaign, Ronald Reagan promised to be active, offering a foreign policy that began with our neighbors. He was unremittingly hostile to Cuba and solicitous of Mexico and the Caribbean. He had opposed the Panama Canal treaties with a blunt expression of traditional American attitudes: "We built it, we paid for it, and we intend to keep it."[7] In office, however, he was not disposed to tamper with the treaty. One trouble at a time. First came the Sandinistas.

Reagan's first secretary of state, Alexander M. Haig, Jr., believed that the United States should take its anti-Nicaragua campaign "to the source"—pressuring Cuba and the USSR. In this case, America's ability to bring superior force to bear on the problem would combine with incipient signs of Soviet economic failure to persuade Moscow that its true strategic interests required it to back off in Central America. Haig's ideas, however, which involved naval demonstrations and ultimately might have led to a naval blockade to interdict Cuban and Nicaraguan shipments to Salvador, never became policy. The president decided that the American people were not ready for a crisis in Central America.[8]

That appeared to leave only a combination of loud rhetoric and a continuation of the late Carter policy of diplomatic isolation and economic restrictions, a policy of obvious failure. Was there a policy that avoided the risks of war yet was more effective than economic sanctions? The Reagan answer was yes, and it was called "covert action"—two of the most infamous words in Washington's infamous lexicon. Theoretically, the United States could employ means against Nicaragua that were "readily deniable." Thus, U.S. interest in harming the Sandinistas would be served, the American people would be spared a direct crisis, and all would be well.

## Congress, the Executive, War Powers, and Covert Action

The president chose this appealing option, and his instrument was the CIA, then headed by the late William Casey. I knew Bill Casey in several capacities. Of him I could say, as others have said, that behind a shambling gait and a self-protective mumble there resided an iron will and a keen mind. Bill approached the CIA, hobbled and disgraced by the scandals of the Vietnam era, with the style of the old Office of Strategic Services (OSS), its forerunner. He was prepared to run off the Soviets from Central America through covert means, and the less Congress knew, the better. Constitutional sharing of power was for future scholars to argue. Before long, he took a small cross-border raiding force, largely consisting of former members of Somoza's National Guard, and began forming them into an army of rebellion against the Sandinistas. This did not, however, go unobserved on Capitol Hill.

Haig had said that covert action in Washington was a contradiction in terms. In the Reagan era, that contradiction was elevated to a doctrine. Before it was over, the U.S. Congress was

211

approving "secret" aid publicly known to be given to the Mujahedin in Afghanistan; Jonas Savimbi in Angola; and, of course, the Contras in Nicaragua. But the Reagan Doctrine never enjoyed much support in Central America. The House and Senate Intelligence committees, the official congressional overseers of the CIA, were informed of these operations, and they weren't happy. Soon a semipublic row developed between the committees and Bill Casey, who viewed their prerogatives with barely disguised contempt. A seesaw voting pattern developed in Congress, one year barely authorizing Contra assistance, another year prohibiting it. The tug-of-war with Casey and Reagan over the direction of our policy was often clothed by congressmen in the high rhetoric of constitutional "balance" between the executive and the legislature, while the Reaganauts spoke of congressional "usurpation" of presidential power.

As we have seen in earlier chapters, there is no perfect or preordained balance between president and Congress on national security, and recourse to the third branch—the courts—has resolved only small parts of the issue. There are only the barest of limits to the divided and overlapping powers specified by the Constitution, and there are the diverse practices of successive generations. The balance has usually been set less by legalities than by politics, more by urgent problems than ingenious theory. In short, the "invitation to strife" issued by the Founders has been answered and attended by both president and Congress. Often the minuet has ended with blood on the floor.

As for war, experience of eighteenth-century government and the Revolution had taught the Founding Fathers that Congress could not run a war effectively; that fell to the executive. But they also resisted an executive whose powers, like those of a monarch, could bring the country to war without congressional consent.

Given the role of force in foreign policy, Congress would usually be inclined to restrain executive warmongering. Despite an international reputation for bellicosity, the people of the United States have always opposed getting entangled abroad and almost never favored initiating hostilities. Their representatives in Congress have nearly always reflected this aversion. Once involved in hostilities, however, popular opinion historically swings overwhelmingly behind the prosecution of force, with Congress falling in line. In the decade prior to World War II, for example, the American people and Congress opposed and blocked FDR's attempt to build up war-making capability to deal with the growing threat of Japan and Nazi Germany. Efforts to fortify the Philippines, train an army (the entire U.S. Army was still smaller on Pearl Harbor Day than the Marine Corps is today), and expand the army and air corps were voted down year after year because the people wanted no war. Even as late as 1940, the renewal of draft authority passed by only one vote, and even that was only a year's extension. Once the war began, however, the pendulum slammed hard over to the president in support of the war effort.

During World War II the executive reigned supreme; Congress, to paraphrase Gilbert and Sullivan, "throughout the war did nothing and did it very well." After World War II, the onset of the Cold War left the executive with much of the hot war prerogatives. Both the Korean and Vietnam conflicts were waged without formal declarations of war. But Vietnam enjoyed congressional support only so long as it appeared to succeed, that is, had clear objectives, acceptable costs, and a probable date of achievement. Once it did not succeed, even had there been a declaration of war instead of the Tonkin Gulf Resolution, Congress would not have continued to support it.

The struggles of the Vietnam era are chronicled elsewhere in this book. Suffice to say that by 1981 the Vietnam debacle had led to vastly increased congressional activity in both the war-making and foreign policy areas. What some were calling the Imperial Congress had acquired new and very large measures of influence over areas formerly near exclusive executive domain.[9] But the problem was not congressional imperialism. My experience with congressional involvement in defense and foreign policy left no doubt that when it went badly wrong it was not because it was an Imperial Congress but because it was a chaotic Congress. No elected official has the time and very few have the knowledge to deal with the level of detail now involved in national security micromanagement. Effectively, congressional micromanagement transfers power from the elected executive and the elected legislature to the unelected and inexperienced staff elite who instruct senators and congressmen alike in the narrow whys and wherefores of competing interests that most of them are far too busy to learn. The result can only be chaos occasionally interrupted by gridlock. In the pre-Watergate era of powerful committee chairmen like Richard Russell and Carl Vinson, orderly policy could emerge from the process because they could make compromises with the executive that they could enforce. After Watergate, with the explosion of committees and subcommittees, there are no longer chairmen powerful enough to enforce agreements with the executive. Instead, there are now more than eighty chairmen whose staffs are micromanaging all parts of the national security policy of the executive. But micromanagement is not the same as forceful congressional involvement. The latter is usually as unwelcome to presidents as the former, but it is an essential function of democratic government.

Thus, by the late 1970s, in the midst of a still-raging Cold War in which the United States appeared to be losing ground in Afghanistan, Central America, the Middle East, and Africa, the balance had shifted to the branch of government least capable of running national security. The Reagan administration, from the president on down, wanted to change that balance. Certainly the rhetoric changed. Practically, however, much remained the same. The Reagan Doctrine, carried out mostly by covert action that was above all things not covert, seemed to offer a neat solution. The executive could retain its control over management, while Congress would be unable to deny funds publicly or disclose embarrassing (or illegal) secrets without compromising the national interest.

However, foreign policy by covert action had, and has, very basic flaws. First and foremost, there is the test of "deniability," which requires secrecy. Great success or great failure will expose it. At a certain scale of support, it simply cannot be "covert."

## The Uses and Abuses of Manuel Noriega

Among America's less than pleasant covert associations, none combined a less attractive combination than Manuel Antonio Noriega of Panama. Unattractive, and given to menacing expressions, Noriega had come from a poor background. His mixed blood and out-of-wedlock birth marked him further as a social inferior

214

in a society that prized both money and "whiteness." But Noriega was not stupid, and he gradually became, at least in his own mind, an "expert" on psychological warfare, especially as understood by the Americans.

The PDF, then in its early expansionary phase, offered him both a career and the social prestige he sought. By the time he came to the notice of General Torrijos in the troubled times following the 1969 coup, his character was well set. He combined an unusual intelligence with a bizarre mixture of beliefs. Noriega's Brazilian "spiritual confidant," Tilha, described him as "a Christian, a Rosicrucian, a Freemason, a Buddhist, a Taoist."[10] All who knew him agreed that whatever his beliefs, his true creed was power; his true enthusiasm, violence. This trait encouraged fear of Noriega, a fear that had only too much evidence to sustain it.

Though filled with those anti-American sentiments that pervaded much of Panamanian society, Noriega allegedly was from his early years on the payroll of the United States, a ready source of both cash and power. He allegedly was paid by the U.S. Army for providing intelligence, and later the CIA put him on retainer to inform them on drug, political, and military intelligence. According to his own legal counsel, he was provided with a "multimillion dollar slush fund" by the CIA. That he also played a familiar game of selling and cross-selling to several clients and that he had a hand in gunrunning, drug selling, and several other forms of "adult entertainment" did not make him unusual. It was Noriega's enthusiastic cruelties plus his well-developed intelligence resources that made him unique: a man deemed worthy of cultivation by the highest levels of the CIA but also, a real management problem.

As Noriega's former political adviser, Joel McCleary, once put it, "Everyone was sleeping with Noriega. Noriega was a lovely hooker. But then he grew old and got a wrinkled ass."[11] Quite simply, as he gained power in his own right, he catered less and less to the CIA, and they in turn valued him less and less.

The amounts paid by the United States to Noriega over the years are not known precisely but are alleged to be in six or seven figures. Some journals have reported that Noriega earned his real U.S. money by skimming technical assistance grants to the

Panamanian military. Whatever is true, he did not need direct
U.S. payments or the strings attached in the circles he fre-
quented. What he did need to survive and prosper was critical
information—personal, political, military. And Noriega's U.S.
training and his closeness to Trujillo gave him the discipline and
access to accumulate and use such information.

We have a great picture of the early, aspiring Noriega in the
late seventies, then a lieutenent colonel of intelligence and, by
virtue of previous services and loyalty, the effective second in
command to Torrijos. Shortly after ratification of the Canal treaties, one of Noriega's close friends and business partners was
indicted in a Miami gunrunning case. These guns were run from
Miami through Panama, under Noriega's nose, to the Sandinistas, among others. At the same time, Noriega characteristically
was reported to be providing other branches of the U.S. government with information about how the Sandinistas got their weapons! According to at least one version, Noriega himself was
supposed to be indicted and arrested on a visit to the United
States, but other elements of the government tipped him off while
arranging to quash the indictment.[12]

In any event, following this close call, Noriega and Torrijos
were anxious to be of service to the Carter administration. An
opportunity presented itself in the sticky business of the exiled
shah of Iran. That formerly valuable American ally, terminally
ill with cancer, had at first been refused medical asylum in the
United States because the Carter administration feared its impact on U.S. relations with Khomeini's Iran. Torrijos offered a
place of refuge—at a price—and the shah did indeed stay for 100
days in Panama before feeling unsafe and extorted. Recalling
these days, Robert Armao, the shah's adviser and friend, depicted
Torrijos as a broken-down drunkard. As for Noriega, Armao described him this way: "It was like out of a gangster movie. He
pulled up in a six-passenger Mercury, a gun rack hooked over the
front seat with an assortment of guns. . . . Noriega was smiling
like a hyena, and he was wearing a double-knit leisure suit."[13]

The physical decline of Torrijos in the last two years of his life
offered Noriega increasing opportunities. He became, by general
acknowledgment, the man who knew best what both Right and
Left, pro-American, pro-Cuban, drug lords, smugglers, and gov-

ernments were doing in Central America. Torrijos himself was said to be unhappy about Noriega's lack of restraint. Essentially, to know more, Noriega had to become more involved in illegal or impolitic activities, hoping that his value as an intelligence source would keep the major players in his debt. On July 31, 1981, however, Torrijos died in a plane crash in eastern Panama after thirteen years of one-man rule. Panama had been deprived of its *"macho caudillo."* A struggle for succession followed in which, as is customary, the most ruthless emerged as the victor: the introverted, back-room tactician and spymaster, Manuel Antonio Noriega.

## The Downfall of American Policy

Noriega, unlike Torrijos, preferred at first to rule through a civilian proxy. Because he was now the boss in Panama, he was again cultivated by the CIA. He now expanded his efforts in doing what he did best, accumulating and selling information to many sources. His importance to the United States grew in direct proportion as the inevitable exposure of the so-called covert action against the Sandinistas drew increasing congressional opposition. That such a rogue was held so valuable by Casey's CIA demonstrated both gross misjudgment by CIA leadership and predictable behavior by the covert operations bureaucracy.

The year 1984 turned out to be crucial. Ronald Reagan's triumphant electoral victory over Walter Mondale overshadowed what was becoming an increasing debacle in his not-so-secret Central American policy.

In January 1984, it came to light that the CIA had been mining—or causing mines to be laid—in Nicaragua's harbors. This was a serious act of war going far beyond what the Senate and House Intelligence committees had understood to be the extent of U.S. covert action. After an uproar, CIA director Casey was forced to apologize on April 26 for his failure to inform the committees. But that was not the end of it. That October, Congress passed yet another of the Boland Amendments, banning the CIA or "any other agency or entity involved in intelligence activities" from spending money to support the Contras in their war against Nicaragua. There were, in all, five Boland Amendments enacted between 1982 and 1986. Each one was a negotiated compromise between congressional liberals opposed to any interference with the Sandinistas and a veto-wielding president determined to drive them from power in Nicaragua. While Reagan opposed all restrictions, he signed the Boland Amendments because, in the words of the Library of Congress report on the legislative history, "it was clearly understood at the time of enactment that the compromise would not cut off all direct or indirect assistance to the Contras." Boland himself viewed the 1984 amendment as far more restrictive: "It clearly prohibits any expenditures, including those from accounts for salaries and all support costs." If his interpretation is correct, then the president and his National Security Council (NSC) staff would be under the prohibition. The plain language of the act would seem to exclude them from the prohibition. Unfortunately, because Special Prosecutor Walsh concentrated his efforts on "getting" his Iran-Contra targets rather than testing these constitutional questions, it is unlikely that the issue will be decided by the Supreme Court in any of the Iran-Contra cases.

Even before the third Boland Amendment, it was clear that the Contra struggle had become too big to sustain covertly but not yet big enough to defeat the Sandinistas. Under the assumption that the president and his staff were not an "agency" under the Boland definition, a sometimes frantic effort was launched to sustain the Contras by financial appeals to third parties—other governments and individuals, some in the Middle East, others in Asia—all of whom wanted to accumulate credit in Washington. Then there was the issue of the arms supplies themselves and how to get them to the Contras.

As we now know, part of the great Iran-Contra scandal had its roots in the NSC-CIA attempt to work around congressional restrictions. The CIA took care to obey the Boland stricture. Bud McFarlane, a colleague and friend from the Kissinger NSC days, took the first steps toward his rendezvous with disaster by assuring Congress that the NSC staff would abide by the Boland restrictions, even as Lt. Col. Oliver North was organizing a "private" ring of support for the Contras.

The marine commandant, Bob Barrow, and I had handpicked Ollie North for assignment to the NSC in 1981. He had an impressive Vietnam combat record and was a standout in his class at the Naval War College. He had proved his great operational value in the intercept of the *Achille Lauro* hijackers in 1985, becoming a personal hero to the president. He had originated the idea of the intercept and pulled together a small team to make it happen. It would have taken months to organize such an operation through the joint staff. North's reputation as an action officer would lead him even deeper into the scandal about to break.

In fact, North's "enterprise" to aid the Contras was a going concern *before* the third Boland Amendment was passed. "Project Democracy," as it was called, also involved using Panama and Israel as alternatives to direct U.S. support for the Contras, an option that Casey suggested in a memo to McFarlane on March 27, 1984. Panama was useful because of its location and Noriega's ties to the CIA, as was Israel because of its network of assistance to various South American regimes, especially in the realm of personal security. Noriega's own personal security adviser, for example, was a former Israeli intelligence officer.[14]

Thanks to the new access to East German files, we now know that both Stasi (East German Intelligence) and the KGB were very active in Washington, viewing Nicaragua in 1984 as a crucial battleground of the Cold War. While much remains locked away, I was given an inadvertent taste of some of its high intrigue that summer of 1984. One evening I gave an official dinner aboard the secretary of the navy's "barge" on the Potomac. In addition to Ollie, one of my guests was my good friend and Cambridge classmate David Walker, a decorated former SAS commando and prominent figure in national security circles of Her Majesty's Government. Six months later, I was astonished to see the tape of a one-hour program on British television called "World in Action," all about that evening cruise. It was a conspiratorial fantasy implying an elitist network of militarists, spawned at Cambridge. The show was replete with video of my barge on that evening and shots of David and me in our student days, along with interviews with Sandinista officials denouncing us. The photography of the social gathering on the boat and decades-old Cambridge gatherings could only have come from an intelligence service supporting the Sandinistas.

While Casey, North, and McFarlane were trying to keep the Contras afloat against a swamping tide of congressional opposition (and possibly in violation of the law, although that remains to be adjudicated), Noriega himself had begun to encounter trouble. In May 1984, the newly self-promoted general "managed" the election of a handpicked president, Nicolas Ardito Barletta—an act of fraud his popular predecessor Torrijos had never needed. Noriega's personal excesses had also begun to arouse serious opposition within Panama. But to Reagan policymakers he continued to offer a convenient and important set of assets to the Contra war.

## The State Department Intervenes

The year 1985 therefore found both the U.S. government and Manuel Noriega driven closer together as the United States tried to salvage its Central American policy while Noriega was only too happy to receive the legitimization of U.S. support as he extended his control of Panama. But the U.S. government is a wondrous thing. Even as officials were asking other governments to help funnel funds to the Contras, some of the same men— perhaps oblivious to Noriega's role—were increasingly disturbed by the Panamanian's behavior.

One of them was the new assistant secretary of state for inter-American affairs, Elliott Abrams. Abrams had been nurtured by the neoconservatives. These well-spoken, sometimes brilliant expositors of American interests numbered, among others, Midge Decter, Norman Podhoretz of *Commentary*, and Jeane Kirkpatrick, ambassador to the United Nations. Many had been Democrats, sound foreign policy thinkers who revolted against the McGovernite takeover of the party. They saw the Central American policy as a test case in turning back Soviet imperialism— with the "freedom fighters" for once on our side. And by 1985, U.S. aid had indeed helped transform the Contras from a Somoza National Guard remnant into an increasingly peasant based liberation movement.

Abrams, a protégé of the late senator Scoop Jackson, helped link the advocates of the Reagan Doctrine to the many former or current Democrats who followed the neoconservatives on foreign policy. As a former assistant secretary for human rights and also, in 1981–83, assistant secretary for international organizations, Abrams believed that U.S. association with the drug-selling, gun-running Noriega would be fatal morally to the Contra cause and indeed to what the United States was trying to achieve throughout Central America.

Abrams's efforts on behalf of the Contras were later to involve him in the complex attempts to raise money secretly from other governments; he became *persona non grata* to important leaders in the Congress who alleged that he lied to them. Lying to Congress by officials seeking to protect presidential policy, while never defensible, has often been defended. McGeorge Bundy, for instance, has praised Robert McNamara for lying to Congress in denying that Kennedy had agreed to withdraw American missiles from Turkey in exchange for Soviet withdrawal of missiles from Cuba (a "most justified deception," he called it).[15] And many Roosevelt officials misled Congress, denying that Roosevelt was breaking the law while he was in fact defying the Neutrality Acts in convoying and attacking German subs in the North Atlantic in 1940. More recently, it has been reported that Bush administration officials, working to enact a tax increase in 1990, withheld data from Congress revealing a far larger deficit than they were telling Congress at the time.[16] No special prosecutor was appointed in these cases.

From the CIA's first dealings with Noriega there were no doubts that he was a treacherous character, but by 1985 his odious behavior was impossible to overlook. In the fall, Noriega was implicated in the murder of a rival who had accused him publicly of drug smuggling: the charismatic Hugo Spadafora. Spadafora's charges, his personal charm, and his rumored connection to the U.S. Drug Enforcement Agency (DEA) were threatening enough. He was brutally assassinated in September 1985 after being tortured in what some alleged was trademark Noriega fashion. And the commission established by President Barletta to investigate the slaying became the occasion for Noriega to force Barletta's resignation. He was replaced by another toady, Eric Arturo Delvalle.

In March 1986, Panama's old nemesis, Senator Helms, held hearings focused on criminal activities in Panama. Helms's purpose was to amend the appropriations bill in order to disrupt the operation of the Canal treaties. He was joined eventually by a liberal democrat, Sen. Bob Kerrey, in demanding an investigation of the role of the PDF—which Noriega headed—in Spadafora's death.

The murder of Spadafora and the extension of PDF control—and corruption—throughout Panamanian society created organized opposition. The National Civic Crusade for Justice and Democracy, consisting of over two hundred well-respected professional and business groups, stripped the remaining civilian facade from Noriega's rule. With the fall of North and Poindexter following the exposure of the Iran-Contra scandal in December 1986, Noriega's American "protection," based on his secret dealings, disappeared as well.

Internal and external opposition now mounted inexorably on Noriega. In June 1987, his own chief of staff, Roberto Diaz Herrera, publicly charged the boss with Spadafora's death and with drug dealings. At the end of that month, the Senate passed Helms's resolution. Public demonstrations against the general's rule began across Panama.

But Noriega had not become the master of Panama through loss of nerve. He had Herrera arrested and put hired thugs in the streets ("the dignity battalions") to intimidate his opponents and stir up anti-Americanism. Having been warned by his few remaining supporters in American intelligence agencies that they could no longer defend his actions, Noriega also sought high-powered public relations help to restate his case and restore his influence. In July, however, the U.S. government suspended all military and economic assistance and, when the year was out, also denied Panama its 1988 quota of imported sugar.

## The Indictment

Now that both State and Congress had acted, the third branch of government, the judiciary, entered the fray. The wheels of judicial inquiry that had spun since that January day in 1986 when two of Noriega's key American drug partners had been arrested in a "sting operation" was now complete. Both the Miami and Tampa district attorneys were well aware of the potential diplomatic

COVERT ACTION AND THE INVASIONS OF PANAMA

consequences of going ahead and also the political consequences of appearing to delay an indictment. For once Noriega's fearsome reputation had worked to frighten some of the key witnesses into cooperating with U.S. authorities and seeking American protection rather than risk another "interrogation" at his hands if they kept their mouths shut and were released. They simply knew too much to be confident that Noriega would let them live.

So it was that on February 4, 1988, both indictments were announced. The local authorities did take the trouble to "inform" the State Department a couple of days beforehand, making it clear their intention to proceed regardless of State's objections. Ronald Reagan, president of the United States, was not informed beforehand.[17]

A burgeoning foreign policy problem—Noriega's rule in Panama—now became an American legal issue as well. The administration and Congress had both fallen out with Noriega before the indictments. But that problem could have festered for some time until the usual diplomatic oil had either eased the friction or else led to additional sanctions. Noriega, with his supreme reliance on his intelligence contacts, clearly hoped that after Iran-Contra his capacity for blackmail and tough tactics would see him through the rough spots. American officials, in his view, had too long a history of association with him and too heavy a stake in Panama to intervene blatantly against him. The judicial indictments, however, made it impossible for the executive branch to "negotiate" the issue without looking like a "cave-in" to a drug dealer, thereby compromising both its "war on drugs" and the operation of justice.

The stage was therefore set for a showdown. But the Noriega story, already so complex, did not have a simple ending. U.S. policy passed through three phases: illusion, disillusion, and finally reluctant action. After the illusion that Noriega could be disposed of merely by an expression of American displeasure, there followed the disillusion: that even with heavy American economic and political sanctions, Noriega would not go. Finally, Noriega's personal disposition and personal debaucheries produced a coup within his own camp. But when it came, the U.S. government was paralyzed by the aftermath of its own absurd shenanigans in Iran-Contra and fearful of congressional prohibition, which ensured the coup's failure. That left only massive force as an option to get Noriega.

## Illusion

The indictments imposed a dual burden on the Panama problem. Washington could not be seen to compromise justice in dealings with Noriega. On the other hand, Noriega's incentives to leave power while still facing indictment meant that he could not expect to remain a free man. The classic Latin solution in which the caudillo retires wealthy to bullfights and displays of his sexual prowess in Spain or on the Riviera was almost certainly ruled out.

Many in the United States and Panama itself believed that Noriega was finished. He had no friends, only enemies multiplying in Washington. The Panamanian opposition brought out the street crowds. The U.S. Southern Command had troops at its disposal literally a block or two away.

Still, you could not beat Noriega unless there was some authority to take his place. In theory, the general was subordinate to the president. Panama's president, Eric Arturo Delvalle, was an unlikely hero. A longtime friend and beneficiary of Noriega's, Delvalle owed his office to the general. He was not popular with either the people or Noriega's opponents. His connections ran to the business community, however, and they clearly wanted Noriega out.

On February 25, 1988, Delvalle "fired" Noriega in a broadcast to the Panamanian people. It was a videotape, Delvalle having taken the precaution of hiding and then leaving the country once it became clear that Noriega would not comply. Early in the morning of the twenty-sixth, Noriega assembled thirty-eight of his sixty-seven legislators in the National Assembly to vote the dismissal of Delvalle for abuse of power and at 2:20 A.M. elected Manuel Solis Palma as Panama's new president.

Delvalle had indeed "abused" his power in that he lacked the capability to carry out his order. There was imminent expectation of American action, for no one believed that a figure like Delvalle could have attempted anything so brash, or rash, without American support. And sure enough, the State Department announced

224

that it continued to recognize only Eric Delvalle as the legitimate president of Panama.

When the rhetorical smoke cleared, however, Noriega was still in power. From February 25 until March 8, the United States did nothing at all. Then it proclaimed that "Noriega must go," and the president imposed partial sanctions, among other things putting Panama Canal revenue into escrow ($6.5 million a month).

Meanwhile, Delvalle had reached the United States. Working with a private Washington law firm, Delvalle tried legally to gain control of Panama's foreign assets. When, on March 2, acting Secretary of State John C. Whitehead (Shultz was traveling) certified Ambassador Sosa as the sole authority for Panamanian property in Federal Reserve Banks, Delvalle's "government" deprived Noriega of access to considerable money—some $40 million—which led to the closing of Panama's banks on March 3.

But was it enough? On March 10, both the U.S. House and Senate voted almost unanimously to impose economic sanctions and encourage restoration of civilian rule. Amid a sense of impending chaos, on March 16, the day after the Panamanian authorities failed to pay public salaries, the inevitable coup was attempted. Some of Noriega's best men were involved, though as some of the survivors complained later, not the U.S. Southern Command. Then, under the command of Gen. Frederick Woerner, the Southern Command stoutly opposed military confrontation with Noriega as being both unnecessary and dangerous to America's long-term position in Panama. Woerner's appraisal was strongly supported by the Joint Chiefs of Staff (JCS).[18]

Noriega had been wise to the coup and with the help of Capt. Moses Giroldi, misled the plotters about his whereabouts, then had them arrested and subjected to the usual special interrogations. Having thwarted the immediate danger to his position, Noriega sought money from the usual suspects, including the Palestine Liberation Organization (PLO), Cuba, and the Soviets, the better to frighten Washington.

Elliott Abrams strove desperately to renew the ebbing pressure on Noriega. He and the upper reaches of State were convinced that the United States could not be seen to fail in a confrontation with the Panamanian strongman. But Abrams was by then badly wounded by charges of lying about his role in Iran-Contra. The

Pentagon opposed any course that would require U.S. military intervention; General Woerner, Admiral Crowe, the JCS chairman, and Gen. Colin Powell, Poindexter's successor at the NSC, argued vehemently against it. They believed rightly that any intervention would mean the deaths of numerous U.S. servicemen and probably many innocent civilians. They also believed (with much less logic) that no operation could be mounted without it being so large as to look absurd as an effort to get one man. The embattled CIA chief, Casey, had died of a brain tumor in May 1987, taking his secrets with him. Exposed as inept in Panama and now rudderless, the CIA was now inert. Abrams was stalled.

Economic sanctions imposed upon a dictator who had already suppressed both a coup and a popular uprising would only impoverish the people. Attempts to deprive Noriega of his legal financial reserves meant little because Noriega's finances derived mostly from illegal sources. Thus, with the shattered illusion that strong disapproval by Washington alone would prove fatal to Noriega, the Reagan administration had to face the awful possibility of taking further action.

## Disillusion

By the spring of 1988, the situation was serious enough to attract Secretary of State George Shultz's personal attention. I had observed Shultz in the Nixon days when he had been Office of Management and Budget (OMB) director and secretary of the treasury. Henry Kissinger had written of his admiration for Shultz's integrity and calm under fire. A big man with the deliberate ways of the college professor he had once been, Shultz's bureaucratic tenacity was legend. As Haig's successor, he overcame a bad start in the Lebanon disaster, befriended the president, and survived years of bureaucratic struggle with his cabinet colleague, Cap Weinberger. A former marine, Shultz was vehemently opposed to Cap's famous preconditions for the acceptable use of American military power, which, if observed to the letter, virtually restricted such power to defend against an attack on the American homeland. Both in Lebanon and later in Grenada, the secretary of state had sounded much more like the secretary of war, while Defense and the JCS, with its leaden feet, often seemed to prefer the doctrine of "deterrence by appropriations"—forces to be accumulated but never used. With some notable exceptions the service chiefs are usually military bureaucrats in the mold of George Marshall, who typically spend 80 percent of their careers in Washington. They are very risk-averse.

Shultz had been careful not to bog himself down in the Central American fiasco. He and Weinberger had opposed, on the grounds of common sense, what little they knew about Iran-Contra. Thus, when the Iran-Contra scandal broke, their integrity and credibility were intact, and they emerged with a higher standing in Congress and the media.

There was an additional complication going beyond the Pentagon's opposition to intervention. A presidential election campaign had already begun, and Vice-President George Bush appeared to many to be vulnerable to the whole tangle of Iran-Contra, the flagging war against drugs, and Manuel Noriega in particular. Rumors and charges circulated about Bush's friendship with a onetime CIA operative who had become a private contractor for the Contra effort. The vice-president's staff had been involved in meetings and briefings that placed them circumstantially "in the know" about the CIA and its Central American connections.[19] In my own view, whatever his staff knew, Bush, like Shultz and Weinberger, was not cut in because it would not have passed his own commonsense test.

Shultz banked on Noriega's understanding that his survival to this point was an accident not likely to be prolonged. It followed that Noriega should seek the best deal be could get while a deal was available and before the weight of U.S. sanctions and regional opposition forced his ouster. Shortly after the coup failed, a State Department official, Michael Kozak, began negotiating with a Noriega representative. The implicit trade, of course, was Noriega' departure in exchange for a dropping of the indictment.

In early May of 1988, the outline of such a deal, which also included a large financial settlement, seemed within reach. President Reagan now had to decide whether the United States would approve. To Reagan, then on the eve of a vital trip to a Soviet summit, Panama was a bothersome diversion.

The choices presented to the president ran the gamut from full intervention to negotiated settlement. Shultz, who wanted decisive military action or a decisive negotiation, found the Pentagon up to its usual tricks. Not only was military intervention of any kind in Panama seen as unwise, but as usual the JCS bureaucracy had drawn up an unwieldy, militarily riskless but politically absurd contingency plan requiring a huge force to deal with an opponent who had at his disposal not more than several hundred professional soldiers. Turning away from this, Reagan, on May 13, approved the outline of a deal dropping indictment of Noriega in return for Noriega's departure—to be accepted by the Panamanians no later than May 15.

It was a decision he would have to make twice. Details began to leak on the fourteenth, perhaps placed by Noriega himself to test the resolve of the Americans. These rumors were followed by a Noriega-inspired story that the deal had collapsed.

In the United States, the deal promptly split the Republican party. Senator Dole, on May 17, got the Senate to vote 82–10 in favor of a nonbinding resolution attached to the 1988 Defense Appropriations Bill that opposed any quashing of the indictments. On the next day, Vice-President Bush said publicly that the United States should "not bargain with drug dealers on U.S. or foreign soil." He feared not only the political consequences of a deal but also Noriega's real intentions, which may have been to compromise his American opponents rather than reach any agreements. Since the CIA-level contacts with Noriega stretched back through Bush's tenure at the CIA, he could not afford to be seen as "soft" on Noriega.

Noriega's seriousness could indeed have been questioned. He had seen what happened to the shah in exile and to Ferdinand E. Marcos. And he had learned often enough in his career that if you waited long enough, the other side might blunder.

Facing the uproar in Washington, Reagan wanted to learn more about the problem and to review the decision. Shultz's executive assistant, M. Charles Hill, was given the delicate assignment of recalling Kozak for briefings in Washington when his presence in Panama, combined with covertly inspired pressure, was essential to keep Noriega anxious. Hill, a professional Foreign Service officer, had an experienced nose for disaster. A refugee from Carter's East Asia Bureau, he had been parked in that haven for State Department types who "did not go along"—the

Arab-Israel Affairs Bureau. Hill had caught Haig's and then Shultz's attention for his yeoman service during the Lebanon crisis. He saw in the Panama policy the same fatal combination of excessive rhetoric supported by underwhelming force that always spelled disaster. The somewhat befuddled Kozak briefed the president, but in fact, as Hill, Shultz, and Abrams well knew, the combination of Washington's political splits and Pentagon paralysis would never carry the day with Noriega.

Reagan's choices were stark but to him fairly easy to make. The indictment was unenforceable unless Noriega could be captured. That meant U.S. lives if intervention was needed; if there was no intervention, Noriega would go on thieving, killing, and running drugs, brothels, and guns under the nose of the U.S. Southern Command. So it seemed eminently sensible to drop the impotent indictments in order to get rid of Noriega without losing any Americans lives in a military effort. He again approved the deal with Shultz's support.

Kozak returned to Panama equipped with an ultimatum that the deal was take it or leave it by Wednesday. Shultz delayed his trip to join Reagan at the Moscow summit, a tactical decision that cetainly inflated Noriega's ego, if not his resolve. The general stalled. In Washington, Hill was convinced that if Noriega had ever wanted to agree, it was now or never. Shouting an answer over the noise of the waiting helicopter upon leaving for Moscow, President Reagan implied that there was no hurry to make a deal. Noriega apparently concluded from Reagan's remark that he was being conned. He promptly backed out of the deal.

Negotiations had failed. A painless exit of Noriega from the scene was foiled by irresolution in Washington and a sloppy public comment by the president. Meanwhile, economic pressure was wrecking the very people in Panama who supported the ouster of Noriega. The military option was out because of Pentagon opposition. So the United States could fall back only upon that sphere of action in which the Noriega connection had originally been forged: covert activity. In short, a coup.

American attempts to overthrow unfriendly governments were a definite no-no to the congressional committees set up during the Watergate onslaught for the purpose of overseeing the CIA. There was, also, Executive Order 12333, dating from the same congressional jihad that forbade activities that could endanger the lives of foreign leaders. In July, when the administration discussed plans to foment a coup against Noriega, the Senate Select Committee on Intelligence balked.[20] Such a coup in their view could lead to Noriega's murder, even if the U.S. role was indirect (i.e., not planned to kill him). It should therefore not be supported. (One member told me that his opposition to supporting a coup was based more on his belief that the CIA would bungle it.)

This was a classic post-Watergate interpretation by Congress that everyone thought absurd. How could the U.S. then even support any coup when by definition its object was to undo a leader who might resist and be killed in the process? An answer to this dilemma was to be provided a year later.

The Reagan administration had shot its bolt ineffectively with Noriega. One by one, its options had been either too little, too late, or prohibited. The economic sanctions, enforced belatedly by an executive order in March 1988 freezing assets, were ruining Panama but not Noriega, most of whose money sources were illegal: The indictment deal was blown by ineptness. The Southern Command and the JCS stood hard against intervention, rightly wondering why eighteen-year-old soldiers should give their lives because of the bungling of NSC, State, and CIA bureaucrats. The CIA could not stimulate a coup that might lead to Noriega's death—so ruled the Senate Select Committee.

## Coup de Main

The newly inaugurated Bush administration first hoped that Panama would remain on a back burner. Secretary of State Baker focused on cleaning up the mess in Nicaragua. He was able to fashion a new consensus that provided new credibility to the efforts of Costa Rican president Oscar Arias Sanchez to bring about a peaceful settlement. The result was a complex series of agreements that led eventually to the disarming of the Contras and the defeat of the Sandinistas in a free election that took place in the spring of 1990.

Noriega, like the Sandinistas, believed that his control of his country would allow him to determine election outcomes. He had done it in the past, and in the general elections on May 7, 1989, he expected his candidates to succeed once more. After all, the general had faced down the Yankees, and that should have made him invincible. Surprisingly, he was willing to allow former president Jimmy Carter and an international team to monitor the poll. Perhaps he believed his own propaganda; perhaps he thought that Carter, author of the Panama Canal treaties, would be forced to give the regime an endorsement. Whatever Noriega planned, the fraud was so blatant that, following Carter's denunciation, no faith was put in the result. The real presumed winner, opposition leader Guillermo Endara, led a demonstration that marched toward the presidential palace, only to be set upon viciously by Noriega's ironically named "Dignity Battalions," or "Digbats." There were scenes of Endara and his vice-presidential running mate being beaten as a "lesson" for all to remember.

Washington's reaction was to send Southern Command an additional 1,700 men to join the other 10,000 already there. Noriega, who had been harassing American troops for some time, was not impressed. Neither was anyone else. It looked like the administration, obviously preoccupied with the Soviet Union and developments in Europe, was about to repeat the illusion of its predecessor. On May 13, the president publicly suggested that the Panamanian people "get Noriega out of there," a naive hope that Bush expressed again with regard to Saddam Hussein after Desert Storm—with equal success.

In early July a more important change occurred. General Woerner, who had complained early in the Bush administration of a "policy vacuum," had been rebuked by Cheney. Now he was abruptly replaced, having been judged not aggressive enough.[21] Maxwell Thurman, a blunt-spoken man of action near retirement, was to be his replacement. This change was announced on July 20.

Gen. Max Thurman is one of the more impressive military men I have known. It was he, with Secretary of the Army Jack Marsh and his assistant secretary, Harry Walters, who had transformed the failed all-volunteer army with brilliant personnel policies— "be all that you can be." I copied many of them for the navy with equal success. We targeted college and tech school–bound men and women willing to trade active and reserve service for techni-

231

cal skills and tuition benefits. These initiatives are now permanent in the army, but many were canceled by the navy as soon as I departed. The nuclear admirals want only long-term enlistment.

By mid-July, American dependents in Panama were ordered to remain on U.S. military bases. Once more the United States started down the already failed route of military exercises and diplomatic complaints. Bush finally suggested publicly that the United States would welcome action by the PDF to "defend democracy," that is, a coup.

But how could the United States act, or encourage an act, to strike Noriega in view of the strict prohibition against U.S. support for any coup that might result in Noriega's death? The answer came soon enough. Major Giroldi, who as Captain Giroldi had saved Noriega from the 1988 coup, had become disgusted by the general's increasingly criminal disposition: his drinking, his drug taking, and his abuse of women. As chief of Noriega's headquarters security, he was in a good position to seize his boss, but his circle of trusted helpers did not extend to units, such as the elite Batallion 2000 or the airborne Machos del Monte. So Giroldi sought U.S. help to block two key roads and airfields.[22]

On October 2, President Bush and his national security advisers were made aware that a coup might be in the offing. But the president and his people had no plan. His new JCS chairman, General Powell, had opposed intervention to overthrow Noriega when he was national security adviser to Reagan for the same reasons as expressed by the JCS (i.e., why should American soldiers die for such a cause?). The new commander of Southern Command, Gen. Max Thurman, had just taken control on September 30. Thurman had put Gen. Carl Stiner, commander of the army's Eighteenth Airborne Corps, in charge of contingency plans, but none of the planned contingencies included assistance for an inside coup.

Powell consulted the JCS lawyers, who warned him that only an FBI or DEA officer could legally seize Noriega. Powell's intelligence adviser, Adm. Edward D. Shaefer, advised that the intelligence community believed that the coup was a phony, a setup by Noriega. As usual, the consensus view of the vast intelligence bureaucracy was wrong. In my fourteen years in government

I found it wrong far more often then correct. Our intelligence community is brilliant in providing pictures and data but a failure in drawing accurate conclusions.

The result was a tragedy of errors and omissions. On October 3, the coup began earlier than expected because Noriega arrived at headquarters an hour ahead of time. Before he could be seized, he managed a telephone call for help; the coup makers were late cutting communications; expected troop reinforcements from certain trusted units did not arrive, as their commanders vacillated.

Giroldi sent two officers to Thurman's headquarters to say that they had seized Noriega, would not give him up, but wanted the United States to block key roads so he could not be rescued. Thurman called Powell for instructions. Powell was not about to begin his term by violating congressional bans on supporting coups. He told Thurman: "You don't have authority to go in and get him [Noriega]."[23] Furthermore, Thurman was forbidden any "show of force." Shortly thereafter, Noriega's commandos, the Machos del Monte, commandeered a civilian 727, landed on the highway near the airport, and seized private cars to speed them, unopposed, to Noriega's relief.

In Washington it was a confusing day. Cheney had been escorting Soviet defense minister Dmitri Yazov on an official visit. Later, he and Powell had presided over public ceremonies marking Powell's assumption of the JCS chairmanship. At one point, the president convened a crisis meeting without CIA representation and tried to establish facts. These were hard to come by, so Bush seems to have decided to follow General Powell. In an absurd bit of logic splitting, Powell decided that congressional strictures could be met if Noriega was voluntarily given into U.S. custody by the coup makers but not if U.S. personnel had to go to the location of the coup and pick him up. Thurman was so instructed.[24]

The result was that Giroldi found himself surrounded by Noriega loyalists. He could not bring himself to kill his superior, and lacking any hope of American help, he surrendered to General Noriega. Giroldi was tortured and later killed in a hail of bullets.

Congressional reaction was predictable and bitter. Ignoring the congressional opposition to support of coups, one after another blasted Bush. Sam Nunn said, "Occasionally we have to foresee that our policy of encouraging a coup might succeed, and we ought to be prepared." Dave McCurdy said, "Yesterday makes Jimmy Carter look like a man of resolve."[25] A verbal brawl ensued between National Security Adviser Scowcroft and Sen. David Boren, the chairman of the Senate Intelligence Committee, over restrictions on covert actions, with Scowcroft blaming committee strictures and Boren the administration's incompetence. As we have seen in earlier chapters, there would have been overwhelming congressional support and praise, regardless of the points of law, if the administration had supported the coup and met with success. Nor could Congress be expected to accept blame regardless of the legislative record. The inescapable reality was that the coup failed because of bad decision making by a new administration. Giroldi had been loath to kill Noriega. The U.S. military leadership had been loath to intervene. The White House had been loath to plan for the consequences of the president's call for Noriega's overthrow (a charge that would be repeated after Bush's call for an uprising against Saddam Hussein in 1991).

General Noriega, however, was serious about violence. He did not believe, based on twenty years' experience with the Americans, that Americans were capable of the deliberate killing that was his own forte. And so, in a showdown, he was convinced that Washington would not dig him out and hunt him down. Giroldi would not kill him, but he would kill Giroldi.

The brutal facts were now impressed on an unwilling Washington. After years of paying and conniving with Noriega, they had created a monster. The president and his team had been stung. Declaring that amateur hour was over, Bush insisted on some real contingency planning. Thurman began tightening operations in Panama in his usual no-nonsense way. He apparently shared Powell's view that if a loyalist like Giroldi was ready to try a coup, Noriega could no longer trust anyone. He was dependent purely on bayonets.

Of course, as the old adage has it, you can do everything with bayonets except sit on them. Toward the end, Noriega seemed to lose control of himself, taunting Bush and driving the president into a corner. On December 15, to everyone's astonishment, Noriega declared war on the United States. Harassment of U.S.

troops increased, culminating in the killing of a marine lieutenant on December 16 and physical and sexual abuse of a naval officer and his wife who had made a wrong turn.

The final meeting in the White House on December 17 that launched Operation Just Cause took place under curious circumstances. This was not a surgical coup but an invasion that was contemplated. Fear of failure and a general lack of confidence that any decent men remained in the upper ranks of the PDF (if any did remain they would have to be insane to count on the United States after what happened to Giroldi) led Powell, Thurman, and Stiner to plan on the swiftest, deepest, and heaviest operation that could be mounted on short notice. That translated into a doubling of the force (11,000 beyond the 13,000 already there); forty-eight hours' notice instead of five days; simultaneous nighttime strikes that would decapitate and incapacitate the PDF. It is amusing to note that in today's Pentagon, with the land services given four times the number of staff positions as the sea services, operations like Grenada and Libya, which are obviously suited to naval operations, are indefinitely delayed until land forces can be given an equal role, while operations suited to joint operations are invariably assigned to the land services. Except for the Seals, the navy and marines were excluded from Operation Just Cause (in my view, correctly so).

Earlier that decisive Sunday, Powell had secured the unanimous recommendation of the JCS for the execution of this very large military operation based on the "unacceptable" situation created by the murdered marine and harassment of the navy couple. Then Powell and Cheney met the president at the White House, where a Christmas party had been in progress. With the NSC present, General Powell argued for the massive force that he claimed could reduce casualties versus a surgical raid to seize Noriega.[26] This of course was a dramatic and ironic reversal of the Pentagon's consistent opposition to the use of force in the Panama crisis. Mr. Bush, no doubt intrigued by this unlikely turn, probed the necessity for such a hammering of the gnat. Powell was persuasive and determined. This was the prudent plan. After lengthy discussion, the president agreed. The Giroldi coup mishap and presidential permission to use maximum force without civilian micromanagement had finally freed the reluctant warriors from their inhibitions in Panama. Nearly two years after his indictment, Manuel Antonio Noriega, commander of the PDF and rogue extraordinaire, was seized by an American army 24,000 strong.

## Hammering the Gnat

Around twelve-thirty on the morning of December 20, the victor in Noriega's stolen election, Guillermo Endara, was sworn in as president of Panama at a U.S. military base. He promptly requested American help to reestablish democratic government in Panama. A few minutes later, President Bush signed an order authorizing U.S. troops to apprehend Noriega and others under indictment. Then Operation Just Cause finally began. It did not resemble either of the commonly discussed contingency plans: the sudden seizure of Noriega himself by a small force or the surprise use of only those troops, already over 13,000, already in Panama.

Panama, unlike Grenada, seemed to offer a perfect opportunity for a set-piece military operation. U.S. forces knew the terrain, the people, and the targets. There had been plenty of time for planning. There was no risk of foreign allies coming to Noriega's aid. There was every indication that the Panamanians were friendly to the United States, and the adversary forces were little more than a well-trained police force.

In the end, however, important assumptions about the operation proved false. First, there was no surprise. Some sources say that Noriega was warned by Cuban, Nicaraguan, or Soviet sources at least two days ahead of time.[27] The U.S. front-line commander, Lt. Gen. Carl W. Stiner, complained that the operation had been compromised, although he retracted his suggestion that a State Department official had warned members of the Canal Commission of the timing.[28] Given the number of C-141s moving in additional troops, it would not have been hard to figure out that something was happening. But Noriega seemed to have counted it as yet another bluff. The PDF was not alerted. Yet there seems to have been some planning by Noriega to evade the "quick grab" scenario; he remained free over four days even as U.S. forces in large numbers sought his whereabouts. And at least part of his troops—those at the Rio Hato Air Base—were ready and did fight hard.

Second, the night attack proved to be a double-edged weapon. Because there was no surprise, the pinpoint attack of the Commandancia, carried out by two AC-130 "specter" gunships firing 105-millimeter howitzers, found no one at home. The three M-113 armored personnel carriers running up Fourth of July Avenue (called by the Panamanians Avenue of the Martyrs after the 1964 riot victims) encountered strong resistance from adjoining buildings. Twenty-one of the twenty-four U.S. soldiers in the armored personnel carriers (APCs) were hurt. (Other troops that did penetrate the Commandancia discovered some of Noriega's secret world: Hitler mementos, $5 million in cash, porno tapes, a voodoo doll with an Endara effigy within, and the dictator's favorite decorating scheme—camouflage). Before night was over, the entire area around the Commandancia was aflame. Many of Noriega's men were not in uniforms, and it was difficult to tell the enemy from civilians.

There was another complication. The Stealth F-117 fighters struck the Rio Hato Air Base some yards off target, reportedly a deliberate decision to frighten rather than kill the troops.[29] They may have been frightened, but they did not surrender. A fierce ground fight developed against all expectations.

Still, the U.S. military action ran more like an exercise than a real war. Noriega's PDF numbered 15,000. Thirty-three hundred of those had combat qualifications, and only a few hundred actually resisted. The simultaneous U.S. attacks, including two parachute jumps, had achieved all of the objectives rather quickly. By the afternoon of December 20, the United States had control of PDF headquarters and all of the strong points, airfields, and roads. The command structure was destroyed. Whatever plans there may have been for guerrilla warfare were stillborn. No hostage taking succeeded. Despite the threats of some house-to-house fighting, the worst fears of any field soldier operating in a major urban area, none occurred.

The U.S. military had to expect and plan for guerrilla warfare. What no one expected and for which no plan existed was the widespread looting of Panama City by the poorer Panamanians themselves. The PDF, after all, was primarily a police force. Its disappearance and the absence of any other police led to riotous scenes. Panama's new government had no force with which to restore order. After two days of chaos, American soldiers and military police finally took control.

General Powell's fears and those of the JCS were realized: Twenty-four American soldiers and hundreds of innocent Panamanians paid with their lives for the knavery of Noriega and the ineptitude of the U.S. government.

America's actions in Panama were justified by the president as necessary to protect U.S. lives (reportedly a CIA agent held hostage by Noriega was rescued), restore democracy, arrest Noriega, and preserve the Canal treaties. All of this had been done to a chorus of denunciation by the Organization of American States (OAS), the usual critics at the United Nations, and some leading Democrats in Congress. It was very much a unilateral action, and it carried unilateral responsibilities.

After the invasion, Panama's government still depended on U.S. forces. The PDF, though smaller and purged at certain officer levels, is still much the same people as before. When, in December 1990, a disgruntled former Noriega favorite in the PDF escaped jail and roused a rebellion, only American troops saved the Endara government. There are still a thousand people living in temporary shelter after their homes were destroyed in the invasion. To sum up, the American military victory has not yet been translated into a lasting political achievement—a democratic Panama able to stand more steadily, if not entirely, without American support.

Noriega was the creature of covert action, but the rules changed just when he was no longer useful, and the new rules made covert action to remove him too difficult for the Bush administration. For that the Congress could take the discredit. For giving Noriega an outsize role, the executive attempt to carry out foreign policy through the CIA because it could not muster sufficient popular support could be blamed. To imagine that loud noises, big ships, and presidential threats could intimidate a formidable thug like Manuel Noriega was the special vice of the State Department. To pretend that Noriega would somehow be brought down in the absence of a credible military threat was the unique delusion of the Pentagon.

It was left, then, to the judicial branch, in this case the Florida grand juries, to propel both the executive and Congress to resolve the Noriega problem decisively. (The grand jury is a recent institution and not widely understood. A grand jury may, as the saying goes, "indict the Bishop of Boston for bastardy" or anyone else, foreign or domestic, whomever they please.) The indictments made a negotiated outcome virtually impossible. And with covert action blocked off, an act of war, with its attendant casualties, destruction, and long-lasting U.S. responsibility, was the last resort. But when war was launched, the president did not trouble about the War Powers Resolution that Congress insisted set the procedures on going to war. And neither did Congress.

# 9

# The Power of Money

The "power of the purse," over expenditures as well as taxation, is the most far reaching and awesome power granted to the federal government by the Constitution. It is the source and substance of all activities of the federal government and of the machinery of government in all its branches. In the most unambiguous granting of power contained in the Constitution, the framers clearly intended to invest the "power of the purse" in Congress alone.

In all democracies, the "power of the purse" is the normal prerogative of the legislature, but in no other democracy has the legislature such power to subject executive budget proposals to such detailed review and such extensive revision in the relating of appropriations directly to policies, programs, and activities of the executive departments.[1]

Article I, Section VIII, of the Constitution provides:

The Congress shall have power to lay and collect taxes, duties, imposts, and excises, to pay the debts and *provide for the common defense* and general welfare of the United States; but all duties, imports, and excises shall be uniform throughout the United States.

Thus, the very power to tax is tied to the need to "provide for the common defense."[2]

More explicit grants of power over defense affairs are contained in clauses 12, 13, and 14 of Section VIII:

Clause 12: To raise and support armies, but no appropriation of money to that use shall be for a longer term than two years.

Clause 13: To provide and maintain a navy.

Clause 14: To make rules for the government and regulation of the land and naval forces.

These three clauses imply a great deal more than they make explicit; as we shall see, it is only since about 1950 that they have been translated into detailed influence by Congress. While the two-year appropriations limit for the army was inserted because of the colonial fear of standing armies, it later became the basis for an entirely different use of the appropriations process: the molding of both defense posture and defense policy.

Section IX, clause 7, is at once an implicit recognition of the executive's powers of expenditure and also the most important single restriction of presidential power found in the Constitution:

Clause 7: No money shall be drawn from the treasury, but in consequence of appropriations made by law; and a regular statement and account of the receipts and expenditures of all public money shall be published from time to time.

That the framers intended this "power of the purse" to be used extensively in the area of foreign and defense affairs cannot be doubted. In "Federalist No. 58," Madison wrote:

[The House] alone can propose the supplies requisite for the support of government. They in a word hold the purse—that powerful instrument by which we behold . . . the people gradually enlarging the sphere of its activity and importance, and finally reducing, as far as it seems to have wished, all the overgrown prerogatives of the other branches of government. This power over the purse may, in fact, be regarded as the most complete and effectual weapon with which any constitution can arm the immediate representatives of the people, for obtaining a redress of every grievance, and for carrying into effect every just salutary measure.[3]

In "Federalist No. 24," Hamilton said:

> . . . the whole power of raising armies was lodged in the *legislature*, not in the executive; . . . there was to be found in respect to this object an important qualification even of the legislative discretion on that clause which forbids the appropriation of money for the support of an army for any longer period than two years—a precaution which upon a nearer view of it will appear to be a great and real security against military establishment without evident necessity.[4]

And in "Federalist No. 26," he stated:

> The legislature of the United States will be *obliged* by this provision, once at least in every two years, to deliberate upon the propriety of keeping a military force on foot; to come to a new resolution on the point; and to declare their sense on the matter by formal vote in the face of their constituents.[5]

In 1789 it was perfectly reasonable to expect that Congress was entirely capable of handling the military and defense responsibilities involved in the exercise of the "power of the purse." The sizes of the armies, the methods of warfare, and the simple problems of primitive logistics were all issues well within the ken of the legislators of the day. Through their own investigations and judgment, they could be expected to determine the kinds of armed forces required for the Republic's defense and the diplomatic policies best to serve the young Republic's interest. Indeed, the largest challenges of the time seemed to be the lower-level question of food, forage, horses, and musket balls.[6]

## Appropriations

The first appropriations act of the new Congress, however, did not include the kind of detailed itemizing that appeared later. Instead, it provided lump sums for four general categories: $216,000 for the civil list, $137,000 for the Department of War, $190,000 to discharge warrants previously issued by the Board of the Treasure, and $96,000 for pensions to disabled veterans.[7]

With the Appropriations Act of December 23, 1791, however,

Congress began the process of narrowing executive discretion by the introduction of a "that is to say" clause. For example, approximately $500,000 was appropriated for the War Department—"that is to say," $102,686 to pay of troops, $48,000 for clothing, $4,152 for forage, and so on. Two years later, the process had gone to the level of such minutiae as an item of $450 for firewood, stationery, printing, and other contingencies.[8] Thus, the period of lump-sum appropriations was short-lived and did not reappear until the later periods of war.

The solidifying of congressional "power of the purse" over military and foreign affairs, like all other aspects of the money power, was determined largely during the monumental struggle between the first secretary of the treasury, Alexander Hamilton, and his Federalists, on the one hand, and the Democrat-Republicans and supporters of Thomas Jefferson on the other, who swiftly gained ascendancy in the House of Representatives. The details of that struggle are outside the scope of this story, but by the time Hamilton had been driven from office and Jefferson had assumed the presidency in 1801, Congress, and most importantly the House, had established a determined grip on the spending power of the executive branch.[9]

Shortly after Jefferson took office, he warned Congress that it would be prudent to appropriate "specific sums to every specific purpose susceptible of definition."[10] He was less scrupulous, however, in his adherence to the constitutional provision that "no money shall be drawn from the Treasury but in consequence of appropriations made by law" when he agreed to accept France's offer to sell Louisiana for $15 million, even though no such sum had been authorized or appropriated. Later, in 1807, while Congress was still in recess, Jefferson ordered the purchase of military supplies for an emergency created by the attack by a British vessel on the American ship *Chesapeake*. "To have awaited a previous and special sanction by law would have lost occasions which might not be retrieved," said Jefferson to Congress when it had convened.[11]

## Authorization

In 1828, when an attempt was made by Congress to reiterate the prohibition on unauthorized commitments, there was an interest-

244

ing exception made for contracts for subsistence and supplies for the army and navy. This exception reflected a certain sanctity in these appropriations that lasts to the present day and, indeed, must be considered a qualification to the congressional "power of the purse" over the military. Unlike weapons, Congress has never canceled orders for food, clothing, and fuel.

In 1837, the House further solidified its position by passing a rule providing that "no appropriation shall be reported in any general appropriation bill or be in order as an amendment thereto, for any expenditure not previously authorized by law . . ."[12]

By 1860, the House Ways and Means Committee had become the most powerful body of Congress. Its tight control over the purse dominated all other committees and gave it a special status under the House rules. It controlled House proceedings, and its chairman was second only to the Speaker in his influence. The problems of government finance up to this period, however, were quite different from those to be encountered from this point forward. Total expenditures as late as the period of 1846–53 averaged less that $50 million annually for the entire federal government.[13]

The Civil War, of course, brought about a tremendous change. The federal budget, for instance, climbed from $63 million in 1860 to $1.3 billion in 1865. During the war itself, the military forces continued to enjoy the benefit of largely unspecified lump-sum appropriations. The authority of the executive branch to transfer funds from one account to another, however, was repealed, and a requirement instituted that each agency must return all unexpended funds to the treasury; furthermore, the obligation of funds in excess of existing appropriations was specifically prohibited. At the same time, the House transferred some responsibilities of the Ways and Means Committee, which heretofore had handled all supply as well as revenue bills, to two new standing committees, the Committee on Appropriations and the Committee on Banking and Currency.[14]

As was noted elsewhere, the exigencies of war often have led to the ignoring of established appropriations procedures. After the firing on Fort Sumter, while Congress was adjourned, President Lincoln, for instance, directed his secretary of the treasury to spend $2 million for "military and naval measures necessary for the defense and support of the government . . ." even though there was neither authorization nor appropriations.[15]

245

In 1876 the appropriations power was greatly augmented by a rules change in the House that allowed substantive riders to be attached to appropriations bills. Thus, the appropriations process came to include general policy as well as financial matters. This action is of arguable constitutionality and has never really been settled. Edward Corwin raises the questions of whether Congress, by such riders, is constitutionally entitled to lay down conditions that bind the president if he signs the appropriation and decides inconclusively that "a logically conclusive argument can be made on either side of this question which, being of a 'political' nature, appears to have been left to be determined by the tussle of political forces."[16]

In 1855, in reaction to the greatly increased power of the Appropriations Committee, jurisdiction over the supply bills for the army, navy, and consular and diplomatic service were taken away from it and dispersed to the legislative committees of jurisdiction. A similar dispersion took place in the Senate. This spreading of responsibility led almost immediately to a loss of congressional control and to considerable confusion. The Appropriations Committee had a fairly unified control and policy oversight, while most of the legislative committees, "having intimate and for the most part cordial relations each with a particular department, launched out into an unrestrained competition for appropriations, the one striving to surpass the other in securing greater recognition and more money for its special charge."[17]

The disorganization in Congress during this period was exceeded by relative chaos in the executive branch. There was no central budgetary authority in the executive branch; the chief of each agency simply submitted his own estimates, usually padded in the expectation of cuts, to the secretary of the treasury, who then transmitted them to Congress. The president had virtually nothing at all to do with the process.[18] Woodrow Wilson wrote in 1885 that the United States had "a financial policy directed by the representative body itself, with only clerical aid from the Executive."[19] Moreover, such spending control as was exercised by the legislative committees during this period seems to have been more apparent than real, judging from the practice of deficiency appropriations, or "supplementals," that were routinely submitted if the original budget request of final appropriations did not meet the needs of the executive department.[20]

The Budget and Accounting Act, drawn up in 1920 with the active encouragement of President Wilson and signed into law in 1921 by President Harding, directed the president to prepare and transmit to Congress each year a budget showing federal revenue and expenditures for the previous and current years and an estimate for the following year. It further set up the Bureau of the Budget to carry out this function for the executive branch. It set up also the General Accounting Office (GAO), under a comptroller general, to assist Congress in its oversight function of the budgetary process.[21]

In anticipation of passage of the Budget and Accounting Act, the House of Representatives, on June 1, 1920, restored full jurisdiction to the Appropriation Committee for all supply bills, which it had originally been granted in 1865. It set up ten subcommittees of five members each, with jurisdiction over one or more agency budgets. The Senate followed suit.

The newly reconstituted Appropriations Committee went at the first Harding budget with a vengeance, taking twenty thousand pages of print testimony and reducing the budget by more than $300 million. The chairman of the Appropriations Committee immediately took on tremendous new prestige. "For the first time since Joseph G. Cannon had been tumbled from the throne of Blaine and Reed, there was an individual in the House who could put on his hat and talk to the President of the United States eye to eye and man to man in the plain blunt language of yes and no."[22]

The exigencies of World War II brought a return to the lumpsum appropriations practices of all previous wars. While surveillance and some line-item supervision was exercised by the Appropriations Committees, the successful hiding of the Manhattan Project illustrated the rather gross scale of the categories appropriated.

In 1946, great changes were made by the Legislative Reorganization Act, under which each legislative committee was charged to "exercise continuous watchfulness of the execution by the administrative agencies concerned of any laws, the subject matter of which is within the jurisdiction of such committee." It required the formation of a Joint Committee on the Legislative Budget, composed of members of the House Ways and Means and Appropriations committees and the Senate Finance and Appropriations committees. This joint committee, under Republican control in 1947, set ceilings on appropriations and expenditures well below the Truman budget submission.

One significant change in the 1946 act was its provision for the hiring of professional committee staffs on a supposedly nonpolitical career basis. This set in motion the greatest change in the institution's history. In 1945 the staff serving the Foreign Relations Committee consisted of one clerk serving on a half-time basis, an assistant clerk, a secretary, and the part-time services of another secretary.[23] Total staff in the Senate was just over 200 and was only 150 in the House. By the time I left the government in 1987, total congressional staff had grown to 39,000 and had become a permanent bureaucracy, just like the executive branch. This huge legislative bureaucracy had taken on its own powers and become an engine for further growth in the executive bureaucracy. In May 1991, for instance, President Bush denounced the fact that "for fiscal year 1989 the Pentagon devoted 500 man-years and over $50 million just to write reports (over 861) responding to congressional queries on such items as plans for meetings, tugboats and accounting for the number of bands." He noted that the Pentagon bureaucrats annually answer 750,000 inquiries from legislative bureaucrats and that the Pentagon today reports to 107 congressional committees and subcommittees.[24] At last count, Congress's investigators in the GAO conducted 450 Pentagon audits and spent $100 million per year on investigating the Pentagon. This is in addition to the 25,000 investigators and auditors working for Congress under the defense inspector general's office. The actual cost of this congressional oversight is estimated at $10 billion per year.

The first attempt at a legislated budget in 1947 died in conference. In 1948, the attempt succeeded in passage; but when its projected $10 billion surplus turned into a $1.8 billion deficit, it became somewhat discredited. When the Democrats took control of the Eighty-first Congress, it was pronounced a failure and buried.[25] By 1950, however, the size of the federal government, and especially its defense establishment, had become so vast and complicated that it really was beyond the capability of one committee, let alone one subcommittee or several, to oversee fully. In 1952, for example, Carl Vinson, chairman of the House

Armed Services Committee, urged acceptance of the Defense Appropriations Bill just as it was reported out by the Appropriations Committee, saying: "They [the subcommittee] deserve the support of every member of this house because they are in a far better position to know the needs and necessities of national defense than you and I, who have not given . . . the bill the complete and detailed study it should have."[26] Vinson, who first came to the House of Representatives in 1914 and who served as chairman of the Naval Affairs Committee under Franklin Roosevelt and later as chairman of the Armed Services Committee, had enormous influence over defense policy, primarily through his control of the authorization process after the 1959 reforms. When asked about the report that he might resign his seat to become secretary of defense at one point, Vinson replied, "I would rather run the Pentagon from here,"[27] a sentiment many attributed to Vinson's grandnephew Sam Nunn when he killed the nomination of his former chairman, John Tower, as secretary of defense in 1989.

After several years of reflection in retirement, however, Vinson had a somewhat different perspective. He said that the role of Congress

has come to be that of a sometime querulous but essentially kindly uncle who complains while furiously puffing on his pipe but who finally, as everyone expects, gives in and hands over the allowance, grants the permission, or raises his hand in blessing, and then returns to his rocking chair for another year of somnolence broken only by an occasional anxious glance down the avenue and a muttered doubt as to whether he had done the right thing.[28]

## The Birth of Micromanagement

In 1959, in a little-publicized action, Congress did more to gain real influence over the defense establishment, and hence the strategic doctrine of the executive branch, than it had done in the previous 170 years.

Until 1959, there had been permanent legislation of a general nature authorizing appropriations for research and development, aircraft, and other items. These general authorizations served as open-ended permission to request appropriations for these programs without further specific legislative action on the part of the Senate and House Committees on Armed Services.

In 1959, under the sponsorship of Sen. John Stennis of Mississippi, Congress passed an act requiring annual authorizations for important weapons systems and activities before any funds could be appropriated. This act (section 4–12(b) of Public Law 86–149) prohibited the appropriation of funds for the procurement of aircraft, missiles, or naval vessels until a legislative authorization from the Committee on Armed Services had been passed. In the years since the 1959 act, research development, test, and evaluation; tracked combat vehicles; the strengths of reserve components; all "other weapons"; naval torpedoes; and the active-duty strength of the armed forces have been added to this authorization requirement.[29]

Thus, today the annual military authorization bill and the annual military appropriations bill provide that the Committees on Armed Services and the Committees on Appropriations hold detailed "posture" hearings, undertaking in each one a sweeping review of the entire range of U.S. military and strategic policy as well as the international political situation. During the course of these hearings, all of these committees and subcommittees go into some detail as to the international climate, foreign policy assumptions of the executive branch, and worldwide military commitments. Each of these bills then provides the opportunity for detailed exploration of the more contentious issues during floor debate. This is, of course, more extensive in the Senate than in the House and always more extensive in both houses on the authorization bill than on the appropriations bills.[30] The authorization bill has come to be the central focus of attention because amendments and restriction may be attached to the authorization bill by a simple-majority vote, whereas it takes a two-thirds vote to do so on an appropriations bill.

When I first walked into the Hearing Room of the House Armed Services Committee to present the navy budget in 1981, in addition to the members and chairman of the committee, I stood before an impressive walnut plaque bearing in gold letters the words from Article I, Section VIII, subsection 14: "The Congress shall have power to make rules for the government and regulation of the land and naval forces." One who had occasion to spend even more time than I before that walnut plaque, Robert McNamara, former secretary of defense, in reflecting upon the process, thought that

> ... the greatest power of all, of course, is the power of Congress to state to the public and bring to bear the pressure of the public upon any administration which is failing in any way to provide adequately for the national defense . . . the role of Congress is, as I have observed it, to lay out the problems as the congressional representatives of the people see them . . . and in many, many cases Congress has changed the initial decision of the executive branch with respect to such appropriations.[31]

Underlying the whole process, in the view of William Elliott, is the assumption "that the Congress may always repudiate any major shift in military posture and, whatever may be the wisdom of such a repudiation, there can be no denial of the constitutional rights of Congress in this connection."[32] While sound in theory, the practice has gone out of control since Watergate. The defense justification required by Congress that I reviewed in 1976 in the last year of the Ford administration was 12,350 pages; the last one I reviewed as secretary of the navy was 30,114 pages! And by the time the 39,000 congressional staffers had finished with it and passed the bill, 60 percent of those pages had been changed.[33] Perhaps the most accurate assessment of the current process was pronounced by the new chaplain of the Senate during floor debate of the defense bill on October 7, 1985, when he prayed, "Father in heaven, I confess not knowing enough about what is happening here to pray relevantly . . ."

The implications for congressional exercise of the war powers of this far-reaching power of the purse in defense affairs were seen in chapter 3. The Johnson and Nixon administrations both laid heavy emphasis on the participation by Congress in the prosecution of the war and, hence, its legitimization through the appropriations process. For instance, on May 4, 1965, President Johnson, in requesting a special appropriation to meet the mounting costs of the war, told Congress that this was "not a routine appropriation. For every member of Congress who supports this request is also voting to persist in our effort to halt Communist aggression in South Vietnam."[34]

In 1970 and 1971, a series of cases on the constitutionality of the war confirmed the legitimizing roles of military appropriations and other collaborative legislation. In the case of *Orlando v. Laird* and *Berk v. Laird*, district courts upheld the principle that even in the absence of an explicit authorization for hostilities, Congress had ratified the escalation of the war by its votes on military appropriations, on renewal of the draft, and on other "joint action" or "mutual participation." The following year, the First Circuit Court of Appeals ruled in the case of *Massachusetts v. Laird* that in a situation of prolonged but undeclared hostilities in which the executive branch "continues to act not only in the absence of any conflicting congressional claim of authority but with steady congressional support, the Constitution has not been breached."

The situation was quite the contrary, however, in the absence of such collaboration through appropriation. For instance, in the summer of 1973, the courts seemed about to take a contrary view, as would seem to have been justified, regarding the legitimacy of pursuing the bombing campaign in Cambodia. Every military appropriations bill from October 1970 on contained a clause expressly forbidding direct military support for the government of Cambodia except in connection with the withdrawal of U.S. troops from Southeast Asia and the release of prisoners of war. These conditions were fulfilled in March 1973, and thereafter the appropriations argument alone could no longer support the executive policy. And as we saw in chapter 3, the executive did not have political strength to obtain any other authority from Congress. Bereft of appropriations to provide support to Cambodia or Vietnam, the paralyzed Nixon administration watched in despair as its allies fell to the North Vietnamese.

The congressional Budget and Impoundment Control Act of 1974, born of congressional frustration with presidential impoundment of funds (including the bombing of Cambodia on credit only one year earlier), served to augment the power of Congress to control spending by setting limits thereon through the budget process. The act set up the House and Senate Budget committees, designed to recommend changes in the executive budget proposals, and the Congressional Budget Office, intended to provide information to Congress on the budget independent of the Office of Management and Budget (OMB)—the Bureau of the Budget, reorganized and renamed by Nixon in 1970. The act also required strict executive budget proposal deadlines for submission to Congress. This act begat a new layer of legislation and another annual interbranch negotiating process over overall spending limits. In light of the large portion of the budget's being "untouchable" (i.e., comprised of entitlements like social security and local "pork" programs politically dangerous to alter), compromise must be found disproportionately in defense and foreign assistance accounts. This act not only added two Budget committees dedicated to monitoring presidential spending (and at least another month of annual delay), but they have grown to rival in prominence the Ways and Means, Appropriations, Armed Services, and Foreign Affairs/Relations committees in matters of national security.

But the combined effect of the 1970 legislative reorganization, the 1973 "Subcommittee Bill of Rights" (formulated by the House Democratic Caucus, it wrested control of subcommittees from the full committee chairmen and gave each subcommittee an independent staff, leading to an explosion in the number of subcommittees and of staff numbers), and the Budget Act of 1974 was to dilute greatly the power of the Armed Services and Appropriations committees over military affairs.

Before 1970, secretaries of the military departments reported to two committees, authorization and appropriation, in each house, and compromises were quickly reached with chairmen who could deliver. By 1984, as secretary of the navy, I was reporting to more than sixty committees and subcommittees, all writing legislation effecting the Navy Department. The armed services and appropriations chairmen were still the most important, but deals based on sensible compromise were frequently not possible because they could no longer deliver.

That same year, 1984, the Senate Armed Services chairman, John Tower, voluntarily retired, the first in memory. He told me that it just wasn't fun anymore. "When I came to the Senate in 1961, Dick Russell was Armed Services chairman, and he made defense policy as a peer of the president. Now, as chairman, I am just one of many that the president may or may not counsel with as the spirit moves him."

The period following World War II brought a great increase in congressional influence through the appropriations process not only in defense but also in diplomatic and foreign political affairs. The greatest single catalyst to this process was the executive-branch policy of containment, resulting shortly after the war in the proposing of massive assistance programs through the Truman Doctrine, "Point 4," and the Marshall Plan. Because of the formidable opposition to such bold policies that was certain to be encountered in Congress, the executive branch embarked on an unprecedented policy of consultation and cooperation with Congress before and during the sending up of these requests. This was the great era of "bipartisan foreign policy." One result was that Congress was brought into the policy-making process in the area of foreign assistance as it had never been on any foreign political issues. The years since have established that temporary expedient as a permanent admission to the process, not a passing opportunity. The history of the foreign assistance program, in its many versions, provides a record not merely of congressional participation but, indeed, of congressional dominance. The policy impact in many cases went far beyond the mere shape or size of assistance programs themselves. In 1956, for example, the Eisenhower administration decided to withdraw from the Aswan Dam project for a variety of reasons. At least one observer, however, described the impending action by the Senate to cut off any aid to Egypt as a determining factor in a decision that was to have grave repercussions for U.S. interest in the Middle East for many years.[35]

As Arthur Schlesinger put it shortly after the end of the Kennedy administration:

> In the realm of hemisphere affairs, Monroe could promulgate a doctrine, Theodore Roosevelt wave a Big Stick and Franklin Roosevelt become a Good Neighbor without reference to Congress; and if Congress disapproved, there was little it could do. But the Alliance for Progress, since it needed appropriations, was at the mercy of Congress every step along the way. No one wished to change the system; but it was hard to deny that contemporary presidents, hedged around by an aggressive Congress and an unresponsive bureaucracy, had in significant respects notably less freedom of action than their predecessors.[36]

Dr. Schlesinger's view, as we noted in the preface, changed remarkably, however, when the Republicans got control of the presidency (see *Imperial Presidency*).

The congressional hold over appropriations for foreign assistance, moreover, drew into the political process the pull and haul of the many interest groups and lobbyists for agricultural, coal, shipping, maritime labor, etc., each of whom saw in foreign aid a new public trough and set about getting conditions and restrictions on the legislation, according to their need.[37]

A less dramatic but sometimes more pervasive appropriations hold over international diplomatic and political affairs is exercised by the budgeting, authorization, and appropriations for the Department of State. Since 1971, however, the Senate Foreign Relations Committee and the House Foreign Affairs Committee have followed the example set by the Armed Services Committee fifteen years before and have required an annual authorization bill for the Department of State, United States Information Agency (USIA), and AID (Agency for International Development). Each of the bills produced since that time has proved to be what the executive branch describes as "a Christmas tree" of restrictive amendments.

In the course of this process, then, the budget, authorization, and appropriations committees currently exercise five distinct but closely related types of control over foreign and defense policy. First, they settle, through compromise with the executive, the total amount of money to be budgeted for all programs related to foreign affairs and defense. Second, they determine whether any funds will be committed for a policy proposed by the executive. Third, they decide the amount of funds to be allocated for such a commitment and, within such allocation, what parts of the program will be funded high and which low or not at all. In the case of the defense posture, this is tantamount to molding the defense posture and, hence, to determining the parameters of the strategic doctrine available to the administration and in the last ten years to the micromanaging of the minutist detail, with the legislation now running to thousands and thousands of line items. Fourth, they shape the nature of U.S. participation in international organizations and in defense organizations. Fifth, they review and pass upon the administrative and policy procedures of the departments in the carrying out of programs under their jurisdiction. In the case of the USIA, for instance, this gives Congress control over the image projected abroad of the United States and of the public affairs policy of the executive branch.

The hearings of the vastly proliferated subcommittees and of the full committees and the reports published by them each contain hundreds of policy decisions and administrative directives. Most of them are actually written into the acts themselves, which run collectively to thousands of pages annually, written by staff and, except for the big issues, unread by most committee members.

Lack of discipline in subcommittee proliferation has led to lack of discipline on the floor. Now everybody wants a piece of the defense action. Between the House and Senate, the number of floor amendments rose from 6 in 1977 to 247 in 1985.

A typical appropriations act is written in technical, legal, and often abstruse language and contains a vast body of statutory authorizations, provisions, restrictions, and conditions. They may typically include statements of the activities or objects for which each line item might be spent; allocations to or limitation on expenditures for subitems under each line item; restrictions or limitations on the number and prices of items to be purchased; prohibition of the use of such purchased items for certain activities; directives concerning international administration; and other substantive legislation. The thirty-two regular and social appropriations acts for fiscal 1960, for instance, required 248 pages of fine print, totaling approximately a hundred thousand words.[38] By 1990 that had exploded to over four thousand pages. Line-item authorization had grown from 3 percent of the defense budget in 1947 to 70 percent in 1981, finally hitting 100 percent in the 1991 budget. Specific program changes went from fewer than twenty to more than two thousand per year.

The chairmen and senior members of the principal committees are usually formidable overseers. Coming from safe districts as a rule, these members often have served decades on the same subcommittees and committees and are usually better informed about certain aspects of their departments and their budgets, which they have been reviewing for many more years, than the cabinet officers themselves.[39] Chairmen Nunn and Aspin, for instance, are wholly deferential to their former colleague, Secretary of Defense Dick Cheney, except on matters involving the Defense Department, where their combined experience is fifty-five years longer than Secretary Cheney's.

There are of course limitations on the effectiveness of the appropriations power as well. The sheer complexity of the process is one formidable shortcoming among others that include the many different types of appropriations bills in which funds are voted, the confusing terminology, the technical jargon, such as NOA (new obligational authority), delivery ceilings, expenditure ceilings, and carryovers. The amount appropriated for any fiscal year does not indicate even approximately what the actual expenditures will be for a program. An appropriation authorizes a department to incur obligations, but the spending may be spread over several or even many years. In addition, there are the annual supplemental appropriations and deficiency appropriations that often are huge, and their relationship to programs voted upon earlier is often very difficult to ascertain. Appropriation for an aircraft carrier, for instance, is made in one year but spends out over eight years.

Another problem is conflict among committees themselves. In many instances the appropriations committee of, say, the House will seek to impose policies on a department that are in direct contradiction to those favored by the legislative committee of the same or the other house. The executive branch, therefore, usually finds itself subject to conflicting instruction and no clear legislative policy guidance. Depending on the chutzpah of the agency head, the legislative disagreements can paralyze action or provide all the running room necessary to do what he or she wants.

Because of these and other problems, there has grown up a perennial problem of delay. It is now the norm that the authorization and appropriations process for the major agencies of the executive branch is rarely, if ever, completed before the start of the fiscal year for which the legislation is intended. During this interim period the executive branch must operate on continuing-resolution authority. In these cases it is faced with a situation described in 1825 by one of my predecessors as secretary of the navy, Samuel L. Southard, who reported to Congress that for nearly half of the year his department acted in "perfect ignorance of the law under which it is bound to act." As a result, "the law is necessarily, not complied with, because it is passed after the act is performed."[40] Legitimate questions have been raised, moreover, whether all of this effort, especially on such bills as the State Department authorization and the foreign assistance bills, is really worth it. A high percentage of the leadership of the committee is often tied up for months in conflicts between and among committees and between the committees and the executive branch over these appropriations and authorization bills. A good case can be made that the scarce time of these committees and their members could be used much more advantageously.

One of the most controversial of the limitations on the appropriations power exercised by the executive branch is presidential impoundment of appropriated funds. The policy has a long history, beginning in 1803, when President Jefferson declined to spend money for gunboats. The practice was exercised from time to time by his successors when they could get away with it. In 1941, President Roosevelt carried it to its next dimension by systematically impounding funds appropriated for public works not directly related to the war effort. In 1949, President Truman created a furor by impounding appropriations for the air force, and President Kennedy did the same when he refused to spend the $180 million appropriation for the RS-70 bomber in 1961. In 1967 alone, President Johnson impounded a total of $5 billion. By 1974, President Nixon had impounded over $15 billion. Cong. George H. Mahon, then chairman of the House Appropriations Committee, said, "The weight of experience and practice bears out the general proposition that an appropriation does not constitute a mandate to spend every dollar appropriated. . . . I believe it is fundamentally desirable that the Executive have limited powers of impoundment in the interests of good management and constructive economy in public expenditures."[41] William Rehnquist, then of the Department of Justice and later chief justice of the Supreme Court, advised in 1969 that "with respect to the suggestion that the President had a constitutional power to decline to spend appropriated funds, we must conclude that the existence of the broad power is supported by neither reason nor precedent. . . ." He found it difficult "to formulate a constitutional theory to justify a refusal by the President to comply with the Congressional directive to spend."[42]

The issue of impoundment was addressed, though not eliminated, by the 1974 Budget Act, which arranged for "deferrals" and "rescissions" of monetary outlays by the executive branch. Under "Title X" of the law, deferrals allow a temporary delay in spending that remains in effect until the president decides to spend the money or either house of Congress passes a resolution forcing him to spend it. Rescissions are requested when no spending is desired or anticipated. The attempts to codify impoundment procedures was not entirely successful. President Ford, in his tenure, requested 330 deferrals and 150 rescissions in less than three years, of which one-third (120) of the deferrals and virtually all (133) of the rescissions were considered policy related.[43] President Carter's rescissions concerning major strategic system's purchase (including the B-1 bomber and what became the aircraft carrier *Teddy Roosevelt*) and Reagan's tens of billions of dollars in deferrals and rescissions came to show that the phenomenon of impoundment would not go away merely by an act of legislation, as is often the case with separation-of-powers issues.

## Sequestration and Gramm-Rudman-Hollings

The 1985 Balanced Budget and Emergency Deficit Control Act (Public Law 99–177, commonly known as Gramm-Rudman-Hollings) vested in the comptroller general of the United States the power to order mandatory cuts in the budget should deficit ceilings under the law fail to be reached. This process, known as sequestration, posed constitutional problems from its inception (as the comptroller general is removable only by Congress, which was seen to be a violation of the separation of powers), yet the method of selecting cuts has remained largely the same since 1985.

Although Congress had the power to renegotiate ceilings on the deficit, a failure to do so would lead to equal arbitrary cuts in budget programs. In theory, the cuts in spending would come equally from national defense and domestic programs. In fact, huge portions of the budget are exempt. On the military side, all contracted spending, including systems under construction and maintenance of the Department of Defense physical plant, would be exempt, while manpower programs and other facilities' maintenance, for example, would be subject to mandatory cuts.

It is on the domestic side, however, that the exempt programs swell in number, with many programs such as these qualifying: Social Security; income tax credits; Medicaid; federal retirement; disability and Workers' Compensation; food stamps; nutrition assistance to Puerto Rico; other child nutrition; family support payments; supplemental security income; the Women, Infants, and Children (WIC) program; and commodity supplemental food programs. In all, between national defense and domestic exemptions, about 60 percent of federal spending does not qualify for automatic cuts, meaning that nonexempt programs (domestically, student loan programs, foster care, and veterans' medical care, for example) would take massive budget cuts under the law. The cuts would be active upon approval of the budget, and no money can be further authorized or appropriated for sequestered programs, save for emergency supplementals.

Aside from the problems of the comptroller general's role, the problem of self-renegotiation of the deficit ceilings has been the largest impediment to the smooth functioning of the legislation. Since the law's enactment, not one of the original deficit ceilings has been met, and sequestration has not yet occurred, although it was used as a threatening device by the executive in 1989 and 1990. If the bill's intent was to instill a fear in Congress of the negative consequences of sequestration, it has been a failure, since no balanced budget has come out of Congress since the appearance of Gramm-Rudman-Hollings. It was finally abandoned in a new budget "deal" in 1990 when President Bush dropped his no new taxes pledge in return for deficit reduction. This deal also became a joke a year later when the combined effects of higher taxes and a deep recession increased the deficit another 30 percent despite a 5 percent cut in defense.

A quite pervasive limitation on the detail that the appropriations power may determine is the wide variety of contingency and transfer authorities permitted by most appropriations bills. Reprogramming, for instance, is a procedure allowed for the shifting of funds within an appropriations item; and the transfer authorities normally permit the president to take funds that have been earmarked for one class of appropriations and apply them to another. Contingency funds have often been used for purposes not even contemplated by Congress when it appropriated the money. For instance, in 1961, President Kennedy established the Peace Corps by executive order. He financed the agency by the use of contingency funds drawn from the Mutual Security Act until Congress finally appropriated funds for the agency seven months later.[44]

By far the most significant restraint on the appropriations power is the de facto limit imposed by ongoing hostilities. During such hostilities, while opposition to nearly any other legislation is within the rights of a senator, voting against defense appropriations is a kind of civil disobedience for members, described by one critic as "a congressional version of not paying taxes."[45] No member can afford to be characterized by his enemies back home as taking the guns away from our boys on the battlefield. For instance, in 1967 an Associated Press survey reported that forty out of forty-eight responding senators opposed President Johnson's policy in Southeast Asia; but later that year only three of these Senators actually voted against a $12 billion supplemental appropriation for the war.[46] One of those who did vote against it, Sen. Ernest Gruening of Alaska, later recalled that President Johnson had said to him, "I don't care what kind of speeches you make as long as you don't vote against the appropriations."[47] Gruening did and was defeated in the next election.

During any hostilities, moreover, lump-sum appropriations become the order of the day. During one year of the Civil War, Congress appropriated $50 million to pay volunteers, $26 million for subsistence, and $76 million to cover a wide assortment of items, all of these to be divided "as the exigencies of the service may require." During World War I, Wilson received $100 million for "national security and defense," to be spent at his discretion, and $250 million to be applied to construction costs under the Emergency Shipping Fund.[48] There was, of course, the example in World War II whereby the Manhattan Project was funded for several years from funds appropriated for "expediting production." Appropriations for the project totaled well over $2 billion, and members of the House Appropriations Committee told one observer that about $800 million had been spent on the project before they even knew about it.[49]

The turmoil and frustration resulting from Vietnam brought a sustained congressional effort to shape foreign and defense policy through appropriations that has resulted in a significantly greater dependence of foreign and defense policies on appropriations, with the result that the executive branch has lost considerable policy control to Congress.

## Ending the War in Indochina

The beginning of the 1970s brought within Congress a new attitude regarding its own efficacy in ending hostilities in Indochina. This, as was discussed in chapter 3, involved the first Cooper-Church Amendment, the repeal of the Tonkin Gulf Resolution, and the early congressional exploration of congressional war powers, all in 1970. However, as the war continued throughout Vietnam, Laos, and Cambodia, both houses turned to the appropriations power in order to effectively restrain the president from continuing U.S. efforts. Although the House and Senate each rejected three military-funds cutoff proposals in 1971 and the House rejected three similar ones to the Senate's one in 1972, by 1973 the makeup of Congress had changed sufficiently to threaten the president's policy in earnest.

January 23, 1973, marked the announcement by President Nixon of the signing of the Paris Peace Accords, which would end U.S. involvement in the ground war in Vietnam, Laos, and Cambodia. At this point, American force levels were just over 20,000 troops. A general cease-fire in Vietnam was effected, with a similar cease-fire put in place in Laos one month later.

The situation in Cambodia was, however, not so favorable, as the Paris Accords did little to settle the war in that country. Vietnam was not in a position to force the Communist Khmer Rouge to cease and desist, as it was in Laos. Indeed, although American ground troops had been prohibited from Cambodia for three years (since the first Cooper-Church Amendment), American air strikes had been used (to great effect) against the Communist insurgency. When the U.S. bombing was suspended on the grounds of a unilateral end of offensive operations by the Lon Nol government in the hopes of a cease-fire agreement, hopes soared in Congress for an end to the fighting. However, when the Cambodian government's gesture was met with a renewed Communist offensive aimed at total victory, the government resumed operations, and the United States followed with intense bombing of Khmer Rouge strongholds. This interruption of Congress's victory celebration prompted a concerted effort in 1973 to stop American air support over Cambodia, the last significant remaining U.S. effort in Indochina. That the Khmer Rouge was different from, and apparently not taking orders from, the North Vietnamese was not the issue. What was at issue was the desire in Congress to get out of Indochina altogether, whatever the outcome.

When it was determined in April that the Paris Peace Accords had been "totally violated" by Hanoi[50] (the CIA had determined that military matériel and personnel had been funneled into South Vietnam through Cambodia), the administration set out to enforce the accords through continued bombing of Communist sanctuaries in Cambodia. However, once Congress saw that American prisoners of war had been returned from Vietnam (per the Paris Accords), the distrust of the president and fear of reinvolvement on a large scale overrode whatever desire Congress had to enforce the accords as signed. As Senate Majority Leader Mansfield put it, the bombing "could have the possible effect of once again involving this country in a quagmire."[51] Moreover, with the Tonkin Gulf repeal coupled with the signing of the Paris Peace Accords, the administration needed more than what the Congress considered specious constitutional arguments to convince the legislature to approve further bombing. Moreover, the administration asked for no further funds for fiscal year (FY) 1973 bombing until March 1973, since it had reprogrammed funds from other defense categories to continue the bombing, a tactic much loathed by Congress. When the request for money finally did come from the White House, a frustrated and war-weary Congress greeted the proposition with considerable disdain, not just for the actions needing funding but because of Nixon's tardiness in bringing the matter to the branch of government that was constitutionally mandated to have *all* appropriations powers.

The key issue in the second FY 1973 supplemental appropriations was the permission of Congress for the Department of Defense to reprogram $500 million, of which about $150 million was to pay for combat operations that had already taken place. While the House Appropriations Committee did strike down a Joseph

P. Addabbo amendment to bar such transfers, it did cut the request to $430 million and reported the appropriation favorably out of committee on May 3.

On the House floor, however, a groundswell of support from the Democratic leadership for a stronger Addabbo amendment led to a prohibition of all Department of Defense transfers for use in Indochina, including the bombing, as well as covering increased subsistence costs and the dollar's devaluation over the year. On May 10, a vote of 219–188 backed the Addabbo provisions.[52]

In the Senate Appropriations Committee, where the credibility of the executive was even more in question by the members, an Eagleton amendment was passed preventing *past and present* appropriations from being spent on combat activities on or over Cambodia and Laos. Furthermore, all transfer authority was cut to $170 million for FY 1973, as the bill was reported out on May 18.[53] And, on May 31, the Senate passed the bill with the Eagleton amendment by a 73–5 margin.[54] In conference, which began on June 5, it was decided to keep the Senate language and ban all past and present funding for use in Cambodian bombing raids. This version passed easily in both houses. On June 27, President Nixon vetoed the House Resolution 7447 while stating that such an act would jeopardize the integrity of the Paris Peace Accords. And when the House could not produce a veto override, the Nixon administration won its final legislative victory before collapse.

The next day, the Senate resolved to press the fight against Nixon and Cambodian bombing, attaching Eagleton amendments to State Department authorization and six other bills in an attempt to force the president's hand, as Watergate was surely weakening his capability to veto additional bills with confidence. In an attempt to offer the president a way to justify his signing of a new version of the second Department of Defense supplemental, the House Appropriations Committee, on June 28, added a delay of forty-five days to the cutoff, setting an August 15 deadline for the Cambodian bombing. House Majority Leader Ford indicated the next day that the president could abide by this deadline, signaling a monumental victory for Congress.[55] Passage of the bill really marked the final defeat of Nixon's Vietnam policy and ultimately the defeat of the United States in Indochina. For once the bill passed, the Khmer Rouge knew they had only to wait until August 15 and victory was theirs. The North Vietnamese also knew with certainty that there could be no enforcement by the United States of the peace accords, and they were free to resume their reinfiltration of the South, even as the South was held to compliance by the U.S. Congress. Chou En-lai told Kissinger that the August 15 deadline forced him to drop his plan to establish a neutral (anti–North Vietnamese) coalition in Cambodia under Chinese sponsorship.

And so did this sad tale unfold, with the Khmer Rouge resuming their offensive with North Vietnamese support the day after the August 15 bombing halt, which led to victory before year end. Thereupon began the most horrible bloodbath in which some 2 million Cambodians perished in the killing fields of the Khmer Rouge.

With the United States averting its eyes and the president in his final epiphany, the Congress completed the defeat by cutting off all financial assistance to South Vietnam, strangling their ability to resist the North and leading inevitably to the fall of Saigon in April 1975.

## Angola

The congressional heel on the executive throat did not ease even after the fall of Saigon in May 1975. In fact, Congress was so determined not to be caught in a similar quagmire that when two anti-Marxist insurgencies arose against the new Communist government in Angola (which had been promised independence following the coup in Portugal in 1974), Congress moved to prohibit intelligence or foreign assistance activities to aid the rebels.

This decision by Congress was a result of what started as low-level CIA activity in Angola, namely, a retainer paid to Holden Roberto, a member and leader of one of the regional non-Marxist rebel groups, the FNLA, in the amount of $300,000 in January 1975. However, as the Soviet-backed MPLA Marxist ruling party gained foreign support, the rebel groups FNLA (backed by China and Zaire) and the National Union for Total Independence of Angola (UNITA) (headed by Jonas Savimbi) began to falter. Southern African leaders, such as Zambia's Kenneth David

Kaunda and Zaire's Sese Seko Mobutu, pressed Kissinger for
assistance, and the national security adviser made it known that
assistance would be sought in July 1975. While U.S. involvement
was small (about $32 million for 1975), Kissinger had apparently
erred in thinking that the Vietnam issue had settled enough to
undertake another foreign venture.

The vehicle for cutoff was, once again, the defense appropriations bill. On December 17, 1975, Sen. John Tunney of California
forwarded an aid cutoff amendment requiring an end to any
involvement in Angola. It passed overwhelmingly in the Senate
and the House.[56] A similar amendment was attached to the 1976
Security Assistance Authorization bills, this time sponsored by
Sen. Dick Clark. The Clark Amendment, as it came to be known,
was not objected to and was included in the bill, which became
Public Law 94-329.

The Clark Amendment and its predecessor posed severe problems for an executive committed to Soviet containment. By the
time of the 1976 action, Angola had been granted independence,
Cuban troops were stationed in the capital and outlying areas,
and the flow of Soviet military personnel endangered the rebels.
Kissinger's arguments about abandoning vigilance against aggression fell on deaf ears, and the president was powerless to
implement *any* policy. Congress had, in Ford's words, "lost their
guts."

President Carter, presumably with a more friendly relationship with the Democratic Congress, included the Clark Amendment on a list of congressional restrictions that he wished to be
reversed, as it made it difficult to respond to Soviet inroads into
Southern Africa. In the International Security Assistance and
Development Cooperation Act of 1980, a provision was added to
allow the president to assist Angola when it was certified by him
that such was in the national security interests of the United
States. But since aid had to be approved first by joint resolution,
the change amounted to nothing, as it merely allowed the president to seek permission to request from Congress needed funding,
a prerogative that he already had. The Clark prohibition remained in force throughout the four Carter years.

President Reagan came to office in 1981 pledged to restore the
foreign powers of the office, which included the repeal of the Clark

Amendment. Although he failed to do so in 1981, four years later came a new opportunity and a new attitude in Congress that allowed him to accomplish it.

By 1985, congressional opinion had shifted to support other anti-Communist insurgencies, most prominently in Nicaragua and Afghanistan. In the Senate, Sen. Steve Symms offered an amendment to the Foreign Relations Authorization that passed easily on June 11. In the House, an amendment by Democrat Samuel Stratton, supported broadly, was attached to the Foreign Assistance authorization. Public Law 9983, with Section 811 repealing the Clark Amendment, was enacted on August 8, 1985, accompanied by a statement by President Reagan that there were no plans to aid the Angolan guerrillas. This proved not to be the case, as millions were taken from CIA contingency funds to support Jonas Savimbi. Gradually, Savimbi gained wider success as his American support became larger and more visible. He was feted by the Republicans on his annual visits to Washington and proved to be a very effective lobbyist in Congress. Then, with the end of the Cold War, the Soviet Union ended its subsidy to the Cuban expeditionary force supporting the government, the Cubans withdrew, and the government agreed to do business with Savimbi. A historic peace agreement was signed between President dos Santos and Savimbi on May 31, 1991. Democracy, free markets, and free elections were agreed to.

## Nicaragua

The debate over funding the military aspects of the resistance movement (the Contras) in Nicaragua came in fits and starts, then ended completely in 1987 after much heated debate within both houses of Congress. With the fall of the Somoza regime in 1979, the Nicaraguan Sandinista revolutionaries began embarking on their Marxist-Leninist goals for that country, with the assistance of Cuban and Soviet military and civilian advisers. The concern in Washington over these circumstances and their possible effects on regional security engendered caution on aid to Nicaragua, which, by 1980, had attached to it numerous elaborate restrictions and eventually was cut off completely.

With the election of Ronald Reagan, the anti-Sandinista atmosphere thickened, fueled by evidence of gunrunning and training by the Sandinistas of Communist rebels in El Salvador and regional expansionist rhetoric on the part of the "revolutionary" government. In 1981, the CIA began operations aimed at reducing the threat of Nicaragua to its Central American neighbors and stopping the flow of arms through Nicaragua to El Salvador. Congress reportedly also approved $19 million in a classified FY 1982 Intelligence Authorization, to be spent by the CIA as it desired. Moreover, the appearance of three groups of anti-Sandinista counterrevolutionaries, collectively known as the "Contras," seemed a useful vehicle through which to influence Sandinista behavior.

The year 1982 marked the first Boland Amendment, aimed at stopping U.S. aid for military activities when supporting the goal of sparking military confrontation between Honduras and Nicaragua or overthrowing the Sandinista government.[57] This amendment, named after the Massachusetts representative, was tacked on to the FY 1983 Department of Defense appropriations and came in the midst of allegations of Contra incursions over the Nicaraguan border. Although another $19 million was secretly approved in intelligence aid for FY 1983, it was becoming clear that Congress was dissatisfied with the way the CIA was operating. Hence, in 1983, Congress took stronger control over the funding by providing $24 million in the defense appropriations bill for FY 1984, thereby making the assistance public and taking the CIA out of the driver's seat in Nicaragua. Another Boland Amendment was added to the bill stating that no more than the $24 million could be used to support the military arm of the Contras or any other organization in Nicaragua. However, as this seemed to restrict the effort sufficiently, no more money was appropriated until 1986. Then reports of CIA contingency-fund spending for the mining of Nicaraguan harbors surfaced. Although sentiment in Congress was embittered against the executive, President Reagan continued to push unsuccessfully for aid to the rebels and to encourage elections and nonincendiary behavior by the Sandinistas.

A "second Boland Amendment," stating that unless Congress said otherwise, no funds available to any agency of the federal government could be used to support operations in Nicaragua, was added to the Department of Defense sections of the FY 1985 continuing appropriations.[58] As Congress did not say otherwise, no military assistance was allowed, leading to efforts by Lt. Col. Oliver North and others to find alternate ways to fund the insurgency, the upshot of which was the topic of the Iran-Contra investigations (see chapter 6). Humanitarian aid continued, and in FY 1987, $70 million was reprogrammed from the Defense Department for Contra military purposes in Nicaragua in addition to $30 million in humanitarian (nonlethal) aid.[59] This act rejected the limits of 1984 and 1985 on Contra funding and involvement, and the CIA was allowed to retake command of the operation. The exposure of the Iran-Contra affair months after this, however, seemed to snatch defeat from the jaws of the executive victory, as military assistance would not again be provided.

The zigzagging of congressional support for the Contras (covert CIA funding in 1981–82, open funding in 1983, no military funding in 1984–85, a total resumption of military funding in 1986, and then a cutoff of military funding thereafter) served to show the fickleness of congressional attitudes and the harmfulness of attempts at congressionally directed "strategy."

Whatever their source of funding, however, the Contra pressures and the Reagan hostility finally forced the Sandinistas into elections pressed on them by other "moderate" Latin American governments. To the amazement of virtually everyone, the elections in 1990 threw out the Sandinistas and elected Violeta Chamorro and a coalition of non-Communists.

## Conclusion

The Founding Fathers expected Congress, being most directly responsive to the people, would be a restraining influence on the executive in military affairs. While there have been periods in our history when the opposite has been the case, normally it has proved to be true. Constitutional theory aside, we have seen it amply demonstrated that the power of the purse is Congress's ultimate power to have the final say in military affairs. The power was used to keep an activist president from foreign entanglements in the 1930s and in ending American involvement in Southeast Asia in the 1970s. Whoever was right or wrong, Congress succeeded in each case because they were supported by the consensus of the American people and the executive was not. Where the power of the purse has not been used despite congressional rhetoric, as in the continuing funding of the Vietnam War during the 1960s and early 1970s and the funding of Desert Shield and Desert Storm, it was because the leadership of Congress was out of touch with the consensus of the people. In those instances, they were unwilling to be recorded voting against appropriations for military action that had popular support.

In molding the programs, policy, and budget of the Pentagon, the Founding Fathers would be both pleased and appalled at Congress's postwar record. They would be pleased to see that Congress has made many wise changes in defense policy against executive opposition. Without Congress, the executive would almost certainly have reduced the reserve components of the services nearly to zero. It was Congress that forced, upon a reluctant executive in the late 1970s, the personnel policies and pay raises that have made the all-volunteer force a success. It was Congress that overruled the executive in 1980 and forced the Carter administration to continue to maintain a force of nuclear aircraft carriers; it was Congress that through six administrations built the nuclear submarine navy under Admiral Rickover, despite frequent vacillation from the executive; it was Congress that forced the most successful aircraft program in postwar naval history, the F-14 Tomcat, upon an executive wedded to the disastrous TFX, and it is Congress that has kept alive the revolutionary V-22 tiltrotor technology. Even in the highly publicized instances of congressional pork-barrel projects that are not really needed by the Pentagon, they serve an intended purpose of keeping a broad distribution of financial benefits and hence public support for defense spending.

But the Founding Fathers would no doubt draw their breath in sharply if they saw the new postwar dimension of the power of the purse in the immense new bureaucracies the appropriations process has created in Congress and the executive branch. Largely driven by a vastly expanded micromanagement of the executive, Congress has spawned a permanent bureaucracy that is the equivalent of three full army divisions with an annual budget cost of $2.5 billion, or $5 million per member. This postwar explosion of micromanagement and of congressional bureaucracy has driven a far larger expansion of the federal bureaucracy, most notably in the Pentagon. There currently are over 560,000 defense department bureaucrats in procurement alone, 130,000 of them inside the Beltway. This bureaucracy has virtually no direct subordination to the elected president's appointees, since their careers, their pay, and their promotions are not affected by anything but the civil service and military pay and promotion rules. Similarly, in Congress the staffs of the committees and agencies of Congress are largely permanent. The vast majority of day-to-day decision making and policy are set by nonaccountable congressional staffers dealing directly with nonaccountable executive-branch career personnel. Taken together, the permanent career staffs of both branches are nothing less than a fourth branch of the government totally unforeseen and unprovided for in the Constitution. This new branch clearly needs to be studied and addressed in the future. But just as we have seen with the struggles between the three constitutional branches of the government, solutions to the governance of the fourth branch will be found not in constitutional legalism but in the unseemly turmoil of politics.

# Notes

## Chapter 1

1. Quote from Rick Atkinson, "Outflanking Iraq: Go West, Go Deep," *Washington Post*, 18 March 1991, p. 1.
2. Richard M. Nixon, *The Memoirs of Richard Nixon* (New York: Grosset & Dunlap, 1978), p. 395.
3. See Paul A. Gigot, "A Great American Screw-Up: The U.S. and Iraq, 1980–1990," *National Interest*, Winter 1991: 36; Judith Miller and Laurie Mylroie, *Saddam Hussein and the Crisis in the Gulf* (New York: Times Books and Random House, 1990), pp. 139–48.
4. Miller and Mylroie, *Saddam Hussein*, p. 46.
5. Ibid., p. 12.
6. Ibid., p. 14.
7. Senator Dole gave an account of this meeting in a *New York Times* Op-Ed piece entitled "Your Move, Mr. Hussein," *New York Times*, 15 January 1991, p. A19. The Iraqis released a transcript of this meeting highly embarrassing to the senators. See Don Oberdorfer, "Was War Inevitable?" *Washington Post Magazine*, 17 March 1991.
8. Iraqi government transcript as published in the *New York Times*, 23 September 1991, p. 19; Glaspie testimony, see *New York Times*, 21 March 1991, p. A15.
9. Bush related this story when he presented the Medal of Freedom to Thatcher on March 7, 1991. Reported in the *Washington Post*, 8 March 1991, p. A16.
10. For an American account of the Saudi positions, see Bob Woodward, *The Commanders* (New York: Simon & Schuster, 1991).
11. *Congressional Quarterly Almanac* 46 (1990): 682.
12. See *New York Times*, 26 January 1991, p. 1, and *Aviation Week*, 11 November 1991, p. 17. The administration preferred to break the totals

NOTES

into two categories: direct support for military activity and economic support for those in need as a consequence of UN sanctions against Iraq.

13. See *Facts on File* 50, no. 2599 (September 14, 1990): 669–70.
14. Woodward, *The Commanders*, pp. 310, 318–20.
15. *Congressional Quarterly Almanac*, pp. 737–38. For a good review of Democratic twists and turns, see *Washington Post*, 3 January 1991, p. A16.
16. *Washington Post*, 15 November 1990, p. 1.
17. Public Opinion data compiled from PA/Opinion Analysis, U.S. Department of State, Bureau of Public Affairs, August 20, 1990; October 4, 1990; November 2, 1990; November 8, 1990; November 27, 1991; December 8, 11, 12, 26, 1990. These contain popular polling data from as many as seven national polls monitored by the bureau.
18. *Facts on File* 50, no. 2607 (November 9, 1990): 830–31.
19. *Congressional Quarterly Almanac*, p. 742.
20. Woodward, *The Commanders*, pp. 335–37.
21. Ibid., pp. 337–39.
22. Ibid.
23. *Congressional Quarterly Almanac*, p. 742.
24. Woodward, *The Commanders*, p. 342.
25. Ibid., p. 346.
26. *New York Times*, 21 December 1990, p. A14.
27. Ibid.
28. *New York Times*, 31 December 1990, p. I, 6.
29. *Washington Post*, 31 December 1990, p. A1, 5.
30. An account of the meeting between Baker and Aziz can be found in the *Washington Post*, 10 January 1991, pp. 23–26.
31. Woodward, *The Commanders*, p. 338. Senator Nunn agreed. See *Washington Post*, 10 January 1991.
32. Woodward, *The Commanders*, pp. 357–58.
33. Transcript of president's press conference as published in the *Washington Post*, 10 January 1991, p. A27.
34. Michael J. Glennon, "The Gulf War and the Constitution," *Foreign Affairs*, Spring 1991: 92.
35. Glennon, "Constitution." See *Congressional Quarterly Almanac* 46 (1990): 739. On December 13, U.S. District Court Judge Harold H. Greene refused to issue an injunction on the ground that only 10 percent of Congress was seeking relief rather than a majority. On that same day, Federal Judge Royce C. Lamberts dismissed a suit brought by a National Guardsman against the war on the ground that it was a political question, not a subject for a legal ruling.
36. Woodward, *The Commanders*, pp. 363–64.
37. These quotations and information are drawn from the *Washington Post*, 10 January 1991 and the *Congressional Quarterly Almanac* 46 (1990): 747–53.
38. Norman Friedman, *Desert Victory* (Annapolis, Md.: Naval Institute Press, 1991); Joseph Englehardt, *Desert Shield and Desert Storm* (Carlisle, Pa.: Strategic Studies Institute, U.S. Army War College, 1991).

274

## Chapter 2

1. Arthur Schlesinger, Jr., "Congress and the Making of American Foreign Policy," *Foreign Affairs* 51, no. 1 (1972): 83.
2. The *Eliza*: 11 S. Ct 113 (1800).
3. Emmet John Hughes, *The Living Presidency* (New York: Coward-McCann, 1972), pp. 34, 40.
4. Clinton Rossiter, quoted in Edward S. Corwin, *The Constitution* (New York: Atheneum, 1967), pp. 12, 13.
5. William Y. Elliott, *United States Foreign Policy* (New York: Columbia University Press, 1952), p. 63.
6. Walter Bagehot, *The English Constitution* (London: Fontana, 1963), p. 220.
7. Dean Acheson, *Present at the Creation* (New York: W. W. Norton, 1969), p. 600.

## Chapter 3

1. Kenneth J. Hagan, *This People's Navy* (New York: Free Press, 1991), p. 39.
2. Ibid., p. 43.
3. Ibid., p. 54.
4. Ibid., p. 54.
5. Ibid., p. 56.
6. Ibid., pp. 102–3.
7. John Stennis and J. W. Fulbright, *The Role of Congress in Foreign Policy* (Washington, D.C.: American Enterprise Institute for Public Policy Research, 1971), p. 23.
8. *New York Times*, 25 August 1971, p. 37.
9. *Washington Post*, 20 October 1971, p. 12.
10. Arthur Schlesinger, Jr., "Congress and the Making of American Foreign Policy," *Foreign Affairs* 51, no. 1 (1972): 83.
11. U.S. Congress, Senate, *Congressional Record*, 88th Cong., 2nd sess., 110: S18409.
12. H.R. Resolution, November 16, 1970.
13. S2956, April 13, 1972.

## Chapter 4

1. Robert F. Turner, *Repealing the War Powers Resolution* (Washington, D.C.: Brassey's, 1991), pp. 138–44.

## Chapter 5

1. In 1900, Secretary of State John Hay had a memorable confrontation with the Senate, leading him to say: "I, long ago, made up my mind that no treaty . . . that gave room for a difference of opinion could ever pass the Senate. When I sent in the Canal Convention I felt sure that none . . .

could fail to see the advantages were on our side. But I underrated the power of ignorance and spite, acting upon cowardess . . . there will always be 34% of the Senate on the backguard side of every question . . . a treaty entering the Senate is like a bull going into the arena; no one can say just how or when the blow will fall—but one thing is certain—it will never leave the arena alive." Thomas Bailey, *A Diplomatic History of the American People*, 7th ed. (New York: Appleton-Century-Crofts, 1964), pp. 487–88.

2. Norman Friedman, *Desert Victory* (Annapolis, Md.: Naval Institute Press, 1991), p. 156; Bob Woodward, *The Commanders* (New York: Simon & Schuster, 1991), p. 371.
3. Henry A. Kissinger, transcript of press conference, June 15, 1972.
4. *U.S. News & World Report*, 12 April 1965, p. 52.
5. *Strategic Review*, Winter 1979, p. 28.
6. Henry A. Kissinger, *Years of Upheaval* (Boston: Little, Brown, 1982), p. 1029.
7. *Congressional Quarterly Almanac* (1979): 411.
8. John G. Tower, *Consequences: A Political and Personal Memoir* (Boston: Little, Brown, 1991), p. 236.

# Chapter 6

1. U.S. Congress, Senate Judiciary Committee, *Congressional Power of Investigation* (Washington, D.C.: Government Printing Office, 1954), p. 2.
2. U.S. Congress, Senate Committee on Government Operations, *Councils and Committees* (Washington, D.C.: Government Printing Office, 1972), pp. 31–44.
3. Joseph Harris, *Congressional Control of Administration* (Washington, D.C.: Brookings Institution, 1964), pp. 251–52.
4. *Guide to the U.S. Congress* (Washington, D.C.: Congressional Quarterly, 1971), p. 248.
5. Ibid.
6. Martin Nelson McGeary, *Developments of Congressional Investigative Power* (New York: Columbia University Press, 1940). p. 7.
7. Harris, *Congressional Control*, p. 253.
8. Harry T. Williams, *Lincoln and the Radicals* (Madison: University of Wisconsin Press, 1941), p. 63.
9. *Guide to the U.S. Congress*, p. 257.
10. Harris, *Congressional Control*, p. 255.
11. Ron Chernow, *The House of Morgan* (New York: Atlantic Monthly Press, 1990).
12. Harris, *Congressional Control*, p. 260.
13. *Guide to the U.S. Congress*, p. 259.
14. *Guide to the U.S. Congress*, p. 248.
15. Woodrow Wilson, *Congressional Government* (Boston: Houghton Mifflin, 1913), p. 303.

16. *Church Committee Report*, vol. 1, p. 2.
17. *Pike Committee Report*, part 1, p. 1.
18. *United States v. Nixon*, 418 U.S. 683 (1974), p. 694.
19. P.L. 95–121 (1978).
20. *New York Times*, 29 May 1980, p. 18.
21. *New York Times*, 10 September 1980, p. 12.
22. *New York Times*, 3 April 1984, p. 1.
23. *New York Times*, 30 May 1986, p. 19.
24. *New York Times*, 17 December 1987, p. 1.
25. *New York Times*, 20 December 1986, p. 1.
26. *New York Times*, 3 February 1987, p. 20.
27. *United States v. Cox*, 342 F.2d 167 (1965).
28. *Nixon v. Administrator of General Services*, 433 U.S. 425 (1977).
29. *Buckley v. Valeo*, 424 U.S. 1, 126 (1976).
30. *United States v. Nixon*, 418 U.S. 683 (1977).
31. *Myers v. United States*, 272 U.S. 52 (1926).
32. 100 U.S. 371 (1879).
33. *Myers v. United States*, 272 U.S. 52 (1926), p. 134.
34. 189 S. Ct. 2597 (1988).
35. *Morrison v. Olson*, at 2618.
36. *Morrison v. Olson*, at 2617.
37. P.L. 94–505, October 15, 1976.
38. P.L. 95–91 (1979).
39. U.S. Congress, Senate Committee on Government Affairs, 95th Cong., 2nd sess., *Senate Report 1070* (1977), p. 26.
40. P.L. 95–452 (1978).
41. *Senate Report 1070*, p. 26.
42. 462 U.S. 919 (1984).
43. U.S. President, Special Review Board, *Report* (Washington, D.C.: Government Printing Office, February 26, 1987), p. V-6.
44. *New York Times*, 15 September 1991, p. 32.
45. *New York Times*, 20 March 1988.
46. U.S. Congress, *Report of the Congressional Committees Investigating the Iran-Contra Affair with Supplemental, Minority, and Additional Views*, 100th Cong., 1st sess., H. R. 100–433, S. R. 100–216 (Washington, D.C.: Government Printing Office, 1987), p. 620 (referred to hereafter as Joint Report).
47. *New York Times*, 10 July 1987.
48. Joint Report, p. xvi.
49. Ibid.
50. *Wall Street Journal*, 24 March 1989, p. A24.

# Chapter 7

1. *New York Times v. United States*, p. 4879 (1971).
2. *Guide to the U.S. Congress* (Washington, D.C.: Congressional Quarterly, 1971), p. 254.

3. William H. Rehnquist, *Executive Privilege* (Washington, D.C.: Government Printing Office, 1971), p. 421: "In denying the House its request, President Washington advised that 'the nature of Foreign negotiations requires caution, and their success must often depend on secrecy; and even when brought to a conclusion a full disclosure of all the measures, demands, or eventual concessions which may have been proposed or contemplated would be extremely impolite; for this might have a pernicious influence on future negotiations or produce immediate inconveniences, perhaps danger and mischief, in relation to other powers.' The necessity of such caution and secrecy was one cogent reason for vesting the power of making treaties in the president, with the advice and consent of the Senate, the principle on which that body was formed confining it to a small Committee on the judiciary." The decision in this case was made on the rather narrow ground that the House had no role in the treaty process. It should also be noted that the term commonly used for such denial now, "executive privilege," seems to be a recent usage.

4. *Marbury v. Madison*, 5 U.S. 137 (1803).

5. Ibid.

6. *Barenblatt v. U.S.*, 360 U.S. 109 (1959).

7. Rehnquist, *Executive Privilege*, p. 431.

8. U.S. Department of Justice, *Memorandum Reviewing Inquiries by the Legislative Branch During the Period of 1948–1950 Concerning the Decision Making Process and Documents of the Executive Branch* (Washington, D.C.: Government Printing Office, 1959), p. 37.

9. Rehnquist, *Executive Privilege*, p. 420.

10. *Detroit News*, 3 March 1971, p. 9.

11. Burton Sapin, *The Making of United States Foreign Policy* (New York: Praeger, 1969), p. 59.

12. Woodrow Wilson, cited in Dean Acheson, *Present at the Creation* (New York: W. W. Norton, 1969), p. 100.

13. U.S. Congress, Senate Committee on Foreign Relations, *Commitments, I* (Washington, D.C.: Government Printing Office, 1971), p. 4.

14. *Nixon v. Sirica*, 487 F. 2d 700 (1973).

15. Ibid., p. 717.

16. P.L. 93–190 (1974).

17. *Senate Select Committee v. Nixon*, 498 F. 2d 725 (1974).

18. Ibid., p. 733.

19. B. Schwartz, "Bad Presidents Make Hard Law," *Rutgers Law Review* 31, no. 22 (May 1978): 27.

20. *United States v. Nixon*, 418 U.S. 683 (1974).

21. Ibid., p. 705.

22. *Eastland v. U.S. Serviceman's Fund*, 421 U.S. 491 (1975).

23. U.S. Congress, House, H.R. Rep. 94-693, 94th Cong., 1st sess., 1975.

24. *Congressional Record* 121 (1975): H39730.

25. U.S. Congress, House Committee on Interstate and Foreign Commerce, Subcommittee on Oversight and Investigations, *Contempt Proceedings Against Secretary of Commerce Rogers C. B. Morton, Hearings*, 94th Cong., 1st sess, 1975.

26. *Nixon v. Administrator of General Services*, 433 U.S. 425 (1977).
27. 419 F. Supp. 454 (1976).
28. 551 F. 2nd 394.
29. 567 F. 2nd 128.
30. 21 U.S.C. 331.
31. *Congressional Quarterly Weekly Report* 38 (May 17, 1980): 1352.
32. *Washington Post*, 30 July 1981, p. A2.
33. U.S. president, "Executive Privilege: Legal Opinions Regarding Claim of President Ronald Reagan in Response to a Subpoena Issued to James G. Watt, Secretary of the Interior" for use by House Energy and Commerce Committee (November 1981).
34. U.S. Congress, H.R. No. 968, 97th Cong., 2nd sess. (1982).
35. Ibid., p. 20.
36. *Congressional Record* 149 (December 16, 1982): H10040.
37. *Washington Post*, 20 February 1983, p. A1.
38. *Washington Post*, 1 November 1984, p. A15.
39. *Congressional Quarterly Weekly Report*, 8 August 1987, p. 1787.
40. U.S. Congress, Senate, Committee on Armed Services, *Nomination of John G. Tower to Be Secretary of Defense, Hearings*, 101st Cong., 1st sess., 1989.
41. *New York Times*, 22 March 1990.
42. *Wall Street Journal*, 31 July 1991.
43. *Wall Street Journal*, 6 November 1991, p. 18.

# Chapter 8

1. Frederick Kempe, *Divorcing the Dictator* (New York: G. P. Putnam's Sons, 1990), pp. 236–37.
2. Quoted in Edmund Morris, *The Rise of Theodore Roosevelt* (New York: Ballantine Books, 1979), p. 12.
3. Quoted in R. M. Koster and Guillermo Sanchez, *In the Time of the Tyrants: Panama 1968–1990* (New York: W. W. Norton, 1990), p. 389.
4. Edmund Morris, *Rise of Roosevelt*, p. 11.
5. Koster and Sanchez, *Time of Tyrants*, p. 393.
6. Gerald Warburg, *Conflict and Consensus* (New York: Ballinger, 1989), pp. 175–83.
7. Ibid., p. 76.
8. Alexander M. Haig, Jr., *Caveat* (New York: Macmillan, 1984), pp. 126–40.
9. Peter Rodman, "The Imperial Congress," *National Interest*, Fall 1985.
10. Kempe, *Divorcing the Dictator*, pp. 1–3.
11. Ibid., p. 7.
12. Ibid., pp. 91–101.
13. Ibid., pp. 99–101.
14. Ibid., p. 187.
15. *Wall Street Journal*, 16 November 1991, p. 17.

16. *Wall Street Journal*, 30 July 1991, p. 16.
17. Kempe, *Divorcing the Dictator*, p. 251.
18. Bob Woodward, *The Commanders* (New York: Simon & Schuster, 1991), pp. 92–96.
19. Kempe, *Divorcing the Dictator*, pp. 27–34, 313.
20. Ibid., pp. 341–42.
21. Woodward, *The Commanders*, pp. 96–98.
22. Ibid., p. 122.
23. Ibid., p. 124.
24. Ibid., pp. 124–25.
25. Ibid., p. 127.
26. Ibid., p. 168.
27. Kempe, *Divorcing the Dictator*, p. 13.
28. *Washington Post*, 13 March 1990, p. 23.
29. Woodward, *The Commanders*, p. 177.

## Chapter 9

1. Joseph Harris, *Congressional Control of Administration* (Washington D.C.: Brookings Institution, 1964), p. 46.
2. Edward Corwin, *The Constitution and What It Means Today* (New York: Atheneum, 1967), p. 26.
3. "Federalist No. 58," *The Federalist Papers* (New York: New American Library, 1961), p. 359.
4. "Federalist No. 24," *The Federalist Papers*, p. 158.
5. "Federalist No. 26," *The Federalist Papers*, p. 171.
6. E. A. Kolodziej, *The Uncommon Defense and Congress* (Columbus: Ohio State University Press, 1966), p. 436.
7. Louis Fisher, *The President and Congress* (New York: Free Press, 1972), p. 110.
8. Ibid., p. 111.
9. For a detailed review of this struggle, see Wilfred Binkley, *President and Congress*, 3rd ed. (New York: Vintage, 1961), pp. 33–82.
10. Fisher, *The President*, p. 111.
11. Ibid., p. 127.
12. *Guide to the U.S. Congress* (Washington, D.C.: Congressional Quarterly, 1971), p. 188.
13. Harris, *Congressional Control*, p. 52.
14. *Guide to Congress*, p. 39.
15. Fisher, *The President*, p. 128.
16. Corwin, *The Constitution*, p. 81.
17. Harris, *Congressional Control*, p. 54.
18. Binkley, *President and Congress*, pp. 205–20.
19. Cited in Arthur Schlesinger, Jr., *The Imperial Presidency* (Boston: Houghton Mifflin, 1973).
20. Harris, *Congressional Control*, p. 56.
21. *Guide to Congress*, p. 44.

22. George R. Brown, as cited in Binkley, *President and Congress*, pp. 270–71.
23. Francis Wilcox, *Congress, the Executive, and Foreign Policy* (New York: Harper & Row, 1971), p. 74.
24. *Wall Street Journal*, 15 May 1991.
25. *Guide to Congress*, p. 53.
26. Cited in Harris, *Congressional Control*, p. 53.
27. Cited in Wilcox, *Congress, the Executive, and Foreign Policy*, p. 90.
28. Cited in Schlesinger, *Imperial Presidency*, p. 207.
29. John Stennis and J. W. Fulbright, *The Role of Congress in Foreign Policy* (Washington, D.C.: American Enterprise Institute for Public Policy Research, 1971), pp. 24–25.
30. Kolodziej, *Uncommon Defense*, p. 445.
31. U.S. Congress, House Armed Services Committee, *Military Procurement Authorization Fiscal Year 1964* (Washington, D.C.: Government Printing Office, 1963), pp. 3–4.
32. William Elliott, *United States Foreign Policy* (New York: Columbia University Press, 1952), p. 66.
33. *Wall Street Journal*, 18 December 1989, p. 10.
34. John Norton Moore, *Law and the Indochina War* (Princeton: Princeton University Press, 1972), p. 629.
35. Richard E. Neustadt, *Alliance Politics* (New York: Columbia University Press, 1970), p. 11.
36. Arthur M. Schlesinger, Jr., *A Thousand Days* (Boston: Houghton Mifflin, 1965), p. 556.
37. Elliott, *Foreign Policy*, p. 48.
38. Ibid., p. 92.
39. Harris, *Congressional Control*, p. 87.
40. Fisher, *The President*, p. 113.
41. Cited in Fisher, *The President*, p. 113.
42. Internal memorandum cited by Schlesinger, *Imperial Presidency*, p. 237.
43. Louis Fisher, "Effect of the Budget Act of 1974 on Agency Operations," in *The Congressional Budget Process After Five Years*, ed. Ralph Penner (Washington, D.C.: American Enterprise Institute for Public Policy Research, 1981), p. 150.
44. Fisher, *The President*, p. 112.
45. John Rothchild, "Cooing Down the War: The Senate's Lame Doves," *Washington Monthly*, August 1971, p. 13.
46. Emmet John Hughes, *The Living Presidency* (New York: Coward-McCann, 1972), p. 222.
47. Rothchild, "Cooing Down the War," p. 13.
48. Fisher, *The President*, p. 112.
49. Ibid.
50. *New York Times*, 24 April 1973, p. 5.
51. *Congressional Record*, 22 April 1973, p. S12004.
52. *Congressional Quarterly Almanac*, 1973, p. 30-H.
53. S.R. 93–160, May 18, 1973.

54. *Congressional Record*, 31 May 1973, p. S10128.
55. *Congressional Record*, 29 June 1973.
56. In the Senate the vote was 54–22 (*Congressional Record*, 29 December 1975); in the House, the vote was 323–99 (ibid., 22 January 1976).
57. P.L. 97–269 (1982).
58. *Congress and Foreign Policy* (Washington, D.C.: Government Printing Office, 1984), p. 35.
59. Military Construction Appropriation Act of FY 1987, P.L. 99–591.

# Index

283

Israel *(cont.)*
Iraq and, 15, 16, 18
Lebanon and, 102–3
Libya and, 114
occupied territories of, 28
terrorism against, 118–19
Isthmian Canal Convention, 206
Italy, 15, 134, 137
Lebanon and, 103, 105, 106
terrorism and, 115, 119–22
ITT, 190

Jackson, Andrew, 78, 79
Jackson, Henry M. ("Scoop"), 29,
77, 133, 135, 138, 139, 145,
146, 148–50, 152, 220
Jackson, Robert, 63, 199
Japan, 23, 30, 134
in World War II, 10, 213
Japanese Red Army, 115
Javits, Jacob, 90
Jaworski, Leon, 164
Jay, John, 59
Jay Treaty, 186
Jefferson, Thomas, 59–61, 65, 76,
79, 186, 187, 244, 258
Jennings, Ivor, 133
Jeremiah, Rear Adm. David E.,
119–20
Johnson, Andrew, 68
Johnson, Lyndon B., 6, 40, 51, 68,
74, 82, 83, 134, 143, 144, 251,
258, 261
Johnson, Rady, 88
Joint Chiefs of Staff (JCS), 39, 100,
118, 125, 139, 140, 142, 151
Grenada and, 111
Gulf War and, 35, 39
Panama and, 225–28, 230, 232,
233, 235, 238
Jones, Gen. David, 39, 100, 151
Jordan, Hamilton, 165
Julius Caesar, 76
Just Cause, Operation, 235–38
Justice Department, U.S., 164,
165, 193, 196, 258
Inspector General in, 171

Kaunda, Kenneth David, 265–66
Keating Five, 68
Kelley, Gen. P. X., 8, 25–26, 106
Kelly, John, 18

Kelso, Adm. Frank, 119–20,
122–25, 127
Kennedy, Edward M., 38
Kennedy, John F., 81, 86, 221, 254,
258, 261
Kent State University, 86
Kerrey, Bob, 222
KGB, 219
Khmer Rouge, 262–63, 265
Khomeini, Ayatollah, 7–8, 13, 15,
100, 115, 216
Kirkpatrick, Jeane, 220
Kissinger, Henry, 6, 39, 84, 85, 88,
92, 113, 135, 139–41, 144–46,
150, 152, 192, 208, 218, 226,
266
Klinghoffer, Leon, 119
Kohl, Helmut, 24
Korea, 134
Korean War, 47, 77, 79, 213
*Korematsu* case (1944), 63
Korologos, Tom, 88, 135
Kozak, Michael, 227, 229
Kraft, Tim, 166
Kroll, Jules, 180
Kurds, 3, 12, 16, 17
Kuwait, 3–5, 19, 32–34
air war and, 39, 52
and arms sales to Iraq, 16
ground offensive in, 52–53, 56
hostages in, 24, 27, 29, 31, 37
and Iran-Iraq war, 13, 14, 48
Iraqi invasion of, 1, 19–22, 25,
27, 28
Iraqi refusal to withdraw from,
40–44, 46, 51, 78

Labor Department, U.S., 171
Laird, Melvin, 83, 88, 138, 139
Laos, 262, 264
Lavelle, Gen., 190
League of Nations, 79
Lebanon, 16, 23, 50, 77, 78, 101–9,
118, 226, 229
hostages in, 174
Marines in, 103–9, 142
Syrian presence in, 28
Lee, Robert E., 187
Legislative Reorganization Act
(1946), 158, 160, 247
Library of Congress, 57, 218
Libya, 76, 112–17, 122–28, 235

Syria, 17, 115, 119
 in Gulf War, 27, 33
 Lebanon and, 28, 102, 103,
  142–43
 Libya and, 114
 terrorism and, 125

Taiwan, 73
*Teddy Roosevelt* (aircraft carrier),
 259
Tercom, 137–38
Terrorism, 15, 114–25
Tet offensive, 80, 83
Texaco, 10
Texas, annexation of, 78, 135
TFX, 270
Thatcher, Margaret, 23, 32, 38, 43,
 111
Thomas, Clarence, 66, 69, 197,
 199
Thurman, Gen. Maxwell, 231–35
Tin Cup, Operation, 30
Titan missiles, 144
Tomahawk cruise missiles, 9, 52,
 55, 129, 132, 136–43, 146, 148,
 149, 151
Tonkin Gulf Resolution, 67, 81–83,
 87, 89, 213, 263
Tornado bombers, 136
Torrijos, Gen. Omar, 209, 215–17,
 220
Tow missiles, 55
Tower, John, 74, 77, 93, 145, 146,
 149, 150, 152, 154, 174, 197,
 199, 249, 253
Tower Board, 174–76
Transportation Department, U.S.,
 171
Treasury Department, U.S., 171
Treaties, 129–56
 with Panama, 206–10, 216, 231,
  238
Trible, Paul S., Jr., 178
Trident missiles and submarines,
 146
Tripoli, 76–78
Trucial system, 3
Truman, Harry S, 5, 47, 53, 73, 79,
 134, 135, 248, 258
Truman Committee, 159–60
Truman Doctrine, 254
Tunis, 76

Tunney, John, 266
Turkey, 27, 30, 73, 221
Turner, Robert, 109
Turner, Stansfield, 209
TWA, 118, 125
Twain, Mark, 205
Twin Pillars, 6

United Arab Emirates (UAE), 3,
 19, 20, 30
United Fruit Company, 207
United Nations, 33, 49, 130, 132,
 220, 238
 Conference on International
  Organization, 132
 and Gulf War, 24, 29, 31, 32, 34,
  36, 38–40, 42, 47, 49, 51–53
*United States* (frigate), 75
*U.S. v. AT&T* (1976), 193, 194,
 198
*U.S. v. Belmont* (1937), 64
*U.S. v. Curtiss-Wright Export
 Corporation* (1936), 64, 132
United States Information Agency
 (USIA), 19, 171, 255, 256
*U.S. v. Nixon* (1974), 164, 168, 191,
 198
*U.S. v. Reynolds*, 186
U.S. Southern Command, 208, 224,
 225, 229–32
Urgent Fury, Operation, 111
U-2 incident, 184

Vance, Cyrus, 151
Versailles Treaty, 130
Veterans Administration (VA), 171
Vietnam War, 2, 11, 12, 23, 39, 48,
 51, 79–89, 209, 211, 219, 266
 appropriations for, 251–52,
  261–65, 270
 Congress and, 161, 213
 covert action in, 202
 France in, 72, 78
 Nixon and, 189
 and War Powers Act, 89, 91,
  96–98
*Village Voice*, 162
*Vincennes*, USS, 10, 14
Vinson, Carl, 214, 248–49
Virginia, University of, 109
Vladivostok summit, 147, 148
V-22 tiltrotor technology, 270

# ABOUT THE AUTHOR

JOHN LEHMAN is an investment banker living in Manhattan with his wife and three children.

He was a senior staff member to Henry Kissinger during the Nixon administration, an arms-control negotiator in the Ford administration, and secretary of the navy in the Reagan administration.

Captain Lehman has flown actively in the naval reserve for twenty-four years.

He is a graduate of St. Joseph's College, Cambridge University, and the University of Pennsylvania. He has written numerous books, including *Command of the Seas*.